cl

Laurence

D W

FORESTS

Credits: The verse appearing in the Preface is from Robert Service's *Rhymes of a Rolling Stone,* published by Dodd, Mead and Co. in 1912 and again by Triangle books in 1940, and used with the publishers' permission. The opening quotation in Chapter 8 and another in Chapter 12 are from *Textbook of Dendrology,* fifth edition, by W. M. Harlow and E. S. Harrar, published by McGraw-Hill, Inc., 1968. Lines by Roy Underhill in Chapter 26 are from *The Woodwright's Companion,* published by University of North Carolina Press, 1983, and used with permission of the publisher. The several extended quotations in Chapter 27, used with permission of the publisher, are from *Live Oaking,* by Virginia Steele Wood, published by Northeastern University Press, 1981, and containing a quotation from J. A. Lawson in *New Voyage to Carolina,* 1709. The quotation in Chapter 5 is from *Bartram's Travels,* edited by F. Harper and published by the Yale University Press, 1958.

Parts of this book were published under the title of *Ecology and Our Forests* (A. S. Barnes, 1972) and *Trees* (Prentice-Hall, 1984).

Dr. Joyce Greene Gellhorn of the Boulder, Colorado, School District and the University of Colorado provided valuable assistance. So, too, did Carol Evens and Sheila Wichita.

Library of Congress Cataloging-in-Publication Data

Walker, Laurence C., 1924–
    Forests : a naturalist's guide to woodland trees / by Laurence C. Walker.
        p.   cm.
    Originally published: New York : Wiley, c1990, in series: Wiley Nature editions.
    Includes bibliographical references and index.
    ISBN 0-292-79112-7 (pbk. : alk. paper)
    1. Trees—United States.   2. Forest ecology—United States.   I. Title.
[QK115.W35   1997]
582.160973—dc20   96-34535

For Emily
  Julie
  Evan
  Rachel
  Clayton
  and all the other children of the world whose futures depend on
  how well we understand our forests.

Contents

v

13   Timber for a King: Eastern White Pine, 99

14   From Monterey to the World: Monterey Pine, 111

15   Woods of Longevity: White-Cedars and Junipers, 120

16   Pioneer Plant for Paper Pulp: Virginia Pine, 130

17   Krummholz and Elfinwood: Subalpine Fir, 134

18   Sandhills and Flatwoods: Slash Pine, 142

THE BROADLEAF TREES

19   Lost Bonanza: American Chestnut, 151

20   Oranges That Are Apples: Osage-Orange, 160

21   Cinderella Cellulose: Trembling Aspen, 166

22   Living Riprap: Willows, 173

23   Toxic Defense: Black Walnut, 179

24   From Cotton to Cottonwood: Cottonwood, 188

25   Species Proliferation: The Oaks, 197

26   Tree Legume: Black Locust, 208

27   Ship Timbers: Live Oak, 217

28   Stink-Bomb Tree: Ginkgo, 228

Preface

*T*he writing of this book came about from a desire to share my personal interest, awe, and reverence for the marvelous adaptations that enable trees to survive and forests to regenerate. I hope the reader finds it serves this primary purpose.

As a forester and an educator of foresters, I trust that it also will provide readers with some understanding of how innate habits that ensure survival after catastrophe often alter species composition in our forests, and how the management of woodlands depends upon these fundamental tree habits.

Professional forestry in America, from its beginning at the turn of the twentieth century to the present, has been subject to severe critique by laymen of the conservation movement. Gifford Pinchot, the nation's first native-born forester and the first chief of the U.S. Forest Service, was referred to by that day's park enthusiasts as utilitarian. In turn, Theodore Roosevelt's "Forester," for so the president called Pinchot, publicly suggested that those people enthusiastic for park setasides were full of "sentimental nonsense." Both he and his detractors had a point.

Not only were those sentimentalists, whose primary interest in forests was aesthetic, unrelenting in their attack on the managers of woodlands, so too were ranchers, lumbermen, mining interests, waterpower proponents, wildlife enthusiasts, and not a few politicians. Yet laymen—as far as natural resource management is concerned—were also those who throughout this century have provided the support in legislative chambers and executive offices that enabled the forestry profession, with an able assist from Providence, to avoid predicted timber famines and to acquire the knowledge necessary for meeting our continued requirements for cellulose fiber. Enlightened public support usually made possible, with happy results, the steering of a middle course between extreme philosophies. To enable the nonprofessional to better understand the things of nature and the nature of things has been a principal motivation for penning these pages. Professional resource managers continue to need the layman's enlightened interest.

Why are some the supporters, others the detractors of the foresters' efforts? In this, as in other disciplines, knowledge is the determinant. Although no one individual or group of people can have all the necessary information for ascertaining truth, particularly in the complex interactions of environmental ecology and economics (both derived from the same term, *oikos* in the Greek and *iconaea* in Latin, suggesting the care of the household or estate), some understanding by the public of the ecological bases for decision-making by foresters should be helpful. As practicing environmentalists, then, foresters are both ecologists and economists when managing the estate.

Since the mid-1960s, a battery of angry environmentalists have attacked the work of foresters. Charges in the courts, the Congress, and the public prints made difficult, if not impossible, wise management of much of the nation's woodlands. These pages do not exonerate foresters for errors in judgmental management as viewed today. Indeed, a hundred years hence they may not be considered errors, for the profession currently is charged by society to provide for adequate timber resources for the future. On some sites that will necessitate removal of stagnated and low-value forests and their replacement with genetically superior stock of commercially important woods. It will mean, too, providing logs for mills in areas all too often economically depressed. On other sites, "special places" may be set aside, even on industry lands, to meet nontimber goals. The forest, too, must provide pleasing landscapes and biological diversity.

Production of timber must be the principal use of some forests because wood is an essential basic raw material. It is also renewable. Other "goods" of the forest, not necessarily of lesser importance for humankind's welfare, are water, game, and forage. Among the "services" provided are wooded landscapes for aesthetic appreciation and places for recreation. The forester accepts responsibility for managing and protecting all of these woodland resources so that they are neither exhausted nor destroyed. Ecological understanding here, too, will help us realize why on every acre, or every block, of forest, all components of "multiple-use" forest management cannot with justification be given equal weight when planning the allocation of financial resources. Fortunately for humankind, wood production is compatible with other important forest-related goods and services.

Indeed, clearcutting may be good ecology if it is a reasonable imitation of nature's way. "Reasonable" is the key here. A fire or storm that devastated 50,000 acres of Douglas-fir in 1870, after which a new stand of timber stocked the area, is not sufficient justification for even a 5,000-acre regeneration harvest by clearcutting (that imitates the catastrophe) today. Nor is it wise, in my opinion, to harvest trees from sites with a high risk of erosion or from those which have special beauty, if the cost of regeneration to high-yield forests is more than the value of the timber removed. That day may come as population expands and increasing standards of living demonstrate the need for greater quantities of raw material. For the present, however, it appears more appropriate to grow timber of high quality on sites that can be dedicated infinitely—as we now reckon—for wood-fiber production.

Currently foresters plan for the time when wood must substitute for metals and other energy-intensive materials. The necessity will occur because, as higher-quality materials become exhausted, production of metal from residual low-grade ores will require increasing amounts of energy. And energy will be more scarce as known reserves of gas and oil are depleted. Thus, foresters shall continue to be responsible for sustainable development of wood resources for future generations.

I hope these pages may give concerned citizens some understanding of the forester's *modus operandi* and a better basis for objection when the knowledge the forester professes to have is not exemplified in practice. That will be reward enough for the hours spent in the preparation of this book.

I hope the suggested "hands on" activities will excite curiosity, whether the reader be a young person or a senior citizen. The author, long associated with the scouting movement as a Boy Scout and a scouter, kept in mind various merit badge assignments in developing these exercises. As an instructor in a professional forestry school, I've given uppermost consideration to the need for field studies at the introductory level. I trust, too, these suggestions will stimulate retirees to "think and do" for their emotional and physical health.

Literature listed at the end of the book serves two purposes: to cite a pertinent reference to material presented and to give the reader an idea of the kinds of books and journals in which forestry information is published.

I will appreciate suggestions made by reviewers, though their barbs will remind the writer of the rhyme of Robert Service, every forester's favorite "poet of the Yukon":

I have no doubt at all the Devil grins,
    As seas of ink I splatter.
Ye Gods, forgive my "literary" sins—
    The other kind don't matter.

L. C. W.
Nacogdoches, Texas
1996

1

The Changing Forest

A thousand poets have described the peaceful beauty of the forest glen. Deep carpets of leaves, golden sunlight filtering through a canopy of green, and the bubbling stream moving down a wooded slope on its long journey to the sea speak of quiet, restful solitude.

In another sense the forest is far from quiet, far from restful. It is the scene of desperate struggles, a battlefield with its dead, its dying, and its proud victors. If one is still, a myriad of sounds emerge: the rabbit's squeal in death, the grinding crash of deer antlers locked in mortal combat, and the girdling nibble of insects eating through living tissues just beneath the bark of trees.

Not only animals are involved in this competition for survival. Trees, too, vie with each other and with other plant forms for their life-giving requirements: water, light, and nutrients. Within a dense forest of a single species, competition may be especially keen among trees of the same age.

Seeds and Their Seedlings

Trees need a foothold. Nuisance weeds of garden and lawn have certain habitation limitations; most tree seeds are more selective of their environment. Some seeds germinate in the mulch-like leaf litter of a moist hardwood forest. Others pop their coats and enlarge into little trees after falling on an old log, while many of the most important trees require a mineral seedbed—the soil scarified and fully open to the light and heat of the sun for seed germination and early seedling survival. True, some seeds germinate in the soot that collects in abandoned chimneys, in the rusted debris of automobile bodies, and in the cracks of sidewalks. Rarely are these the trees of economic value to man— more likely they behave as pests.

1

Even before seeds alight on the land, there is the problem of dispersal. Some go by air—willows and maples are examples; others, like the hop hornbeam, travel by water; while some "hitchhike" on mammals and birds. Witchhazel seeds are scattered by propulsion, acting like bullets. Cedar berries and mesquite beans are transported great distances internally by birds and cattle. The spread of mesquite in Texas, for instance, followed the great cattle drives.

. Before the seedbed is prepared and seed dispersal occurs, there must be seed production. Before that, obviously, flowers and fruit must form.

Light, nutrients, and soil moisture have their roles. Interactions of these environmental components influence the carbon:nitrogen (C:N) ratio of the living tree, which is the secret of flower bud formation. Increase nitrogen by fertilizing or eliminating competing trees, increase carbon production by stimulating photosynthesis (exposing more leaves to the light), or wound trees by girdling the bark so that carbohydrates move downward with difficulty through the living inner-bark (called the phloem), and buds evolve into flowers. So, too, conifer trees about to die go "cone crazy," their proportions of carbon and nitrogen being disturbed as though they "think" that perpetuation of the species is all important.

Flowers do not automatically become seeds. Insects and fungi that attack flowers take their toll. And if male and female flowers are incomplete—both not in the same organ—simultaneous ripening is especially essential. Lack of synchronization, by even a few days, of pollen dispersal by staminate flowers and reception by pistillate flowers results in seed losses. For some species, sexes are separated by trees and if male-bearing trees are too distant from the female, obvious difficulties arise. If seeds do develop, other insects and fungi destroy many.

So now the seeds are in the ground. Some, such as longleaf pine, germinate shortly after seed-fall. Others, like loblolly pine, lie dormant several months during which time mice, mourning doves, and fungus molds effectively reduce the supply. Squirrels collect acorns and hickory nuts over large areas and cache them away for a "rainy day." Floods, snow, and drought effects are not tallied in the statistical records of seed traps, the simple pans that collect samples of seeds as they fall, thus hinting to a forester the adequacy of the catch for a new stand of trees.

On Roots

The forest is not a carefully managed nursery; weed-trees, insects, fungi, and mammals are not controlled. As the tree seeds arrive, so do weed seeds. Ragweed or tree weed, the difference is little in the effect of competition for soil moisture, nutrients, and light in the life of the little plant. The struggle continues for the life of the tree; those with root systems most able to absorb moisture, adsorb nutrients, and grow rapidly to keep their crowns in the sunlight are most likely to survive.

Roots that grow down to great depths are called tap. Lateral roots grow radially from the base of the tree. Most trees have some of both types, but those endowed with a finely branched, rapidly extending lateral system are most apt to win the skirmish. Taproots, desirable for stability, have relatively little effect on a tree's capacity to take in moisture and nutrients.

Once seeds germinate and seedlings begin to grow, continuance is not automatic. Grazing and browsing wildlife and domestic animals, ice storms, floods, drought, insects, diseases, and fire reduce the number of trees on the lands. Forests that begin with 100,000 seedlings on an acre may, at age 75 or final harvest time, have as few as fifty.

Ecological Succession

The ability to compete varies. Many trees grow rapidly in their younger years, racing to the sky lest, it seems, others overtop them. Several kinds of conifers, especially the pines, and hardwoods, such as yellow-poplar and paper birch, are characteristic. These species generally do poorly and succumb quickly once overtopped. Other species—some hickories, oaks, and hemlocks—endure heavy shading as they slowly make height growth. Differences in the capacity to survive and grow when overtopped are principal factors in the ecological process called forest succession.

To visualize forest succession, suppose we stand in the middle of an extensive southern forest composed principally of shade-tolerant oaks and shade-intolerant pines. An oak acorn is relatively large and furnishes considerable stored food for its germinating seedling. These heavy seeds provide the nourishment for the sprouting rootlet to reach the moist mineral soil, even through deep litter. A winged pine seed, in contrast, is small and light, furnishing only a limited food supply for the developing rootlet. That little root must be in contact with mineral soil shortly after it forms in order to survive.

Now that the stage is set, let us clear a 100-acre block of forest, removing the organic debris that covers the soil. A fire often does this. Now, what will happen with the passing of time?

Within the first few years, pines may occupy the area as wind carries seed from the surrounding forest to the seedbed that, for most species, is exposed mineral soil. Organic humus serves for a few kinds of trees. After twenty-five or thirty years, the pine saplings have formed a closed canopy over the land, and a deep layer of pine needle litter begins to accumulate on the forest floor. The pines, by this time, have created an environment in which they cannot perpetuate themselves. Even if here and there a seed might germinate where a deer had scratched the litter to expose the soil, the seedlings that might develop would not be able to withstand the shade and root competition of their parents.

During this time, however, oak seedlings begin to appear here and there beneath the pines, thanks to the activity of busy but forgetful squirrels. Germination requirements met, and the shade posing no serious problem, the oaks slowly push upward. While they may not overtop to harm the pines, they are important components of the canopy, remaining long after the pines have been killed by insects, disease, or old age. After a century or so, only a few hard-

pressed pines may remain in an otherwise pure oak forest. A serious disturbance, such as another fire or logging, could start the process of natural succession over again. If no disturbances occur, the oak forest, able to regenerate in
its own shade, remains as the climax forest. Disturbances are the rule, so climax
forests—those vegetation types that, when man and his axe are kept out of the
woods and fires do not occur, continue to perpetuate themselves *ad
infinitum*—are the exceptions.

The rather orderly change that occurs in forest species with the passing
of time in the course of natural succession is a more or less predictable sequence
in a given locale, although much more complicated than implied by this example. Foresters and other land managers are especially concerned with this
process, for their activities directly influence the rate and course of succession.
On many sites in the South, for instance, pines are the preferred species, and
foresters must "hold back" the succession to economically less desirable kinds
of trees through a variety of harvesting and weed-tree control practices. Laymen, too, appreciate the forest all the more when viewing it in terms of these
dynamic and complex successional trends.

A Little Knowledge Is . . .

Laymen, on an occasion I recall, especially appreciated an understanding of
ecology because of a politically critical situation in North Georgia when a
government agency was being accused by a big city newspaper of mismanagement of lands. Government foresters, the newspaper claimed, had marked for
harvest a virgin forest. True, the trees were large—many more than 3 feet in
diameter—and for this reason perhaps should have been left for others to see
and enjoy. However, they were not old, nor was the forest virgin.

With a spade, I readily found the old plow sole about 12 inches below
the present level of the soil. Above that plowed zone, an over-burden of topsoil
had accumulated, washed into the cove from the surrounding hillsides. This
was, in reality, an abandoned farmer's field. Farmers had left the mountains
in an agricultural depression years before and moved to the towns of the
Piedmont. On that freshly abandoned land with its mineral soil exposed (or on
the fertile over-burden of a year or two later, also with mineral soil exposed),
white pine seeded in. Its growth was often more than 3 feet in height each
year for many years, and the tree diameters often exceeded ½ inch a year in
radial growth.

Under these pines, hemlocks seeded in. Hemlock, like oak, is tolerant
of shade and does not require mineral soil for seed germination. Its seeds sprout
and the fine root works its way through the pine duff to adequate sources of
moisture. The hemlocks, too, grew well and, where pines here and there had
died, extended their crowns into the canopies. Subsequently, many of the
hemlocks were the largest trees in the woods. Adding to that the denseness of
the stand, it was reasonable for the newsmen to consider this dark, damp conifer
forest of giant trees a remnant of the past.

This we knew: the nature of their germination habits and the relative

An ecological transition. A large, decadent jack pine, with the upper half of its crown dead, will pass from the stand of trees as the more shade-tolerant spruce and balsam fir encroach and eventually dominate the forest. The pine, a remnant of a virgin stand in Minnesota, was 186 years old and 16 inches dbh when photographed (USDA Forest Service photo).

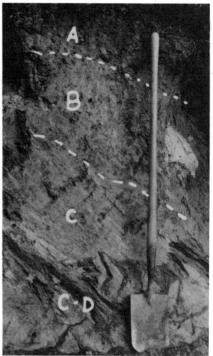

FIGURE 1-1. A roadside cut is a good place to study and map the profile of the soil.

tolerance of the two species to shade meant that the pines had to precede the hemlock, regardless of which trees were larger years later at the time of our visit to the site of the disputation.

Later you'll learn about increment borings for determining the ages of trees. These cores were taken, but only for trees less than 2 feet across, for my increment borer could only drill 10 inches into the trunks. The pines we knew were all of the same age, the 10-inch tree beginning life at the same time as the 40-inch stem. The latter simply grew faster. And the hemlocks had to be younger. It turned out that the "virgin" forest was but 60 years old: the extraordinarily superior site encouraged extremely rapid growth.

Forest succession is of special concern to park and wilderness managers. The preservation of a climax forest type, such as Sitka spruce, while not without difficulties, is much easier to accomplish than maintaining a temporary type indefinitely. The latter situation, as in the mixed pine—hardwood forest in the Big Thicket National Preserve in southeast Texas, requires continual efforts to combat the strong successional tide.

Visitors to the Big Thicket—where rattlesnakes are reputed to grow so old they have whiskers—enjoy mostly the large pines that overtop the oaks and hickories by 50 feet or more and stand over a dense understory of jungle-like shrubs and vines. Yet, if nature is left alone and no disasters occur, these pines will pass out of the picture, for none are known to exceed 140 years of age in that locale. Indeed, most succumb before reaching 100 years. With only the jungle-like mixed mesic forests, the Big Thicket will have lost much of its scenic splendor. Should you ask why, then, are these conifers in these virgin forests, we must answer: "You've been hoodwinked. These aren't virgin, but because of timber harvests in the 1900s, the 1920s, and the 1940s, the lands today have pines that entered in openings unwittingly made by cut-out-and-get-out loggers of yesterday."

The chapters that follow tell about the struggles of trees to survive: how some have adaptations to certain environmental characteristics and others have been encouraged by foresters to extend their ranges, for the good of man, by man's imitation of what he has seen in nature. She is the teacher. He applies her lessons.

🌲 🌲 🌲 Projects for the Amateur Naturalist

1. Count seeds. Build three seed traps out of cardboard, 3.3 feet on a side (¼₀₀₀ acre) and place at 10-, 30-, and 50-foot intervals from the base of a tree. During the season of seed dispersal, periodically count, record, and chart the seed dispersal. Then convert the data to an acre-basis by multiplying by 4,000.

2. Effect of trees on soil improvement. Dig a 1-foot hole in the ground under an old forest and in an adjacent open field. The trees alone should be the only difference in the sites. Note differences in earthworm populations, insect populations, fungus growth (use a hand lens), organic matter in the soil, and the friable—or lack of friable—soil structure. Anything else (see Figure 1–1)?

3. Discover starch in plant parts. Boil in water, soak in alcohol, and rinse in water crushed leaves, twigs, or seeds. Then apply diluted iodine and observe color change. The darker the blue the greater the quantity of starch. Use white bread as a control or "check."

THE NEEDLELEAF
TREES

Also called evergreens (though baldcypress is deciduous) and polycotyledonous—meaning many seed leaves (though northern white-cedar has but two seed leaves). Commercially, these are the softwoods (though southern pines produce hard wood) and botanically the naked-seeded gymnosperms (though ginkgo—not a needleleaf—is a gymnosperm).

2

Westward Wood

Douglas-fir

When Archibald Menzies, Scottish physician and naturalist, stepped off Captain Vancouver's good ship at what is now called Nootka Sound in Vancouver Island, he witnessed a sylvan setting that would, in time, transform the lumbering industry of the entire New World. The isle on which he and the explorer landed would be named for the British naval officer. The tree that they saw would bear the name of the scientist, *Pseudotsuga menziesii*.

Taxonomic "Confusion Worse Confounded"

But that is a relatively new title—or the discovery of an older one—for this important tree of western North America. A generation ago the species name was *taxifolia*, because of its yew-like (taxus) arrangement of needles (folia) on the twig.

Sometime after the visit of Vancouver's sails, about 1825, David Douglas, another Scot, was sent by the Royal Botanical Society to study the tree that Dr. Menzies had earlier described. From this venture, the great stem, to some appearing as a hemlock, to others a fir, to others a spruce, and to still others a pine, got its common name.

Douglas's tree does look like a hemlock, hence the generic name, *Pseudotsuga*, latinized from Greek and Japanese for "false hemlock." Its appearance as a fir gave rise to the appellation of "Douglas fir," later hyphenated because the tree is not a true fir. Such belong to the genus *Abies*. The blue-green foliage of the Rocky Mountain strain encouraged some to call it a spruce, even confusing it with the vegetatively propagated Koster's blue spruce; the wood sells abroad today as Oregon pine. For 150 years, it has carried one of these common names. On the lumber market it also has been tallied as western larch

Old-growth Douglas-fir in the Olympic National Forest (USDA Forest Service photo).

or, amazingly, southern pine—the latter having much denser wood. Add to its trade names yellow fir and red fir because of the color characteristic of certain specimens of wood. Some give it these names because of the softness of the wood. That, of course, depends on ring width, controlled by rate of growth, and ultimately the quality of the site on which trees grow.

The appearance of strains or varieties hasn't helped taxonomists and budding foresters recognize Douglas-fir. The trees on the Pacific slope more typically exhibit yellow-green foliage, in contrast to the Rocky Mountain variety aforementioned. Rocky Mountain Douglas-fir trees are also smaller and have smaller cones, and on those cones are smaller bracts that are reflex, in contrast to the straight bracts and larger-size cones and trees in the forests of the Pacific Northwest.

European authorities haven't helped to clear up the semantics. They've widely transplanted the tree and, in doing so, have given it three names, including big cone spruce. Big cone spruce isn't really a spruce: taxonomists place it in the same genus as Douglas-fir.

If the reader has patiently borne, till now, this taxonomic narrative, he or she may rest. It is recorded here principally to show the "confusion worse confounded" to which so important a tree may be subjected. Indeed a tree of little value and of minor range would not likely be entitled to such study and concern.

Reforest-and-Stay-Put

Pseudotsuga menziesii was the principal reason lumbermen moved west from the Lake States at the time of the cut-out-and-get-out policies of the wood-using industry there. That mass migration of men, mules, and machinery took place about the turn of the century. At that time, other bulls-of-the-woods moved south, many with their ox teams, to ride herd on the loggers, there called flatheads, and to exploit the southern forests.

But it was the Douglas-fir that attracted men and money to the Pacific Northwest and the Inland Empire. By the mid-1920s, lumber cut from trees of the coastal forests of the Pacific slopes surpassed that milled from all of the woods of the nation's southlands.

While southern forests were almost totally harvested by the mid-1930s, the virgin stands of the Inland Empire and western Oregon and Washington were yet plentiful. So tempting was the call westward that lumbermen, some well aware of the potential for natural regeneration of southern pines in the red clay hills and sandy terraces of the South, nevertheless cashed in—for as little as two dollars per acre—in order to invest those dollars on land and stumpage in the region of the Douglas-fir.

Discovery of plywood manufacturing techniques, development of the cooperative mill—in which laborers and only laborers own stock—and the use of the species for pulping were unique incentives that drew men west to work the woods. Lumber, timbers, pilings, railroad ties, cooperage for barrel manufacturing, mine props, boats, and planing-mill products (like doors, window sashes, and cupboards) were other products to stimulate the economy in a depression-torn time and place.

Harvesting the virgin forests continued unabated and with little concern for future wood supplies until the mid-1940s. By then, planning for sustained yields on these lands had become important, for there were few other places one would be able to go when loggers had cut-out-and-got-out here.

No greater chapter has been written in the annals of conservation history than that recorded for the tall trees and tough men of the area. Industry and government teamed to learn how to regenerate new forests even while much of the virgin yet remained. Some of the most intensive management practices in the world, such as fertilizing seedlings with specially designed slowly dissolving pellets, balloon and helicopter logging so as to avoid scarring the soil and causing erosion, and the selection of genetically superior strains from which to collect seeds for future forests are being tested while an abundance of wood is still available.

When Clearcutting Is Not Evil

Intensive management in this locale and for this species requires clearcutting the forests. If selection harvests are made, the world's most important timber species is replaced, not with its own kind, but with trees of lesser value. These may be stems of western redcedar or western hemlock which, able to seed-in and get established under the canopy of the Douglas-fir, take control of the site when released. Douglas-fir, being less tolerant of shade, even its own, is unable to continue as a part of the forest biome. Other species that enter the forest, depending upon the density of the Douglas-fir stand, the quality of the site, the availability of seed sources, and their coordinated ranges, include Sitka spruce (famous for WW II plywood aircraft and pianos), redwood, ponderosa pine, white pine, larch, and true firs.

With control of the dense brush that promptly takes over the land following fire or logging, ecological succession then continues with Douglas-fir, proceeds through the hemlock-cedar stage, and concludes—if within its range—with silver fir as the climax type. That is the forest that here would continue *ad infinitum* if man, fire, and storm were fenced out of the woods.

On Imitating Nature

Once the openings are made, the winged seed, ripening at 2- to 3-year intervals (in some zones 6 to 7 years), will find its way to the scarified mineral soil. If seeds land in deep organic layers, drying out of the sponge-like soil may prevent germination or cause death of germinated seedlings. Seeds, produced on trees as early as age 25, may sail on the breeze for distances of ½ mile. In their first 10 years, seedlings that arise from them may grow 12 to 15 feet; in 80 years they will be ready to harvest. Volumes then likely exceed 50,000 board feet per acre, enough wood to build 10 houses for the yet unborn families of the land. That sounds like a long time, but it is only ¼ or ⅕ of the age of the trees now being cut—and these, too, began as seedlings in openings made by fire or storm. Foresters simply endeavor to imitate nature.

Ironically, while the openings are important to get seed distributed and germinated, too much sun is disastrous. Especially on south-facing slopes, sunscald and desiccation take their toll of unshaded seedlings. Often slats, shakes, or shingles are stuck in the ground on the sunny side to provide some shade. When trees are hand-planted, workers place them on the shady side of fallen logs and logging debris.

Whether the fact that stumps live long after trees are cut—although they do not sprout—has any effect upon the life and vigor of seedlings is not known. The stumps live probably because of roots grafted to residual standing trees from which they receive sustaining nutrients, carbohydrates, and water. Trees in pure, even-aged stands when young, initially have a taproot. Later laterals develop to enable trees to retain vigor under some climatically difficult situations.

When Fire Is Not Evil

The reader has no doubt read of prescribed burning as a tool in forest management. In the Douglas-fir region, it is an important technique for ridding the forest of logging slash that is a serious fire hazard if left to gradually decay. Care must be exercised lest *P. menziesii* seeds coming to rest on the organic layer of the surface soil be killed from too much heat. When that occurs, bracken fern, fireweed, and thistles take over the site. On the other hand, the persistence of needles on logging slash for more than several years may be a retardant to excessive losses from desiccation, enabling young trees to compete favorably with the herbs and shrubs that gain a hold upon the land.

When Red Alder Is Not Evil

Red alder trees are important components of forests in the Pacific Northwest. Often considered weeds, they usually enter the ecological successional picture as a result of catastrophe because they are more intolerant of shade than even Douglas-fir. These small, short-lived (60 to 80 years) trees produce seeds that spread great distances at 4-year intervals, beginning at just 10 years of age. Red alder trees sprout, but only when young.

Prior to man's intervention and his preparation of felling sites by clear-cutting, red alder trees were usually restricted to moist drainages. On other sites, Douglas-fir outlives the alder when the two species mix and where wildfires leave enough coniferous seed to replenish the land. Logging and fire together, however, reduce Douglas-fir seed availability and, consequently, red alders encroach on the conifer sites.

This is not necessarily bad: red alder has actinomycete bacteria-inhabiting nodules on its roots, similar to those of the legumes. These microscopic organisms have the ability to "fix" atmospheric nitrogen, changing it to a form available to plants. Hence, Douglas-fir may do well where red alder had been growing previously on the land. A similar response is noted when commercial nitrogen fertilizer is "fed" to young trees.

Ecological Associates

The best stands of Douglas-fir trees in the Pacific Northwest are found in deep, rich, well-drained porous loam soils. Occasionally inferior stands occur on loose volcanic-derived soils. Those are warm and dry sites. In the far west, stands occur at elevations ranging from sea level to 5,000 feet, while in the Rocky Mountains, the typical site is at about the 10,000-foot elevation and, in contrast to the far west, in relatively arid situations. There it is in association with ponderosa pine.

On coarse-textured soil—gravels, sands, and disintegrating pumice—Pacific madrone, a short, broad-leafed tree, accompanies Douglas-fir. In California, tanoak is a common associate. On well-drained sterile sites, white pine may have the honor; while on newly formed alluvial soil along river courses, it may be black cottonwood. Many of these better sites likely will be cleared for food crops (apples and potatoes are examples) rather than continued as forests for the future.

We have mentioned, in passing, the economic importance of these forests. Perhaps ⅕ of America's total commercial harvest comes from them. Stems are often 180 to 250 feet tall (385 feet is the tallest recorded, though possibly a myth), 4 to 6 feet in diameter (8 to 10 feet is not uncommon, the maximum is 15 feet), and 700 years of age (1,375 years is the oldest known). While what the forester calls financial maturity will prevent us from waiting so long for trees to grow to such sizes in second-growth stands, it is comforting to know that the wood for which man once moved west will, likely for the life of man, move east to fulfill the fiber needs of a strong nation and its ever-striving people.

🌲 🌲 🌲   Projects for the Amateur Naturalist

1. The dynamic forest. See how long it takes for trees to seed-in on a field after abandonment by a farmer, on a road or roadside following abandonment, or following a timber harvest. Chart the time, the kinds of trees, and their growth rate.

2. Fire history of a forest is written in the stumps of felled trees. Find some stumps in a forest or urban development and look for decay, discoloration, or crystalline sap that runs with the annual growth ring and around, what was at the time of the fire, the outer edge of the tree. Date the time of burning by counting rings until, and since, the fire(s) occurred (see Figure 2–1).

3. Control pollinate a tree for seed production. Place clear plastic bags tightly over separate male and female flowers. Obviously, this must be for trees with imperfect flowers (that is, male and female flower parts not in the same

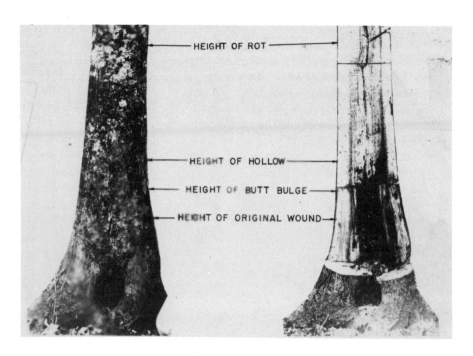

FIGURE 2–1. The wound, probably caused by fire and subsequently used by wildlife and infected with disease, affects the wood far from the entry point (USDA Forest Service photo).

FIGURE 2–2. Male pollen-disseminating catkins (left) and bagged female strobili of a southern pine.

organ). Bagging must precede the ripening of flowers. After pollen has been released from the staminate (male) flowers and collected in the bag, a sample is removed and carefully inserted (best by a syringe or hypodermic needle) into the bag over the pistillate (female) flower. The pollen dust should make contact with the pistil. It should then germinate and fertilize the egg (ovary) in the flower (see Figure 2–2).

3

Dwarf and Giant
Longleaf Pine

Among the finest stands of southern pines found by early lumbermen were those of longleaf, the hard yellow pine that, until the mid-twentieth century and for over a century, enjoyed a world-wide reputation. Strong, even grained and durable, the straight, clear stems could be hewn into square cants that were oxen-logged to water and floated down rivers to every Gulf and southern Atlantic port for shipment to destinations throughout Europe. Exporting all-heart timbers 12″ × 12″ × 80′ to European ports as far away as Greece for shipmasts, many a Gulf Coast producer could boldly proclaim on his letterhead: "longleaf pine structural timbers for the world market." Although little of this strong, hard, stiff wood is now going abroad, today's silvicultural knowledge makes possible regenerating forests that, in a decade or two, could recapture the status of *Pinus extraordinarius*.

Extraordinarius is not the species' Latin name, it's true, but it should have been. Indeed it was misnamed *palustris*, meaning swamp, probably because an early botanist noted some poor stands in the spring on poorly drained sites covered with water perched on the clay hardpan not far below the surface of the soil. During most of the growing season these, too, are dry soils—so droughty in fact that scrub oaks compete with the longleaf pine to the latter's exclusion. The most favorable site for *P. palustris* is not the swamp but, rather, the high and dry sandy hills that gave rise to "hill pine" as one of its thirty or so common appellations.

It's on these hills—perhaps just a foot or so above the surrounding flats —that quality longleaf pine can be grown for the use and pleasure of generations to come. Pleasure, too, for, to many a woodsman, no other tree in the forest has the majestic form, the tall gently tapering stem, the long graceful needles

A stand of pole-size, second-growth longleaf pine, established as a result of fencing against cattle-grazing and hog-rooting damage, and prescribed-burned for brown-spot disease control. Note the saplings, the same age as the larger trees (Georgia Forestry Commission photo).

at the ends of twigs dancing lightly to the cadence of the slightest breeze, and the open park-like canopy that's home to quail and turkey.

Books could be filled with the story of those magnificent longleaf pine forests, products of centuries of growth and the enterprise that converted them to timber for the old world, housing for the new, and naval stores for the wooden ships of two continents. With the earliest colonists came instructions for extracting pitch and rosin from wood by stacking "fat" pine in great domed piles, covering these with earth, and roasting the wood with carefully controlled fire. From the earliest days these naval stores were key exports from the southern colonies. Now sulfuric acid sprayed on "faces" stimulates the flow of gum that is collected in plastic cups at the bases of living longleaf pine trees. And Savannah still sets world prices for these products.

As water-powered and, eventually, steam-driven sawmills replaced the broadax and the manual pit saw, longleaf pine continued to be the lumberman's first choice. Even more so, the industry spread across the South to supply export demands and the housing needs of a growing nation. Limited at first to local requirements, the domestic industry burgeoned as railroads opened markets in the growing Northeast and Middlewest. Often building its own railroads as it moved, the industry marched across the South to tap the westernmost stands of longleaf pine in Texas before 1900. Although other pines were utilized when longleaf became scarce, the virgin forests of this species continued to produce lumber and timbers that set standards of excellence that had no equal among the world's tree species. But by 1940, the original longleaf pine forests existed only in memory.

The Grass Stage

Among the unique characteristics of this tree is a temporary nanism, or dwarfing, in a grass-like stage. So like grass are these ground-hugging tufts of needles surrounding the bud at the soil surface that the inexperienced may mistake the little trees for a stiff-bladed bunch grass. The short-shoot habit of growth in the seedling years has been attributed to competition by plants (including other longleaf pines) for moisture and perhaps nutrients. It has also been attributed to an inherent seedling trait under rigid genetic control and to an auxin, or plant hormone, produced in buds during early stages of development. All are no doubt valid reasons for the grass stage. Certainly environment influences the amount of time seedlings remain "in the grass." It may be 3 years or less, where soil moisture is adequate and plant competition negligible, to 25 years on dry, xeric sites with dense overtopping crowns of scrub oaks and ground cover of wire grass.

One old tale has it that seedlings remain in the grass stage until taproots reach moist soil horizons. But that theory won't hold water because the roots of this species reach water early. Not infrequently, taproots are a foot deep and lateral roots may number fifty within the first year of life—both in the presence and absence of vegetative competition. Controlling competition by hoeing out excess seedlings and deadening useless brush, however, does encourage height growth. A rule of thumb is that the trees begin height growth when the dwarfed stem has swelled to an inch in diameter at the root-collar, and not before. And when that ground-line size is attained, height growth exceeds 3 or 4 feet a year.

So in a region where forest floors are swept by fires nearly every winter, longleaf pine alone protects itself by clinging to the ground during those early years when most vegetation is so vulnerable to fire damage. Then, well-rooted and with ample food reserves, it spurts upward, not as a slender, thin-barked shoot, but as a thick stem surrounded by bark and a dense, continuous array of long needles. Not completely fireproof, it is true, but so nearly so that thousands of seedlings survive fires during the first few years of height growth. After the stems are 10 to 15 feet tall, they become the nearest thing in nature to an "asbestos tree," able to survive with few adverse effects all but the most severe fires.

How does longleaf pine achieve this near miracle of a sudden burst of height growth after years of no elongation? The question has had serious study by plant physiologists and by foresters who, unable to insure the young seedlings continuous protection from fire, would be happy if this delay in growth could be dispensed with. Dry weather, poor soil, and competition by other plants may extend the grass stage to 20 years. So can defoliation by fire or disease. Give the tree plenty of room, good soil, and enough moisture, and you may cut it to 3 years. But eliminate it you cannot, for it is as much a part of the genetic makeup of longleaf pine as are its long needles, its huge cones, and its tall, clean stems.

Growing Straight and Tall

Having developed a monopoly on sites that are burned frequently, *P. palustris* could afford an intolerance of competition beyond that of any other southern pine. As young trees rarely survive beneath the shade of their parents, seedling and sapling stands are often pocked with openings where the competition for moisture and perhaps nutrients by seed trees excluded their offspring. In developing stands, advantage lies with the tallest trees. Most of those that do not keep pace die from suppression. While crowns of dominants rarely touch, their lower limbs die and drop off, mainly because of shade cast by the foliage of their own upper crowns. Primarily dependent for growth upon photosynthesis in needles exposed to full sunlight, longleaf pine is designed from top to bottom to expose its foliage and to discard the parts of its crown that can no longer serve usefully.

An efficient producer of cellulose in pure stands, longleaf pine has a handicap when in competition with other species in the mixed forest. This extreme intolerance of competition is sometimes a problem to foresters, but it also accounts for much of the excellent quality of longleaf pine. Leaving the grass stage with a rush, the stem is thick and stiff enough to avoid most deforming accidents of early youth. Strongly phototropic, the main shoots grow straight toward the zenith in their vital struggle to keep a place in the sun. Usually too far south for the ice loads that disfigure more northerly pines, and rarely deformed by competing species, the trees retain the slim straight figure that makes them valuable for timbers, lumber, poles, and piling. And as they grow, their intolerance promptly prunes off the physiologically inactive lower branches, leaving the clear trunks that delight artist and lumberman.

A Needle Blight

A disease, too, keeps longleaf pine in the grass stage. Brownspot needle blight, caused by a fungus present in most soils, infects the needles near the ground. The straw-yellow spots of diseased tissue, turning brown and running together, eventually kill the needle. Three successive annual defoliations are necessary to kill seedlings, but infection of half of the needles may severely retard growth. Bordeaux mixture is an effective fungicide, but the low price of wood prohibits its use. So foresters turn to fire.

Until they understood this disease, foresters in their solicitude for seemingly vulnerable seedlings sometimes aggravated the disease by eliminating fires. Eventually they learned that with fire protection the disease spreads, seedlings stagnate, and many are lost. Controlled fires, however, were found to have salutary effects, destroying spores along with infected foliage and freeing the new needle growth from major infection for a couple of years. Two controlled burns, two years apart, are usually sufficient to launch a generation of seedlings into the sapling stage of rapid height growth.

Prescribed fire, carefully controlled and bounded by plowed firelines, is the order of the day—or night. One prescription may call for ignition at 3 o'clock on a winter afternoon when the temperature is about 50°F, the relative humidity is above 50 percent, no more than two days have lapsed since a rain of ½ inch or more, the wind is steady and out of the north at 6 to 10 miles per hour, and the fuel moisture is at 10 percent. So precise is a properly prescribed fire that a Bull Durham cigarette paper wrapped around the bud of a seedling is not even charred, yet all the needles will be consumed to within a couple of inches of that bud. That ring of needle stubs around the bud affords insulation.

True, the ends of the needles are blackened or burned away, but, like the astronauts' reentry shield, they help absorb the heat and provide protection during the few seconds it takes the fire to pass over. Cool fires, running with the wind, are needed to do this trick. Slow-moving fires, those pushed against the wind, build up temperatures lethal to bud and cambium as well as to needles.

Needles alone are expendable. From the bud, new ones promptly sprout to form lush-appearing vigorous foliage to manufacture carbohydrates by photosynthesis.

So ages before fire fighters learned to wait out hot spots with their faces to the ground, this tree was taking advantage of the fact that heat rises.

There is a paradox: prescribed fire, a tool of management, has laid bare the soil, allowing reinfection with spores carried by rain splash. That is why sometimes two burns to reduce the disease may be necessary to assure a healthy, well-stocked longleaf pine forest.

Predator Pests

Animals also retard establishment of quality stands. Town ants (unfortunately, as far as this author is concerned, they're also called *Texas* leaf-cutting ants) clip needles, dragging them to their underground colonies, or "town" nests, to be chewed into bits and inoculated with a fungus that lives upon the needles. The fungus "garden," a pure culture, is apparently the only food of *Atta texana* (that name again).

Piney-woods rooters, progeny of once-domesticated pigs, consume seedling roots in their quest for concentrations of starch. The food reserves of grass-stage seedlings, stored mainly as starch in the thickened taproot and as nutritious as a parsnip, provide a longleaf lunchroom for these razorback hogs when acorns are scarce. Lean and long-snouted, they visit these conifer cafeterias only after oak mast is gone from the lowlands. One big old boar is reported to have pulled from the ground 800 grass-stage seedlings in a 10-hour day. Another report tells of destruction of 6 per minute. Many of these hungry hooligans working overtime could soon alter a plan for the land. (Some foresters, it is said, entice the country sheriff to deputize the best-known hog thief to round up stock on longleaf pine lands to be regenerated. When the word is out, via banner headlines in the rural weekly, hopefully owners will trap and claim their own.) Southern woodsmen are not overly skeptical that, fried down, a razorback will "yield a pound of lard and a gallon of turpentine."

Cattle, too, must be corralled lest trampling during grazing of these "multiple-use" lands destroy seedlings. But how does one corral pocket gophers, those soil-burrowing vegetarian rodents that resemble stout mice and have strong claws for digging. Making extensive soil tunnels in their search for starch and the resinous flavor of pine roots, they may consume—from the bottom up—50 percent of the seedlings in a new forest. One "family" has "thrown out" (wasted them, didn't even eat them!) over 200 on an acre in a single year. And then there are the rabbits that bite off seedling tops, cotton rats that clip stems at the ground line, and pine mice that work from below in holes in the ground.

Mourning doves and rodents eat seeds, too. So also do hordes of migratory birds—robins, flickers, blackbirds, grackles, and many others. A classic example is in central Louisiana where vast clearcut longleaf pine lands remained idle for up to 50 years. No matter how seeds were disguised in attempts to reseed the land by man, the birds always found them. Not until the technique for direct-seeding was developed in the present generation were these lands put back to work. The toughest problem for foresters to solve was how to keep the birds from gorging on the valuable seed. Fish and Wildlife Service scientists discovered safe repellents and U.S. Forest Service researchers kept trying until methods for applying the chemicals were found.

To accommodate all these freeloaders takes a lot of seed. From whence does it come?

Seed for the Sowing

About once in 10 years longleaf pines produce an abundant seed crop. The weather must be just right to adjust the carbon:nitrogen ratio of primordial tissues to stimulate formation of flower buds. Then the elements must behave properly to give rise to male flowers ready to disseminate pollen and females ready to receive the pollen for fertilization of eggs in the conelets a year later. The ability to "mate" must occur within a few days. If not synchronized, empty seeds, or cones lacking in seeds, result.

Synchronization is further jeopardized because different trees are involved. Male flowers—properly called strobili for the conifers—are usually found on the lower branches and females on the upper. Thus, wind currents transport the fine, yellow powder-like pollen to neighboring trees rather than to branches and strobili immediately above. Self-pollination, like poor synchronization, leads to hollow seeds. And there are more than 24 months in which all these and many other problems may occur; it takes that long for the primordia of flower buds to grow to mature seed.

The pollen flight may be great; on one East Texas Easter Sunday, the air was smogged with yellow dust. Fire towers were useless, and as the day was "high danger," all rolling stock was employed to scout from the ground for smoke.

In longleaf pine regeneration, the holidays are useful pegs on which to hang events: pollination at Easter, seed-fall at Thanksgiving the following year, and seed germination at Christmas a month later.

The New Forest

Long a problem species to foresters baffled by their inability to replace harvested stands, longleaf pine has in recent years revealed enough of its ecological secrets to justify vast programs for its perpetuation. As each lesson is learned, it is incorporated into systems that can now assure repeated crops of this tree of excellence.

To increase the number of seeds produced in those infrequent crop years, foresters employ a modified shelterwood harvest system. Releasing selected seed trees—those that are straight, healthy, and with a history of prolific cone production—further enhances vigor and absorption of soil nitrogen and water and allows more sunlight to penetrate the crowns. This adjusts the ratio of carbon and nitrogen in the tree's physiology and thus improves the chances for flowering. After the seed crop is assured, all but the five or six seed trees per acre are removed; these are kept for insurance in the event of later crop or stand failure. Logging scarifies the soil. Tearing up the rough—as we call the ground cover of wire grass and broom sedge in longleaf pine forests—is essential because seeds must be in contact with mineral soil in order to germinate. Disking, scalping, or prescribed burning also removes grass and herbaceous plants to expose mineral soil where logging does an inadequate job.

If the new stand of seedlings is well-distributed, loggers then harvest the seed trees. Leaving them longer than for stand establishment and insurance causes stagnation and loss of seedlings within the "magic circle." That circle has a radius of at least 55 feet. Thus, seedlings and seed trees of P. palustris are mutually exclusive.

And, for these tall timbers, the sky is the limit. While the natural range for longleaf pine is receding due to fire *exclusion*, overcutting of an earlier era, and the host of other predators outlined here, this natural resource is renewable. And foresters now know how to renew it.

🌲 🌲 🌲 Projects for the Amateur Naturalist

1. Count seedlings that germinate from seeds naturally distributed from a "wall" of forest trees. How many are in a square foot at the base of the trees in the wall, how many at 10 feet, 20 feet, and so forth, into an open field? Chart the data (see Figure 3–1).

2. Obtain a county soil survey from the Soil Conservation Service. It's free. Every county in the nation has an SCS office and most counties have a soil survey publication with the soils mapped on aerial photographs. Select from the photomaps three distinctly different soils and, in the field, dig holes to observe the reliability of the recorded descriptions.

3. Determine the site index, based upon soil characteristics, for longleaf pine using the table (see Table 3–1) developed by a Duke University professor and his students. Tables like this come in handy where no trees are on the land, as on abandoned farm land.

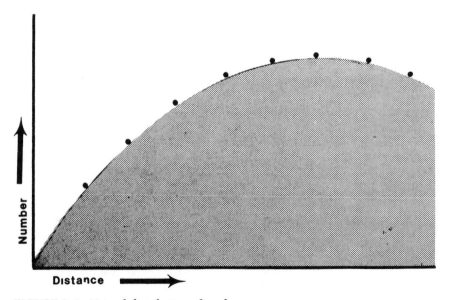

FIGURE 3–1. Natural distribution of seeds.

TABLE 3–1. Site Index

Subsoil characteristics	Depth to mottling		
Texture	Inches		
	18	30	48
		Site index	
Sand	59	62	67
Loamy sand	60	63	69
Sandy loam	62	66	71
Sandy clay loam	64	68	74
Sandy clay	67	70	76
Light clay	69	72	78
Heavy clay	71	74	81

4

Tall Timbers
Coast Redwood

*I*nconsistent as it may seem, coast redwood is both one of the largest living things and, botanically, one of the most primitive of trees. To those who cherish the letter of Darwinian theory, this leaves a lot of questions to ponder. Solutions are not evident.

Redwoods are of ancient lineage; as many as forty fossil forms have been catalogued. They are also the tallest trees. Stems 200 to 260 feet are not uncommon and a tree 368 feet tall perhaps holds the record.

Coast redwoods are old, too, but they are far from the oldest living things. Both a cousin, bigtree, and bristlecone pine have greater tenure. Trees aged 400 to 1,800 years are old, in contrast to 3,000 for bigtrees and 6,000 years (according to one account) for bristlecone pines—all three being residents of California (which makes their bigness difficult for a Texan to write about). As a rule of thumb, old trees in virgin forests are 80 years old for each foot in diameter: 12-foot-diameter stems have held on for 1,000 years.

Sequoias Are Not All Redwoods

Ages of redwoods in the written accounts are often exaggerated. In the oral accounts this may be attributed to the confusion in the minds of many between redwoods and bigtrees. The confusion was most pronounced at the time, in the late 1960s and again in the late 1970s, of the discussions on the establishment and enlargement of the Redwoods National Park. Beyond the locale involved, most folks thought the argument was whether or not to save the bigtrees, since both belong to the genus *Sequoia* and both are large trees.

Sequoia sempervirens, our present concern, grows at sea level in a fog belt along 450 miles of the northwestern California coast, extending inland only

An old-growth coast redwood stand in the California fog belt (USDA Forest Service photo).

25 miles. Its maximum elevation is about 2,000 feet. It is a commercially harvested species, stands often measuring 150,000 board feet to the acre. One stand tallied 480,000 feet (1,000 board feet is a board 1 inch thick and 1 foot wide and almost ⅕ mile long). In contrast, *Sequoia gigantea* (or you may find it catalogued *Sequoiadendron giganteum*) is found in the high Sierra Nevada

Mountains at elevations from about 5,000 to over 8,000 feet and well beyond the reach of the Japanese currents carrying the air that upon contact with the cooler land mass becomes "clouds on the ground."

That fog belt is apparently the secret to the success of S. *sempervirens*. The ground is always moist, hence effectively excluding wildfire intense enough to kill these stems while providing abundant water for sustaining such massive trees. Few of them live beyond the fog belt, the cloud being a blanket extending ordinarily to elevations of 2,000 feet and lifting daily in the summer around 10 A.M. Incidentally, fog reduces waterloss from tree needles and contains high amounts of carbon dioxide, favoring photosynthesis year round for this ever-green tree. (Although a close relative to S. *sempervirens*, which means always green, oriental metasequoia is deciduous. Landscapers plant metasequoia widely as an ornamental.) Only rarely have redwoods grown vigorously beyond their natural range in the United States: two have done well in Augusta, Georgia, and others are reported vigorous in England. I've seen fine stands more than 50 years old doing well in New Zealand and Australia.

Four Factors of Site

Foresters frequently refer to the four factors of site, those attributes that together—or sometimes singly—wholly control the growth of plants and the ecology of an area. These are climatic, physiographic, edaphic, and biotic. Redwood provides a good example of the interrelationships of these factors.

The fog, rainfall, humidity, and warm temperature that make the redwood country rather moist characterize the climatic factor. The western exposure and the position on the slopes of the Coast Range relate to the physiographic factor. The existence of these mountains is of course the reason that the air is saturated with water and that the daily fog occurs in the growing season. Were the highlands leveled, warm and cool air currents would not meet there but, rather, the dominant current would proceed eastward.

Destruction of those mountains by water erosion, rock slides, and the gradual decomposition of the rocks to form soil characterize the edaphic factor of site. Soil formation is expedited because of the heavy rains and constant dissolution of minerals in the seepage of water through the ground. Natural erosion over millennia has resulted in the formation of alluvial river bottoms of deep soil, mostly silt and clay—like miniature deltas in the broad coves of the weathered range. Were the mountains not there and the climate more moderate, the soil would most likely be coarse sands, typical of the shorelines, or less hydric clays of marine sediments geologically lifted and subsequently dried.

The biotic factor in addition to the redwood trees themselves, of course, involves competing plants—shrubs, herbs, grass, mosses, fungi, lichens, and microbial flora. All play their role in maintaining or excluding S. *sempervirens* in the moist soils of the lower western slopes of the Coast Range. Animals, too, like the elk that browse the redwood seedlings, are part of the biotic factor.

A Conifer That Sprouts

Natural provisions for maintaining redwood forests are generous, and, as a result, 90 percent of the wood in a moist alluvial "bench" will be S. *sempervirens*. The trees sprout prolifically, one of the few conifers to do so; from these sprouts arise new forests following catastrophic storms or the rare fire. Half of all redwood trees are probably of sprout origin.

Twenty-year old sprouts often reach 50 feet in height and 8 inches in diameter at breast height (dbh). In 50 years they are merchantable for lumber and plywood. It is a tree moderately tolerant of shade and, if suppressed, will recover and grow well when released.

Sprouting is not the only way to begin a new forest. Seeds are produced abundantly and annually. Unfortunately, however, the percentage of sterile seeds is high, often exceeding two-thirds of the crop. Low germination percentages probably reflect the polyploid genetic nature of the species. Polyploids—in contrast to typical diploid reproductive cell character—contain duplicate chromosomes that often are related to vegetative propagation or asexual success and sexual infertility.

Once the forest begins to grow—from seeds or sprouts—growth is rapid. Terminal shoots extend 2 to 6 feet each year. Soon the bark thickens so that mature trees are well insulated from the heat of a wildfire, should dry weather occur and a holocaust result. Hot fires do, on occasion, cause large cavities called goosepens at the base of trees. Fires of light intensity, however, do little injury to redwood trees—once they are beyond the sapling stage—but, rather, aid in controlling weed plants that compete for the limited sunlight reaching through the canopy of the rain forest.

Light burning also effectively reduces the thick litter layer on the forest floor that must be removed if the seeds that fall later are to germinate. That organic layer, often ½-foot thick, precludes the establishment of new forests because the one-third of the seeds that are viable must come in contact with mineral soil if they are to sprout.

The roots that form are deep and wide-spreading. That and the buttressing of the trunk are especially useful in providing stability for these tall timbers that, one would suppose, would be so easily toppled in the wind. And, too, the irregular, short, conical crown, a very unattractive top for so majestic a bole, doesn't get in the way of more wind than necessary. The branches with their foliage do not function like a sail.

The Shortest Distance Is Up and Down

Rough windstorms are not common in this mild climate. Yet redwood forests often appear like giant matchsticks carelessly dumped from their box, crisscrossed in haphazard fashion on the natural landscape. The ground appears this way because over the centuries trees have toppled here and there as the centers of gravity for individual stems shift slightly. And because the wood of these trees is resistant to rot and decay, they accumulate. That typical character of the woods will make some kinds of recreation in the new Redwoods National Park a difficult chore. Hiking paths will need to be cut like stairs into the prostrate trunks. Up and down, up and down will go the hiker, not to mention the laborer whose assignment is to build and maintain the trails.

Why not go around the trees? That would add miles to a hike, for, in one measured case, it was 205 feet (almost ½₀ mile) from the base to a place where a fallen tree had to be cut to reopen a road. At that point, the tree was 16 inches in diameter. Three-hundred-foot trees have diameters of 8 to 12 feet, and a diameter of 20 feet is on record for a tree 364 feet tall. That trunk has enough wood in it to build 50 five-room frame houses.

Wood of Redwood

The fact that the trees resist rotting is the asset that makes them a demand item in the lumber markets of the world. Caskets, coffins, cigar boxes, boats, shingles, flumes, and pipes (aqueducts, that is) are fashioned from the heart-wood. Redwood is sold in southeastern markets for house siding, in competition, price-wise, with southern pine. If not painted, the wood will bleach on western exposures and mildew on the east side. The defacing mildews are easily controlled with fungicides mixed with the staining preparations. Softer than yellow pine, redwood is subject to erosion of the grain by water and wind-borne sand when used for exterior siding.

Second-growth trees, unhappily, produce wood that is considerably less durable when in contact with the soil and subjected to the elements. However, second-growth trees, happily, have both harder and stronger fiber than that of old-growth, virgin timber. That is an encouragement for the perpetuation of those forests not now in the National Park, the several state parks, and the many memorial groves. (Of the latter, philanthropists have contributed considerable acreages for their establishment. Through the memorial groves winds the Ancient Redwood Highway, the Avenue of the Giants, en route from San Francisco to Portland.)

Without that incentive for the forester to manage lands that produce tough wood, western hemlock would take over and replace the redwoods. Hemlock, much more tolerant of shade, perpetuates itself under its own canopy—sometimes to become the climax forest. Western hemlock, however, is often considered an inferior tree for wood products. I say often, for not to qualify the comment angers suppliers of this wood to the markets of the West.

Tribute to the Chief

Redwood forests are also encroached upon by Douglas-fir, Sitka spruce, grand fir, tanoak, and madrone. It depends on the strength of the influence of the factors of site as to which will likely succeed in capturing the land from the chief of the forest, Sequoia.

Another Chief Sequoyah lost his land in an invasion almost as subtle as

The way they once were: a redwood tree with a stump diameter of 14 feet which scaled 15,000 board feet (USDA Forest Service photo).

the encroachment of trees and shrubs in the wilderness. He was the talented Cherokee half-breed who developed an alphabet for his people of the Appalachian Highlands. Their land was claimed by others. In his honor the botanical genus in which we find the redwood has been named.

🌲 🌲 🌲 Projects for the Amateur Naturalist

1. Using a diameter tape and hypsometer, measure diameter, breast height (dbh), and total height of trees.

2. A tape and a hypsometer may be constructed as follows:
   a. Tape—using a tailor's tape measure, mark off with contrasting ink every 3.14 inches. These points on the tape equate to inches in diameter of a circle. Hence, a tree 30 inches in circumference is 9.5 inches in diameter [c = 2πr]. Foresters measure diameter at 4½ feet from the ground, called breast height.
   b. Hypsometer—A Merrit hypsometer may be made from a yardstick or piece of lath, marking the stick at 3.79-inch intervals, each interval denoting 10 feet of tree height. The hypsometer is used as in Figure 4–1. (Theoretically the 66-foot distance is along line Z.)

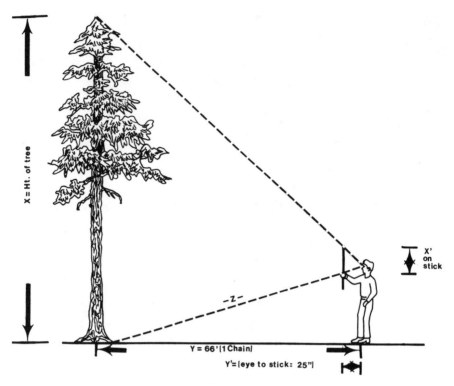

X = Ht. of tree

X' on stick

Y = 66' (1 Chain)

Y' = (eye to stick: 25")

-z-

FIGURE 4–1. Using a Merrit hypsometer.

3. Count pollen. Mount a clear sheet of sticky plastic on a dark surface 1 × 1-foot square. Place in the open during pollen dissemination. Then sample the surface, perhaps 1 square inch or 0.1 square inch, using a hand lens or a microscope to count the grains.

5

Murky Bottom and Droughty Land

Loblolly Pine

Great forests of large loblolly pines, laced with fingers of broadleaf hardwoods astride the rivers, faced the hardy English subjects as they stepped from settlers' boats. The shores of future cities like Charleston and Savannah, later to be hewn from those forests, mark the sites of these debarkations. For those landings the years were 1608 and 1733, respectively.

The trees were of course unnamed when first observed by white men. Shortly they would be called loblolly, an American dialect word for mudhole, for the sites in which they grew appeared as murky as the thick gruel the pioneering travelers ate on the wooden vessels of the sea. The porridge was called loblolly in old England.

Game and other wildlife scampered, sang, and chirped in these woods. Red-cockaded woodpeckers made their homes there, as they do now, in hollows of those living pines with soft, spongy interiors. The fibrous core is caused by a fungus; the resulting decay is termed red heartrot. Ornithologists say the red-cockaded is the only woodpecker to carve its nesting lodges in living trees. As the Fish and Wildlife Service lists the bird as endangered, foresters labor diligently to protect disease-ridden trees so the bird will have a home.

Here in these southern woods, too, was the ivory-billed woodpecker, probably now extinct except for the possible survival of a few pairs in the mountains of Cuba. The New World forest into which the explorers roamed provided the vast acreages of pines and hardwoods required to support a pair of these birds. The largest of North American woodpeckers, ivory-bills demand vast tracts never disturbed by man for their far-ranging ventures.

Early explorers of these southern forests included William Bartram, son of the British king's royal botanist, John Bartram. The year of 1773 saw Bartram's departure by horse from Charleston's coast, exchange of his mount for a canoe,

A superior loblolly pine selected for breeding. Note its straightness, self-pruning habit, and dominance over other trees the same age (USDA Forest Service photo).

and his plodding on foot to tally the vegetation of the Crown's colony. "This World," he wrote in a doxology of praise, "as a glorious apartment of the boundless palace of the Sovereign Creator, [exhibits no] more glorious display of the Almighty Hand."

The "display" that attracted the naturalist's attention included loblolly pine, the tall timbers in the gruel. Along with the wetlands, he encountered infertile sandy soil where "dissolved vegetables," the organic matter mixed in the fine white sand, served "as a nursery bed to hatch . . . the infant" pines. The gray sticky subsoil gave rise, according to Bartram's account, to a "vast growth of timbers." These higher, drier lands were also clothed with loblolly pine (*Pinus taeda*).

A century would pass before someone else would take note for posterity of the forests at the western extremity of the range of loblolly pine. Until 1834, Mexicans controlled East Texas' redlands and yellow sands: few words were sent to the United States about the dry-site loblolly pine of this region.

To the west of the Texas pineries, through a transition some attribute solely to rainfall patterns, one then enters the post oak belt. In the southeastern corner of the Hill Country, interwoven with the oak lands, crowns of loblolly pines suddenly come into view. These are the "islands" of Bastrop pine, a race of drought-hardy short-boled loblolly pine so in contrast in site and form to the obelisk-like, wide-girthed stems described in the opening lines of this chapter. Locally they are called the Lost Pines.

Loblolly pine seems not to have been given a common name throughout much of its range by the time of the Civil War. In some locales, folks called it bull pine or Rosemary pine because of its giant size and the fragrance of the resinous foliage. Old journals suggest the species was erroneously named long leaf or called long straw.

Trees of the species display a rounded crown of spreading branches through which the wind makes a characteristic moan. Tight scales on the bark indicate slow growth, while loose, flakey, sloughing bark tells of rapid growth. When growth is good, expanding girth cracks the bark like a stout man's shirt pops its buttons. Some foresters refer to loblolly pine as windfirm, in spite of its lack of a deep taproot.

Indian Influences

Indians' ancient cultivated fields, ritual grounds, and deserted settlements often regenerated to loblolly pine following abandonment. But the Indians altered the forest more dramatically by fire. They burned the woods with regularity, flintstones sparking the tinder to clear the understory brush. Low-lying vegetation hid the deer, camouflaged the enemy, and obstructed travel. No doubt the overstory often went up in flames as well, the conflagrations causing drastic changes in forest cover types. Loblolly pines naturally seed-in where the mineral seed-bed lies exposed and full sunlight reaches the ground. Seeds on winged flight may travel a quarter mile, descending like a helicopter to come to rest on cleared and burned-over land.

In time hardwood climax species intrude. Lest removed by fire, man, or storm, the loblolly pines remain as sentinels over the land. Their guardianship may last for more than a century unless natural causes or lumbermen intercede. They leave the scene with lightning strikes, insects, and diseases, thereby making room for the shade-tolerant hardwoods sure to follow.

Virgin Forest and Second-Growth

In times past, thick-barked loblolly pines endured much longer than they do today. Virgin forests contained perhaps but five stems to the acre, each averaging 5 feet in diameter and each nigh unto 200 feet tall. Some survived 300 seasons in clearings made by the aborigines' fires. Though growth was slow, these few trees on an acre were protected in the open, park-like forests by the absence of adequate fuel for their destruction. Today's managed stand, in contrast, at 50 years of age may have 60 stems per acre and average 14 inches in diameter and 100 feet in height. Today trees that size are already economically mature, ripe for the logger's chain saw.

Twelve thousand board feet in an acre of old-growth compares to 6,000 feet in a forester's managed woods. Why the difference? Old-growth stands visited by armored knights and their sailing colleagues and lumbermen of 100 years past were over-mature. Growth was immeasurable, 50 to 100 years were required to add an inch or two of increment. Trees fully occupied the site. Understory hardwoods sapped the soil of its nutrients and water so that little cellulose could be added to the boles of the pines. Only as the old giants succumbed to "acts of God" could growth on neighboring trees be accelerated.

Rarely will a loblolly pine stand contain trees from cotyledon-leaf seedling-size to aged monarchs. At first, species composition changes little, the pine invading the old-field, clearcut, or burned-over land. Though many pioneer stems gradually pass out of the stand, some loblolly pine individuals maintain dominance from seedling through sapling stages and on to poles, standards, and mature timber. Meanwhile new seedlings of shade-tolerant hardwoods invade and eventually replace old shade-intolerant pines. Only as the last of the pines die do the climax broadleaf trees seem to suddenly and fully fill the canopy.

Clearcutting Is Good Ecology

Loblolly pine is usually managed in even-aged stands, using seed-tree or clear-cutting methods to regenerate the forest. If the number of seeds is inadequate for natural regeneration, foresters often sow seeds from the air or with farm-type implements. These seeds, collected from ripe cones, are treated to repel rodents and birds.

When seeds are ready to fall or before beginning to direct-seed a site, seed germination and seedling survival are encouraged by scraping or burning the land. Or the site is furrowed with a plow. Anything that scarifies the soil will enhance the catch, sometimes enabling the establishment of 25,000 seedlings on an acre. Crops of seeds may exceed a million per acre; indeed that many may be required to restock the land where the site has not been prepared by scalping or fire.

Some folks confuse clearcutting with the lumberman's high-grading in the virgin forests. High-graders felled the biggest and best trees. Later loggers returned to again remove the finest stems. Often a third cut followed. By then only the least desirable trees remained for producing the progeny to fill the openings in the woods. Genetically inferior forests obviously resulted.

Patiently foresters today search for the finest individuals in the woods. From them the fine, powdery, yellow male sperm grains are collected in plastic bags. This "super-tree" pollen is then injected into plastic coverings surrounding the female flowers of other high-quality trees. Artificial pollination thus develops new families. After several generations, the wood-using industry counts on having trees superior to those harvested by pioneering lumbermen.

Early American lumbermen gave no thought to reproducing the forest. They really considered it impossible; no new merchantable forest would ever grow again where the harvest had been so complete. They were wrong, of course. But their error was not, as often alleged, because they were so selfish as to have no concern for the future. Rather, it was because they did not know how to regenerate the species.

Clearcutting, in contrast to high-grading, imitates nature. Just as storms of hurricane force or hot fires pass over the land to expose the mineral soil and to enable the ground to receive full sunlight, total tree harvests do the same. In either event, nature's methods or the logger's enterprise, a new forest of pioneer species follows, provided there is a source of seeds. Clearcutting, unlike high-grading, anticipates regeneration of the forest. It is a legitimate silvicultural system, a method brought from France and Germany by America's first foresters.

Phenology

Since many trees proceed from flower to seed within a few months, the long process for loblolly and some other southern pines rates comment. In North Carolina, for instance, female flower buds form in September, influenced by the tree's nutrition and position in the forest (open grown or tightly knit). Flowers of both sexes develop the following March, though frost may have an inhibiting effect. Males occur low in the trees' branches, females high, so that wind as well as gravity influences pollination. Pollen falling by gravity from male flowers to pollinate female flowers on the same tree tends to result in hollow, sterile seeds. Wind, in contrast, carries male sperm-producing spores from one tree to the flowers of another, effectively crossing genetic strains of the species.

Pollination occurs a month after flowers begin to appear. Prolonged rain is the major obstacle to successful distribution of the ripe powdery grains. Conelets grow between May and October, a period during which insects take a heavy toll. Then the organs lie dormant until the next spring when fertilization of the egg by the pollen disseminated a year earlier takes place. The yearling cones now grow rapidly until October. Seeds then begin to emerge from the ripened cones and throughout the winter fall from the opened "burrs." Many seeds come to rest on grass and leaves, there to supply feed for birds, rodents, and insects. Those that fall on proper seedbeds send down roots and push up little seed needles, called cotyledons, in the spring of the year.

Patterns of growth through the seasons of the year tell of a tree's phenologic characteristics. As we have noted how seeds develop, we now consider shoot growth.

As a rule of thumb, loblolly pines break dormancy in late February to early April, depending upon latitude. Growth usually ceases in October, yet dormancy may be but only for a few days in the winter.

Photoperiod, the botanist's term for day length, usually accounts for beginning and ending of dormancy in the fall and spring. As the growing season progresses, tree growth slows. This need not be related to photoperiodicity, but could be caused by the depletion of growth-promoting substances, or growth-inhibitor accumulation. Even when abundant water enables continuous growth, trees seem to take short intermissions to rest, then to begin anew with a fresh spurt. New terminal shoots, exhibiting vigorous flushes of branch and top elongation, may under favorable weather conditions be put out as late as mid-November.

Unlike uninodal pines (white pines, for instance, put out one flush of growth or whorl of branches each year), loblolly pine is multinodal. In one case, seven flushes of growth took place in a season. Each flush produces a circle of branches; and each succeeding one for the year grows a little shorter than the one just preceding. With experience, the observer simply counts the number of the large whorls that precede a long flush on a tree's bole to determine its age.

Habitat

Loblolly pines prefer the more moist sites, attaining maximum growth on poorly drained clay and clay loam soils. The species is often vigorous at the edge of swamps. Yet it often inhabits dry uplands, sandy hills, and rocky outcrops. Old-fields abandoned from agriculture provide ideal seedbeds for reforestation.

Three criteria limit natural regeneration of the trees. First, seeds from parent stems are required. Feather-like wings carry seeds great distances. Second, they must come in contact, upon falling, with bare mineral soil. Grass, pine needles, or leaves covering the land hinder germination. The small seeds store too little starch and nutrients to provide adequate sustenance for a root that must grow through dry leaves and grass to the mineral soil. Finally, full sunlight enables carbohydrate production and growth to commence. Some seeds germinate under canopies of brush and large trees, and some seedlings even appear where grass or debris cover the ground, the seeds somehow falling in crevices that allow contact with mineral soil. But within a few years these seedlings die unless released from the shade of overtopping foliage.

While loblolly pine competes unsuccessfully with shade-tolerant hard-wood trees, it has replaced longleaf pine throughout much of the lower Coastal Plain because of its relative tolerance to drought in the deep sands in which the latter species previously was dominant. While fire at just the right time provides an assist for regenerating longleaf pines, fire at the wrong time prevents stands from regenerating (Chapter 3). Then longleaf pine fades from the scene and loblolly pines take over the land. The latter species has greater tolerance for uncontrolled fire throughout most of its life and less sensitivity to the timing of wildfire.

Four distinctly different climatic conditions prevail within the natural range of loblolly pine: East Coast, central Florida (though the tree is not abundant there), mid-continent of Arkansas and East Texas, and the Lost Pine zone of east-central Texas. Inadequate winter rains in Florida and low late-summer rainfall in Texas cause poor survival of new seedlings in the respective regions. High summer rainfall along the Carolina and Georgia coasts encourages ready reforestation. In the Lost Pines situation, where loblolly pines presently occur at appreciable distances from the principal habitat zone for the tree, drought hardiness appears inherited. There annual rainfall amounts to about one-half of that of the Atlantic Coast.

Yet, the Lost Pines survive as a forest because of the rocky, non-agricultural land on which they grow. Survival under droughty conditions there, where some 30 inches of rain falls each year, also may be associated with the friable clay subsoil lying not far below the surface. That water-holding horizon probably provides available moisture for plant growth equivalent to twice this much rain falling on deep sandy soils of the loblolly pine forests to the east.

To the east of the Lost Pines is the Big Thicket, a moist jungle of a myriad of broadleaf species in which loblolly pines pierce the sky. Indians called the forbidden land the Big Woods. Impenetrable, and thus the residence of outlaws, pioneers learned about it after crossing the Sabine River at Orange, traipsing through the swamp at Blue Elbow, hiking through the strands of open-growing longleaf pine, and then encountering the briars and ty-vine that served as natural fences for the exclusion of men in the vast low swale. It is the same today. This wet, formidable land is a high-quality site for *P. taeda*. Some speak of it as virgin, though loggers have likely sawed through all of this land at least three times since 1880.

Several virgin stands of loblolly pine still speak of the past. They are all in the Southeast. Maximum ages are about 160 years. They date in some cases to white settlement, in others to disastrous fires at the time the United States government forceably moved the Cherokee Indians to Oklahoma territory. It is conceivable that the woods were ignited by federal soldiers during the roundup or by the angry Indians in retaliation and to confuse the troops. The pines then seeded in. Less severe fires have occurred periodically, holding in check the climax hardwood trees and brush that, in nature's economy, would take over the land.

The drought-tolerance of some strains of loblolly pine makes it a preferred species for land reclamation where coal and minerals have been surface-mined.

These sites, like severely eroded and abandoned agricultural lands, are often especially droughty. The tight soils with poor moisture retention, once well below the surface, now lie at the surface and form the root zone. Rainwater rolls off of the site as runoff; little water infiltrates into the surface of these compact strata now at the surface.

Many of the loblolly pine forests in the Piedmont province—the foot of the Appalachian Mountains—in the southeastern states have replaced cotton patches, tobacco lands, and cornfields. For perhaps a hundred years farmers literally "mined" these fragile lands to grow their crops. Nothing depletes the soil like these three crops. Clean cultivation, row-cropping, and the demand for plant nutrients soon exhausted the supply of available "plant food." The erosive nature of the silts and clays, expedited by down-the-slope plowing, produced gullies in the furrows. With periodic torrential storms, raindrop impact created little Grand Canyons. Plowed-over in the next cultivation, the damage was simply hidden: the next rain, perhaps just a shower, carved the land. Discouraged farmers moved away. Those farmers cared about the loss of soil, but mules have all four legs of the same length and each man's two are of equal dimensions. Plowing on a contour by animals so created exhausts the bodies of both man and beast. It's a tough job: any means to ease the task, like plowing with the direction of the slope, gained favor.

Uses of the Trees

Pioneers drained the resin from loblolly pine trees for a variety of uses, though streaking today is confined to slash and longleaf pines. The latter two species hold to more restricted site conditions, the range of which is usually to the south of the broad zone that is the habitat of loblolly pines.

Rosin, made from the gum, was once an ointment, a preservative for ropes, an impregnating sealant for roofing paper, an ingredient of ink, and a caulk for ship-timbers. It is a by-product of turpentine distillation, called tar in olden times (hence North Carolinians are tar heels). A cord of pitch-soaked wood produced 50 gallons of "tar."

Turpentine distilled from the sap was used for lamp oil and naval stores, painted on posts as a preservative, and coated on seeds to repel birds. Strangely enough, "turps" once was given people as a laxative, painted on animal wounds, and added to lye ash in soap-making.

A hundred years ago the loblolly pines were believed to modify the atmosphere and thereby diminish the effects of malaria. Just how is not clear. I rather suppose that where loblolly pines were found on drier land, they were not considered the same as the tree found in murky bottoms where mosquitos breed. Folks of the time knew not the mal (bad) aria (air) relationship to the anopheles. They did recognize warm moist air as somehow connected to the fevers that repeatedly attacked certain individuals. So moving to the Piedmont hills from the damp coastal swamps appeared to be a remedy for malaria, even though here, too, the pines would be loblolly.

Today, the wood is usually marketed as shortleaf pine or southern yellow pine. Except for the amount of resin in the wood, telling any of the hard pines of the South apart is a difficult task. Only the most astute wood technologist ventures to distinguish between them and to identify the species from a sample of a board.

Mills now use loblolly pine for paper (mostly for brown packaging boxes called kraft and in newsprint, which is bleached kraft), for rayon fiber, for lumber, and for plywood. Plywood, first made from this species as recently as the early 1960s, presently serves the construction industry throughout much of the United States. Large quantities are sent abroad in export trade. The wood-using industries' fiber requirements make loblolly pine, the tall boles first encountered by the early settlers, the most important forest tree of the eastern and southern United States.

So, the story of loblolly pine is the story of timber use and timber abuse by often well-intentioned exploiters, the forest's restoration by man and Providence, and its future when managed by foresters or set aside for posterity to view.

🌲 🌲 🌲 Projects for the Amateur Naturalist

1. Graph on cross-section paper the relationship of diameter to height for 50 trees. Note the changing slope of the curve (see Figure 5–1).

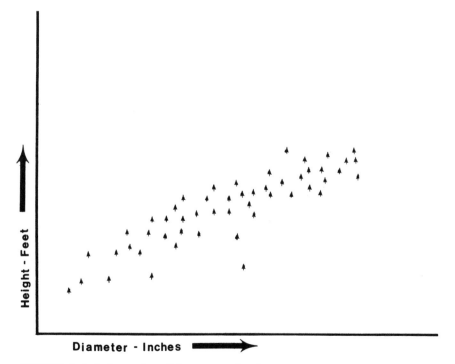

FIGURE 5–1. Relationship of diameter to height.

2. In a pine forest of any species, observe the occurrence of broadleaf trees. Are they
   a. evenly distributed in the forest,
   b. totally absent,
   c. present only in openings in the pine canopy, or
   d. present only when the pines are at certain ages? From an ecological view, why is this so? Incidentally, all of the answers could be correct.

3. Locate bird nests in or under trees and relate their occurrence to the kind of forest. For instance, red-cockaded woodpeckers nest almost exclusively in living pines with rotted cores, and sapsuckers feed in pecan orchards.

4. Phenology (change throughout the seasons). Select three trees, each of a different species. Each day, throughout a year (or at least from March to September), note changes in bud development, flower formation, seed development, seed-fall, leaf formation, autumn coloration, leaf-fall, and bud hardening for winter.
   a. Using an accurate rule or mechanic's micrometer, record and graph measurements (see Figure 5–2),

                               or
   b. Write a description of these observations,

                               or
   c. Trace plant parts to show changing phenology,

                               or
   d. Photograph plant parts, showing change with the seasons.

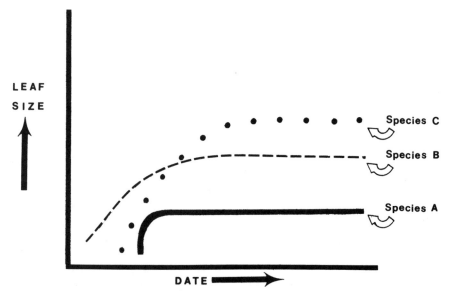

FIGURE 5–2. Changes in leaf size.

6

Ancient Wonders
Bristlecone Pine

*T*his is the story of the oldest known living things among both plants and animals. Unlike the giant sequoias in which houses are carved and through which highways run, bristlecone pines (*Pinus aristata*) are scrubby trees.

A stand of bristlecone pines rises just a few miles from Death Valley, land of the lowest rainfall in the hemisphere, averaging 2 inches each year. But what a contrast in elevations! Death Valley, almost 300 feet below sea level, is the lowest point in the hemisphere. Some 11,000 feet above sea level, less than 15 miles to the west of the valley of parching fame and desolation, are bristlecone forests. There on the summit, rain clouds from the Pacific Ocean, flying at high elevations, release moisture. Precipitation annually amounts to 8 inches, most falling as snow.

Other bristlecone pines occur high in the White Mountains of the Inyo National Forest. There, at 10,000 feet, at the north terminus of Death Valley, are trees exceeding 4,000 years in age. One is tallied at over 6,000 years; another, dead now for a thousand years, lived to witness 3,000 changes of the seasons.

Trees of the Past

Determining the ages of these sylvan Methuselahs requires increment borings. Cores of wood are extracted with a Swedish tool commonly employed by foresters to age trees and to learn rates of growth. For old stems like these, the technique is sophisticatedly called dendrochronology.

Dendrochronology, perhaps introduced by da Vinci, affords us a look at climates of the past as well as at the annual rings that tell the ages of trees. Thin rings indicate slow growth, brought about by adversaries in nature such

An ancient bristlecone pine forest, the Patriarch Grove, at the 11,000-foot elevation in California. The dead portions of the trees have been sculptured by wind, sand, ice, and fire into monuments of beauty (USDA Forest Service photo).

44

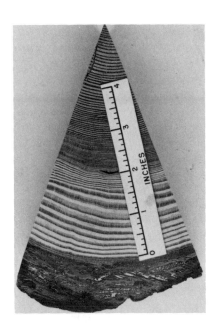

Growth rings of a cross section of a conifer. Note variation in width and the fire scar.

as drought and cold. Wide rings tell of favorable rainfall and long, warm growing seasons. Wind speed is shown by the separating of wood along the ring interface, while charred wood buried deep beneath the bark tells—as we read the rings—the years in which fires raged.

Scientist Edmund Schulman of the Laboratory of Tree Ring Research at the University of Arizona, while looking for evidence of climatic changes, was drawn to the White Mountains of east-central California. Trees found there were believed to be more drought-sensitive than bristlecones in other places in California and the five other southwestern states in which they grow. This is because storm clouds moving inland from the Pacific release water on the main thrust of the Sierra Nevada, higher mountains located on the Pacific side of the White range. The White Mountains are consequently in a "rain shadow" of relative aridity—catching about 12 inches of precipitation annually.

If vegetation persistence in low rainfall areas leads to drought sensitivity, why have the trees not died over the millennia of time? Apparently the sparse ground cover and the scanty amount of accumulating litter provide little fuel for wildfire. This is fortunate because the bark is thin and a poor insulator; while the flammable resin in the wood—though a relatively poor producer of sticky oleoresin chemicals—enhances resistance to moisture and consequent retarding of wood rotting. Further, needles persist for 20 to 30 years, in contrast to 2 to 3 for most conifers, and this assures continuing photosynthesis even during years of unusually high moisture stress.

Tree ring chronologies exceed 7,100 years. Each growth ring is assigned a calendar year in which it was formed. Cores taken in living trees have the outermost ring as a control with a known date, while wide and narrow rings, common to all radii and to different specimens, enable cross-dating among samples. Variations in weather from year to year throughout time prevent duplication of sequences of wide and narrow rings for a particular locale. Thus a tree dead 1,000 years ago, but that lived for 2,000 years, would have ring sequences of its last 1,000 years similar to those of the first 1,000 years of a living tree now 2,000 years of age. By this means, ancient beams in adobe houses found in archaeological digs may be fairly precisely catalogued as to the period in which the trees, from which they were hewn, had lived.

Cross-dating this way may pose a problem. Missing rings are associated with slow growth on dry sites, where 1,100 rings in 5 inches of radius may be normal. Such rings, when absent on only a portion of their circles, may be "found" when more than one core is taken or when the whole cross section of a stump is examined. Some trees, side by side, may exhibit variations in ring patterns.

As rings show in charcoal, which doesn't rot, dates can be fixed for trees excavated from pyroclastic flows attributed to gas deposits that excluded oxygen. Such "fired" wood results when volcanoes erupt and trees are buried in the rubble. Then falling ash that defoliates nearby trees, resulting in narrow rings, enables scientists to date seismic activity.

Archaeologists use radiocarbon dating to check on ring counts, and vice versa. C. W. Ferguson, a dendrochronologist, noted that a long-dead, single small specimen, at death about 400 years of age by ring count, is approximately 9,000 years old by Carbon-14 dating. That dead log was virtually undisturbed by disintegrating elements for a long, long time. Since the tree-ring record is for only 7,100 years, a gap of almost 2,000 years needs yet to be filled with accurate sequences of ring widths to show by dendrochronology what C^{14} *beta* disintegration has revealed.

Scientific successes have their dilemmas. Dates derived for bristlecone pine by C^{14} techniques and by actual ring counts show that at 4,000 to 3,000 B.C., material dated by *beta* disintegration counting is about 800 years too recent. Was the carbon dioxide content in the atmosphere different? Is solar energy variable? Was the climate unlike that which we have now? Or is C^{14} dating less reliable than tree-ring counting? More work with bristlecone pines hopefully will provide the answers.

Trees for the Future

P. aristata (meaning prickles, not aristocrats) generally grows in high alkaline soils derived from dolomitic limestone. The more moist north-facing slopes have denser stands and more ground cover than those of southern aspects. In much of the natural range, west slopes get a little more rain, but they also have higher temperatures to evaporate that moisture in the afternoon. Hence, older stands are most likely to be on protected northern exposures.

Many forests of bristlecone pine (also called foxtail and hickory pine) have been set aside in California and Nevada for scientific study and observation by laymen. Hopefully, these biologic antiques can endure the tampering of man as well as they have the trampling of wildlife, the competition of vegetation, the holocausts of fire, and some of the world's worst weather.

Old bristlecone trees may appear to be dead. An initial examination reveals a skeletal, light gray snag exposing fine-grained wood bleached by centuries of summer sun. Closer surveillance may find a green branch—sometimes a single one not far from the ground—that has provided sustenance for the remaining live cambial layer and the root. It has been suggested that this facility for drastically reducing the living portion of the tree is nature's way of allowing life to continue with minimal requirements. Consequently, these trees can "withstand" the bullet-like blasts of hail in winter gales and other adversities severe enough to drive life out of every other part of the tree. Finite man hopes and trusts nature's way will suffice for another seventy times seventy years.

🌲 🌲 🌲   Projects for the Amateur Naturalist

1. Determine edge effect of woodlands on trees (their growth rate, species, and so forth) and on lesser flowering plants at the edge and within the stand. (Indian paintbrush grows on the roadside in the open but not under a canopy of trees.)

2. Determine the age and rate of diameter growth for trees that have been cut—either in a harvest, a storm, or construction cleanup—by counting annual growth rings and measuring their width (in number of rings per inch).

3. Collect pine and other winged seeds of various species. Subject each to various electrical fan speeds from various distances. Record flight distances and observe whether the seeds in their flight behave as a helicopter, fixed-wing plane, or a bird.

7

Redcedar Riddle

Eastern Redcedar

Certain plants grow only in soils of specific chemical and physical nature. That is a common observation. Many plants, however, adapt themselves to a wide range of soil conditions and, once established, through their own influence, may alter the chemical as well as physical properties of the soil in which they grow. Thus, some plants increase soil acidity while others decrease it. Both eastern redcedar (*Juniperus virginiana*) and common juniper (*J. communis*) alter the pH of old-field soils. The first species raises the pH of the upper part of the mineral soil and lowers it at a depth of 6 inches, while the latter lowers the pH at both depths. Analyses show soils under redcedar often less acidic than those under certain hardwood forests.

Eastern redcedar pioneers in ecological succession. This is especially true for the Cumberland Plateau of eastern Tennessee where soils are derived from both limestone and shale. There, the species follows broomsedge and associates with a number of shrubby trees, including redbud, dogwood, hawthorns, and persimmon. Redcedar is essentially a heliophyte, requiring much sunlight. This is recognized by the thick foliage on the periphery of the crown or on the sunny side, and by the absence of foliage beneath the canopy on the shady side or when the tree grows in dense shade. Young trees are more shade-tolerant than old ones.

In rolling glades, eastern redcedar most frequently occupies south-facing slopes, leaving north-facing sites to a slightly less xeric type, such as scrub oak—black oak—hickory, or to a mesic white oak—red maple—sugar maple association. Glade communities also develop from hardwood stands as the deciduous trees pass from the overstory and the formerly suppressed redcedars receive more sunlight. Shallow soils are taken over by redcedar more quickly than are rich deep soils, as most hardwoods, particularly many oaks, demand much soil moisture to enable sustained presence on shallow soils. Hence, the deciduous species pass out early. Too, the permanent wilting-point for the soil is reached sooner in shallow than in deep soils of equivalent texture.

Eastern redcedar occurs more frequently on fine-textured soils than on those of coarse texture, possibly because of the drier nature of sandy soils. However, because of its drought hardiness, the species commonly occurs in granitic soils and rock outcrops.

The berries of redcedar provide good food for game, and the trees serve well for game cover. The abundance of redcedar along fence rows attests to its palatability for birds, particularly robins and waxwings. In an experiment with a Bohemian waxwing, 900 berries were passed through the bird in 5 hours. The origin of stands in Tennessee, Texas, and Florida have long been attributed in large part to birds, particularly migratory ones; and in the Tennessee cedar glades, robins have a winter haven. A report has it that a herd of cattle moving from the Texas cedar brakes into Kansas gave rise through manure droppings to a small stand of juniper in a treeless prairie.

Cedar Sites

It is a common belief throughout the central and southeastern states that the occurrence of eastern redcedar—really not a cedar but a juniper—is indicative of soils high in lime. In the Ozarks, *Juniperus* may become established in acid soils of low calcium content and actually bring about a decrease in acidity and an increase in calcium content of the upper soil layer as trees subsequently grow and develop. Although soils of the Ozark highlands have their genesis mainly from limestone of various degrees of purity, the surface layers at least generally analyze low in calcium and distinctly acid.

In the Piedmont, too, soils under young redcedar trees have 3 times the volume of open pores and 20 times the permeability to water of adjacent soil in the open. Further south, calcium under redcedar is twice as much as under legumes and grass in the same field. Similar distinctions occur for other *Juniperus* species in the cedar brakes of Texas and can be expected for the cedar glades in the Nashville basin of Tennessee.

Limestone soils on which the redcedar type occurs are generally shallow. These shallow soils are alkaline. Deeper soils from the same parent material have surface layers that are more severely leached and therefore acidic, while the subsoils are usually alkaline. Cedar glades in Tennessee are not restricted to limestone areas since the entire Central Basin is calcareous; but, rather, stratigraphy of rocks influences plant communities by controlling drainage. Only plants that are able to endure spring saturation and autumn droughts and that, therefore, do not compete with mesic species survive. These forests frequently occur where fires have been excluded for lack of fuel, especially on calcareous sites in which rapid decomposition of organic matter and incorporation into the mineral soil takes place because of the activity of abundant soil fauna and flora.

Eastern redcedar trees occur within the red and white pine (*Pinus resinosa* and *P. strobus*) plantations of the Northeast. Individuals, naturally seeded in,

Spire-like Rocky Mountain redcedar, truly a juniper, in the Badlands of North Dakota (USDA Forest Service photo).

grew in old-fields at the time of pine planting and have grown up with the pines. In older plantations, redcedars have nearly disappeared from the stands because of their slow growth rate and consequent overtopping by the pines. Soil conditions, aside from the redcedar influence within the pine plantations, appear fairly uniform, particularly with respect to surface litter of undecomposed needles and the humus layer just beneath.

The plantations, especially those over 35 years old, have a thick mat of pine needle litter and a thin layer of fermenting or partially decomposed material distinctly delimited from the mineral soil. Foresters note, however, that the litter and humus layers directly beneath the redcedar trees differ considerably from the prevailing condition, a difference accentuated by the fact that earthworm work is more extensive under the redcedars than under the pines. The litter layers beneath the redcedars are thinner than beneath the pines, and under the cedar organic material is mixed with the mineral soil. One notes this especially on moderately deep, well-drained, brown podzolic sandy loam soils of glaciofluvial origin.

Measurements Follow Observations

Striking differences occur in physical and chemical properties of the surface soil beneath redcedar and pines in these plantations. Such distinctions doubtless relate to the chemical composition of the tree foliage. Another graduate student and I found this some years past in a New England old-field.

Ecologists recognize three groups of tree species based on calcium content of the foliage. Eastern redcedar falls in the highest group, its mature leaves containing more than 2 percent calcium, whereas the red and white pines fall into the lowest group, with leaves containing less than 1 percent. Redcedar leaf litter, through its influence on calcium content and pH of the surface soil, either brings about or maintains favorable conditions for earthworm activity. As a secondary influence, earthworms incorporate the leaf litter in the upper 2 to 3 inches of surface soil, greatly increasing its organic-matter content. This results in lower volume-weight—like specific gravity, the relative weight of a given volume of soil, and an increase in pore volume—the amount of space taken up by air and water. Also improved are moisture-equivalent (a technique for estimating the amount of water retained one day after a soaking rain), air capacity (the volume of the soil that is neither solid nor liquid, just gas), and infiltration rate (the time it takes water to pass into the surface of the soil).

Earthworms often confine their activity to the area directly beneath the redcedar trees in these forests. In the Connecticut red pine plantation, we found no evidence of earthworms beneath the pines.

So, this ecologic riddle is resolved: the earthworm activity, created by the high calcium levels of the *Juniperus* foliage—an enticing meal for night crawlers—results in porous soil of a crumbly nature. *Lumbricus* just won't eat the nonnutritious, cellulose fibers of pine straw. The worms take into their systems both organic matter and particles of mineral soil. These are glued together by digestive juices and cast out as conglomerates the size of small peas. So rapidly does it occur that the soil will be bare under the redcedars while three inches of pine straw accumulates under adjacent pines. Consequently, the earthworm casts—the mixture of plant material and mineral particles—reduce the volume-weight of the soil. This, too, increases the pore space into which water infiltrates, enabling moisture retention for subsequent tree and worm consumption beyond the normal time such moisture would drain through pure mineral soil. For these reasons, stands of redcedar trees may have as their highest use providing cover on the land for watershed protection.

The greater volume of pore space under the redcedars means more air space, too, for oxygen and other gases necessary for living organisms—the micro- and macro-fauna and -flora as well as tree roots—in the soil. That's why they say that the soil, as a medium for plant growth, is dynamic, ever-changing, and much alive. As the soil that supports the forest is ever-changing, trees like redcedars exhibit a dynamic character.

🌲 🌲 🌲 Projects for the Amateur Naturalist

1. Spade the soil under several kinds of vegetation—several species of trees, grass, and a cultivated field—and count populations of earthworms. To what do you attribute the difference? [Go fishing if the count is high.]

2. Measure the rate of water infiltration into soils (1) under hardwoods, (2) under pines, (3) supporting grass, (4) of freshly plowed land, and (5) where footpaths or picnic areas are worn. A number-10 juice can, open at both ends, makes a good infiltrometer ring, the measuring device. Carefully pound, with a hammer on a piece of 2 × 4 resting across the opening of the can, the can into the soil for one-half its depth. Then pour a quart (or liter) of water into the can. Note with a watch the time in minutes and seconds it takes for the water to disappear into the soil. (Infiltration rates are undependable until a day or so after a ground-soaking rain.) The difference in infiltration rates for the vegetation types will amaze you.

3. Using a soil pH kit, purchased through a farm supply store, test soils under various forest types for acidity or alkalinity. Note the kinds of trees supported by "sweet" (high pH or basic) and "sour" (low pH or acid) soils. Is the soil pH the same under and beyond the crowns of junipers like eastern redcedar?

8

Enduring Giants

Giant Sequoia

"**A** feeling of reverence comes over one upon entering a grove of these patriarchs whose gigantic red trunks are like the supports of some vast outdoor cathedral. The emotions aroused by the silent ageless majesty of these great trees are akin to those of primitive man for whom they would have been objects of worship." This statement from a technical text on dendrology describes well the grandeur of the giant sequoias that stand as sentinels of the Sierras.

Sentinels of the Sierras

There at 5,000- to 8,000-foot elevations on moist western slopes midway up the great range stand big trees that arose from minute seeds about 4,000 years ago. They are the second-oldest known living thing. (Bristlecone pines are the oldest.) Giant sequoia, also properly called bigtrees, are among the tallest trees, exceeding 275 feet. (Only redwoods, Douglas-fir, and the Australian *Eucalyptus regnans* rise higher.) They are the largest trees in diameter, some exceeding 30 feet. One of the largest, almost 300 feet tall, is over 37 feet in diameter 8 feet above the ground. These are the trees through which roads have been carved (the famous one photographed on picture postcards fell in the 1960s) and a ranger's residence hollowed out. And men of destiny like Generals Sherman and Grant and Presidents Lincoln and McKinley have been honored by individual trees being given their names.

Sequoia, Chief Among Trees

Botanists call the genus to which these trees belong *Sequoia*, latinized for the exceptionally intelligent Cherokee Indian chieftain Sequoyah of alphabet fame.

Giant sequoias in the Sierra-Nevada Mountains (USDA Forest Service photo).

Hence, the common name giant sequoia and the scientific name *S. gigantea* for this species. Technical treatises of various vintages also refer to these timbers as *S. washingtoniana* and *Sequoiadendron giganteum*, the latter term separating bigtree (another common name) from the genus to which redwoods (*S. sempervirens*) of the California coast belong.

Bigtrees of California's high Sierra Nevada Mountains are now almost all reserved in national parks and forests. Hence, there is little need for management to perpetuate the species for commercial use. Rather, there is concern to perpetuate the living stems from the compacting effects of human feet and tire treads upon the soil in which they grow. A most precarious balance of nature provided for the Methuselahan age, but that balance can be upset almost as easily by the curiosity of man as by his ax.

For example, to protect the soil from compaction, some park managers use trenching machines and bulldozers to remove the earth from around trees to depths of 6 feet or more, fluffing it loose, and then replacing it. The more porous soil is a healthier environment for the growth of the fibrous roots. These feeders, inhabiting the soil to depths of more than 3 feet throughout an area of a couple of acres for a single bole, are also readily destroyed by the clearing of lesser vegetation or by disturbing the litter under them. Roots of shrubs and herbs maintain adequate pore space for air and water to be transmitted to the bigtree roots, while litter serves as a mulch to protect the soil beneath from excessive drying, flooding, freezing, or heat.

Other than man's predation, the only natural enemies of giant sequoia are fire and lightning. Fires injure, but seldom kill. Fallen logs and trees are burned out, but the soft, thick bark is almost as resistant to flame as asbestos. A better insulator of heat one is not likely to find in the vegetable kingdom. As the bark is not a good conductor of electricity, lightning-struck trees are more likely to explode than to be killed by a charge that is carried to the ground and which—for many species—girdles the tree en route. Insects and fungi, though present, seem not to be common agents of destruction, and this helps to account for the considerable longevity of bigtrees. Some entomologists think the tannin dust in the bark acts like insect powder. Nor is old age a cause of death: generally the tree, typically a 6,000-ton mass, simply topples from a gradual shifting of the center of gravity. When injured, a heavy nonresinous sap oozes out to seal the wound. And the thick bark insulates the living inner-bark from extreme cold.

When blow-down does occur, associated species, rather than other big-trees, often fill in the openings. Sugar pine, firs, and incense-cedar are typical, all of which are more tolerant of shade than the principal component of the forests and, hence, become established under the dense crowns of bigtrees. And, too, germination of the seed of these three conifers readily occurs in the duff on the forest floor often 1 or 2 feet thick, while the sequoia requires the placement of seeds when mineral soil, rather than organic material, is exposed to receive them.

Big Tree, Little Seed

Seed production is unique for bigtrees. Only after a century of growing do flowers form from buds. Then in a single year, those flowers produce and disseminate pollen, the eggs of the female are fertilized, and growth to full-size cones occurs. Full size is not maturity: a second year is required for the embryos to develop and for seed within the cones to mature. Then the cones may remain green and the seeds within them healthy for as long as 20 years. Few seeds are shed until the cones die or are cut by squirrels from branches high in the trees, but "harvesting" of some cones by rodents occurs annually, depending upon the scarcity of seeds on firs and pines nearby.

Significantly, perhaps, our largest tree produces one of the smallest seeds, reminding one of the biblical mustard seed, so small and yet so potentially full of greatness. Three thousand weigh only an ounce. Frequently a discouragingly low 15 percent germinate, but these the wind may blow the equivalent of two city blocks to regenerate the forest.

Bigtrees, in contrast to the coast redwoods, do not sprout from roots, stumps, or the trunks of fallen trees. Regeneration must therefore be from seeds.

A Riddle

A mystery of nature is the dark-red powdery pigment released with the seeds. Dissolved in water, it is a nonfading writing ink—perhaps used by high-country Indians for body and fabric dyes. Some foresters believe the pigment, about ¾ tannin and ¼ water, is associated with germinative capacity of the seeds. In fact, seeds are sometimes stored after being coated with the dust; 20 years later, viability will not be affected.

Those seeds that germinate in the mineral soil—exposed by fire or where the deep litter is disturbed by the wind-throwing of trees—promptly put down a taproot. This may exceed a couple of inches in the early spring, even before the snow melts. Later laterals develop to provide a root system sufficient both in stability and in ability to absorb moisture and to adsorb nutrient elements.

Seedlings are not home free. Birds peck seed coats hanging on newly germinated plants. Cutworms girdle some near the ground. Wood ants sever others, carrying the needles to their underground nests. Squirrels and chipmunks eat tops.

Durability of the wood of bigtrees, like their redwood cousins, is exceptional among the world's woods. Trees lying on the ground a thousand years are relatively sound. The wood is also brittle and, for that reason, was never highly prized for merchandizing. Harvesting trees in the early days of logging required construction of beds of slash and loose soil into which the skilled fallers would drop the tree to avoid splitting and splintering it. Loggers also built scaffolds above the butt swells—perhaps 12 feet up the trunk—and welded together cross-cut saws, two rugged woods workers tugging on the handles at either end.

Tall Trees, Tough Men

Loggers during the short time in which bigtree forests were open to commercialization were pictured as "diminutive men, like ants in a cornfield ravaging the . . . forests."

Those great masses of wood were so unwieldy that waste is said to have exceeded one-half of the merchantable material. Dynamite often replaced saws as a means of breaking logs into transportable sizes; this resulted in much splitting of the fragile timbers. Sometimes a burl—for a decorator's dream of a tabletop—was the purpose of felling a tree that was otherwise wasted. The highly polished figure in the wood is among nature's most ornate designs. From single stems—and their branches—400,000 to 600,000 board feet could be sawed, enough boards to fill 280 twenty-ton freight cars or to build 150 five-room homes.

Had it been necessary—and were it now desirable—to reintroduce big-trees into the highlands, foresters would select basins on the moist, western slopes for reforestation. There, sheltered by mountain crests from heavy winds and surrounded by white firs, the sequoias would be protected. That is imitating the natural ecology, for under these conditions windfall is rare, drought is infrequent, and fire is of little significance. There, too, soil is mesic, neither too wet (hydric, as in a swamp), nor too dry (xeric, as on a sandy beach).

Climb and Climate

On these slopes, however, a variation of over 50°F may occur from one year to another at any particular time. As a rule of thumb, temperatures drop somewhat less dramatically on the west faces of the Sierra Nevada Mountains than on those with east-facing exposures: 4 degrees for each 1,000-foot rise in elevation. Temperatures play an important role in tree growth; a daily average of 8 degrees above normal, for instance, can cause growth to begin a full month earlier than usual. That is significant in this land of short growing seasons where tree rings, counted with hand lenses, may number 100 to the inch.

Moisture's role in tree growth is less obvious; in fact, it's a fooler. Because most, if not all, precipitation falls in the form of snow, wet years reduce growth. Here is how. The snow piles up, the soil stays cold, the roots remain dormant, and the inception of growth—diameter, crown, and root—is retarded. Don't count on this theory holding if after a winter of heavy snow, when it is still piled high on the ground, abundant spring rains melt the snow and, thereby, warm the soil. Then, in spite of the high soil-moisture level, tree growth commences. But that is rare.

Variation in snow depth is as much as 3 to 4 feet from northern to southern extremities of the range of bigtrees. Growth is hence greater, because the season is longer, in the southern sector where the lesser amount of snow melts earlier.

Ancient World, Old World, and New World Meet

It is sometimes said that dinosaurs in Miocene times played among the bigtrees in various parts of the world. In most places the trees disappeared with the great beasts. Fossils of 12 species have been found on four continents. Kindred trees occur, particularly in China, in addition to the redwood, the natural range of which is as little as 200 miles from the Sierra site of the bigtrees.

The New World's sequoias were first noted by white men, according to reports, travelling west from Salt Lake to Monterey, California, in 1833. Later a man named Tharp made claim to considerable acreage and, to validate his ownership, carved his name and date in a fallen log. The 1858 inscription is legible today.

In the intervening years men have labored, mostly in the political arena, to preserve these monuments to immortality. Chief among them were Judge Walter Fry and John R. White, early superintendents of the national park created for the protection of the bigtrees. Another was John Muir, a practical sentimentalist whose diaries and sketches while travelling, camping, and cooking with the Basque sheepherders opened to the flatlander a view on paper of the land beyond the range. The efforts of these men were timely, for one-fourth of the total giant sequoia acreage has been saved. Perhaps 4,000 years from now, if people still prowl the earth, they may, as their forebears do today and as the Roman pagan did in his day at the entrance to the sacred groves of trees, inscribe above the portal, "God is in this place." The alternative is the Greek, *Ichabod*: "The glory has departed." May it not be.

🌲 🌲 🌲   Projects for the Amateur Naturalist

1. Chart the climatic history of an area by the annual growth rings in several trees. Keep in mind that thinnings or partial harvests stimulate growth of residual trees for a few years and, thereby, may be a climate riddle. Generally, wet years encourage wide rings, drought the opposite.

2. Plant tree seeds or seedlings (see Figure 8–1). Both may be obtained *gratis* from state forestry agencies. Determine if the seeds you use have been stratified (if that species requires it). Follow planting instructions provided with the seedlings. Treated seeds and tree seedlings may also be purchased inexpensively from commercial supply houses and nurseries.

3. Observe browse lines in forests and parks. They need not be from large mammals. Rabbits cut small trees low to the ground. See if you can locate rodent or larger animal tracks at the bases of small or large trees. Perhaps they were left by the hind legs of small fauna. Do you see tell-tale teeth or tear marks on the vegetation?

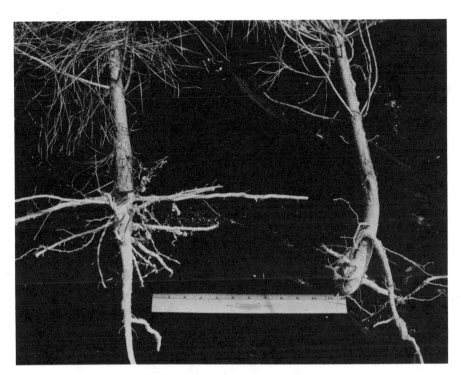

FIGURE 8–1. Tree planters need to be careful about root placement. Growth of the tree on the right will suffer (USDA Forest Service photo).

9

Up from the Ashes

Sand, Pond, Pitch, Jack, and Lodgepole Pines

Wildfires, caused by lightning and ignited by Indians and early pioneers, have been occurring and recurring through the ages. Civilized man, viewing forest fires as destructive, unnatural events, applauds the heroic efforts of fire fighters to control these holocausts. So it's surprising to learn that some trees owe their existence to fire. Without heat, sand pine, pond pine, and pitch pine in the East, jack pine in the Lake States, and lodgepole and Bishop pines in the West would not continue as ecological cover types.

Those trees produce cones year after year, seemingly for no use. The seeds are locked in until fire heats the cone, softening the resinous seal that confines the seeds behind the bract. Tiny cracks in the "glue" allow the cone to dry out. The internal stresses force the scales to open to allow the winged seeds to flutter to the ground. From those seeds and from the ashes of a conflagration come the new forest.

Foresters label this opening of cones due to heat exposure a serotinous characteristic, while Webster's broader definition, referring to delaying action, is also applicable to these cones. Now we examine the habits of a few of these species.

Tree for a Sandy Land

Sand pine, a species with dense wood, is native to the deep sandy soils of the Ocala National Forest in peninsular Florida. Seeds are held in cones until high temperatures cause the "burrs" to open by melting the resins that seal the scales. Usually supplied by fire, the required heat sometimes is generated by the sun's reflection on the light-colored beach sands of open woods.

The Big Scrub, a relatively pure stand of over 200,000 acres, grows on a

Sand pines in the Florida peninsula are often mature when only this large, at perhaps fifty years of age.

gigantic flattened dune. Other southern yellow pines such as longleaf and slash occasionally occur within the Big Scrub when finer soils of greater moisture-holding capacity, and hence less subject to wildfires, are interspersed with the coarse sands. Moreover, even on wire grass sites, where sand pine usually occurs, longleaf pine is better able to endure wildfire. Some individuals are exceptions to the rule. Because cones of sand pine trees found within the longleaf pine type open more readily without heat, some foresters believe the less fertile soil on the typical sand pine site may be a cause of the serotinous nature of the species there.

Other silviculturists attribute the usual mutual exclusion of these two cousins to the special adaptation of longleaf pine to endure frequent fires by the development of a grass-like seedling stage. During this period a tuft of needles protects the tender bud when calamity strikes. Then later, a burst of growth spurts the seedling past the sapling stage in just a few years, and finally a thick heat-insulating bark is formed when trees are only 15 to 20 feet tall (Chapter 3).

Sand pine, growing more regularly and with vulnerable thin bark, its limbs low, dense, and prone to crown fires, is adapted differently. Individual stems perish from fire, but whole forests endure. From earliest time, conflagrations, borne sometimes on hurricane winds, have periodically left miles-wide swaths of devastation from one end of its sandy domain to the other. Yet without the adaptations by which longleaf pines protect themselves, as often as fires pass through, sand pine revegetates the burns and dominates the scrub country. In Ocala's Big Scrub, evergreen oaks follow pines in ecological succession where fire has been excluded.

(Oddly, in West Florida, in the old Choctawhatchee National Forest, now Eglin Air Force Base, another strain of *Pinus clausa* (from the Latin, closed) is characterized by cones that open without the need of heat. Those trees, in contrast, grow in mixtures with other pines and hardwoods, an improbability if they were serotinous trees.)

Flowers and, subsequently, cones develop when trees are only 5 years old. But the closed burrs, hoarding each year's crop of seeds against the day of need, persist on trees for many years; and even after 5 seasons, 20 percent of the seeds are sound.

Such cones, when fire spreads through the woods, gradually open so that a few hours or days later—when the ground has cooled—as many as a million seeds fall on an acre. In the exposed mineral soil and with the lack of competition, seeds germinate within 2 to 3 months unless large, red harvester ants, white-footed deer mice, centipedes, mourning doves, or chewinks get to them first. "Damping off" (a disease caused by a soil-inhabiting fungus), root rots, and wiggling microscopic nematodes also take their toll of freshly germinated stock. However, considering that there are about a million seeds per acre, feeding these flora and fauna is not a serious matter.

Foresters effectively imitate nature in prescribing controlled burns for regenerating sand pine forests. Slow-moving, hot fires, burning against the wind in autumn, are effective, while the explosive nature of the fuel, and especially the debris on the forest floor, restricts the use of head fires—those running with the wind. The fire must not crown in the treetops, for then cones in the upper branches—where they'll likely be—are consumed. Skilled foresters accomplish with little damage what wildfires do in their destructive way—releasing seeds to insure that another forest of sand pine will dominate the Big Scrub.

What does all this heat do to the soil? Probably little. Although the sun radiates high temperatures to the surface soil in sand pine lands, no evidence has been found of nutrient depletion or structural damage as a result. The small amount of organic matter normally mixed with these coarse sands is lost by the heat of oxidation, but it is ordinarily insignificant. Nor do high soil temperatures injure trees; rather, the species seems to have an unusual ability to efficiently carry on photosynthesis where heat is intense, and this may be the reason sand pine is successfully established on hot sands where other conifers fail.

Fire is not absolutely essential to regenerate sand pine stands. Clearcutting may suffice, whereby logging slash (the tops of trees) that contains cones is left on the ground. The sun's rays that reach the white sand reflect upward, heating the cones that soon release their seeds.

Geologists figure the unconsolidated sands of poor water-holding capacity in the Big Scrub were moved from the Appalachian Mountains during the Pleistocene period, transported to the Florida peninsula by offshore currents, and washed and sorted there. The soil, a term remotely applicable, is also low in plant nutrients. There is no grass in many areas, just rosemary and poor grub forbs. Even animals, micro and macro, avoid the Big Scrub, for here the sands reflect the glare of the burning sun to char the less fit. Yet sand pine grows. A Yale forestry professor of an earlier generation must have had sand pine in mind when he told his students, "Give me a bed of marbles and adequate water and I can grow southern pines."

Tree for a Swampy Land

Another example of a serotinous species is pond pine, a tree that stands in wet ground most of the year. A recent classifier called it *Pinus serotina*, although until a couple of decades ago it was called *P. rigida* and considered a variety of pitch pine that grows on dissimilar sites.

Pond pine is usually found in pure stands in the pocosins (Indian for swamp-on-a-hill) and bays of the coastal Carolinas. It is probably climax vegetation in the ecologic scale in these wet swampy sites, for it is maintained in the absence of fire and regenerated as a consequence of fire. Hence, stands may be two- or three-aged, a few seed-bearing trees surviving each holocaust. Wildfires disobey statistical predictions of occurring every 15 to 20 years. Rather, they are synchronized with nature's droughts, only periodically tinder-drying the usually wet and, hence, fireproof organic soils of peat and muck to flammable conditions. And then, what fuel! The advancing ground fire not only consumes the litter and grass upon the surface but also devours soil, tree roots, and everything else in its path.

Pond pine of the North Carolina pocosins. Open cones of a serotinous tree are in the inset.

While fire may benefit pond pine, it is also its chief enemy. As much as 18 inches of the fibrous surface soil may be consumed in a single severe conflagration, leaving a hard, impervious soil layer at the surface. Reforestation is then impractical.

Aside from fire, pond pine alone captures the poorly drained sites because other pines cannot long endure low soil aeration levels. Its root system easily penetrates the upper foot of mineral soil beneath the wet peat deposits.

This tree has another advantage. In addition to being serotinous, it sprouts. Following fire, new stems originate from dormant buds hidden under the bark at the base of the tree. Heat triggers a hormonal mechanism that causes those buds to break dormancy and grow rapidly into new tree stems. Tied to an old healthy root system, nourished for years by the tree whose above-ground parts have just been killed by fire, the new stem may be old physiologically, though a count of growth rings may show its youth.

Some of these Carolina bays and bogs appear to have a toxic quality that inhibits growth of species competitive to pond pine. It seems to be similar to that found in English heaths, where gliotoxin, a fungal growth produced by a *Penicillium*, affects trees. Foresters are sure that its occurrence is not directly related to fire in the swamp.

Tree for a Barren Land

Another serotinous conifer is pitch pine. So sensitive are its cones to heat and moisture that once open, they may close again in wet weather before all seeds are released for dispersal by wind. Seldom found in pure stands, *Pinus rigida* is the principal component of the "scalp locks," short ridges supporting a narrow growth of trees, extending to the "forehead" of a draw in the Southern Appalachians. It is also the evergreen of a heterogeneous hodgepodge of habitats that includes the barrens of southern New Jersey. Note its name! *Rigida* describes the stiff cone scales that protect the seed, until fires have passed, from animal robbers while the burrs hang upon the tree.

It is to the "plains," ecologically complex components of the Jersey pine barrens, that our attention is drawn here. Growth is so poor that dominant trees 65 years old may average less than 11 feet tall. Here we see no normally developed trees.

The virgin forests were probably never lush, but foresters speculate nonetheless that acceptable stands of pine once covered the land. Why the trees of the plains of the Barrens are yet runty, although under fire protection for 50 years, has been the subject of many a scholarly dissertation.

However, pitch pine has other eggs in its survival basket. As its wide occurrence suggests, the roots tolerate many kinds of soils, provided they are acidic. The thick bark, affording even better insulation as the years pass, has a clever way of protecting the vital bud of its newly germinated seedling. While the first roots get a foothold in the soil, the stem grows prostrate on the surface, holding dormant buds in a zone where surface-fire temperatures are lowest. Then following fire, those buds sprout, producing a "seedling" at the crook at the ground-line. Green foliage also may poke through the massive bark higher up the stem of a veteran of 80 years.

In the New Jersey plains, repeated fires prior to the 1930s kept the vegetation low and largely of sprout origin. Many stumps that still sprout exceed 80 years in age. With fire exclusion, hardwoods invade and replace the pines, temporary species in ecological succession. Perhaps in time—100 years or more—the improvement in the soil by the annual incorporation of hardwood leaf litter may enable these lands to again grow acceptable trees of the forest. A further speculation is that, in some future day, these woodlands will need to be acceptable aesthetically, for it will be to escape the cities of the East that man will seek out the nearest wood.

Perhaps the best evidence of pitch pine's ability to survive the vicissitudes of its harsh sites is its generally poor form for lumber and, consequently, its low esteem in the eyes of the forester. Fire-scarred, gnarled, and knotty where adventitious limbs have sprouted after defoliation—a "scalp lock" stand over bedrock on a Southern Appalachian ridge; a sentinel pine on a southwest-facing slope in Pennsylvania; a struggling stand on an outwash sand-plain in New England; a 10-foot-tall scrub stand in the Pine Barrens of South Jersey—pitch pine reflects a tenacious hold on life. And for that reason, if for no other, it remains high in the affections of many sensitive people.

Tree for a Desecrated Land

Jack pine, widely found in Canada, dips down into the Lake States and here and there in spots of the Northeastern United States. Trees of the species have been widely planted in the Northeast. Jack pine spans three-fourths of the North American continent, ranging from Nova Scotia to the MacKenzie River in the north, and south to Michigan, Wisconsin, and Minnesota. Once despised as worthless, this serotinous conifer of the north has become a valued timber tree in recent decades.

No one knows how much of the Lake States' area was in jack pine before the heyday of lumbering in the pineries there. Its abundance is believed to be much greater now than when the pioneer lumbermen began the "cut-out-and-get-out" movement in the last half of the 19th century. Modern industry, adapting to trees of smaller size, considers it a valuable raw material.

Fire was a dramatic force in expanding the acreage of *Pinus banksiana*. Whole towns were wiped out, important industries displaced, and giant stands of virgin red and white pines, covering hundreds of square miles, were consumed. Jack pine then claimed the land.

Aside from its serotinous cones, jack pine does not exhibit fire resistance. Its bark is thin in early years, and when tops are killed it does not sprout from stumps. Nor is it always fully serotinous; some of its cones, especially in the Lake States, open when first mature. However, its ability to spread a multitude of seeds on freshly burned land has made it abundant in second-growth forests where more desirable pines are scarce.

While the lowly jack pine, once a weed in any woodsman's wordbook,

A forest wall of jack pine adjacent to a harvested opening in the Lake States. The white-barked trees are aspens (USDA Forest Service photo).

controlled the dry, sandy, infertile soils, occasional stems slipped in among the valuable red and white pines on the better sites. There they were ignored in the harvests by Paul Bunyan's men. Luckily so, for they served as the progenitor of the pioneer species, replenishing the land following the great conflagrations of those days—both before and after logging. Jack pine was killed too, but its cones, often produced yearly and when stems are still young, provided the needed seeds to start a new forest.

So persistently are cones held to the stem, that they may be completely overgrown and buried by the trunk or branch to which they are attached. Even the seeds in these cones are viable and, if released to find their way to the forest floor, will germinate. Consequently, not only were burned-over jack pine woods reforested with jack pine, but also the lands previously in white and red pines. It is said that jack pines "exploded over the Lake States" in those days.

Tree for a Rocky Land

Indians, and later white men, extensively used lodgepole pines for lodge poles. Prehistoric in American lore, the still-continuing practice could only occur because of fire. Throughout the range of lodgepole pine, from Alaska to southern Colorado and California, dry lightning fires frequently occur. When lightning strikes tall trees in dry soils, when fuel on the forest floor is tinder, when wind is high (a usual characteristic of these mountains), and when no rain falls to quench the thirst of the hungry flame, language lacks a fitting descriptive term for the resulting holocausts. But ecologically, there is a way out. For these tall, straight, small-crowned, slow-growing cylindrical stems bear serotinous cones that open as long as 20 years after forming on a branch when subjected to extreme heat.

A Rocky Mountain botanist at the turn of the century told of a camper building a fire at the base of a solitary lodgepole pine, killing the tree. Several years later, a strip of green extended from the tree's base for 700 feet. Ten to fifty feet wide, the green was that of thousands of seedlings of this species parented by that tree.

Generally lodgepole pines enter ecological succession on sandy or gravelly soils, but if fire has taken its toll of mature trees, and seeds are available, these trees may invade northern muck and peat bogs generally reserved in nature for spruces and firs. For the same reason, these pines occur where ponderosa pine, Douglas-fir, western larch, and white pine encroach, or at higher elevations where subalpine fir is chief. Even so, in time—perhaps 100 years—the species naturally assigned to the particular site will reinvade. In the meantime, lodgepole pines hold the land together in stands as dense as the proverbial "hair on the dog's back," providing wood for 2 × 4 stud mills, pulp, excellent utility poles, and cabin timbers. Its crossties, serving the railroads when ribbons of steel were first laid across the land, still remain squared and bedded in those roads.

In those days, too, many road companies were deeded, by the federal government, every other section—a square mile—for a distance of six miles

A typical dense stand of lodgepole pine in the Colorado Rockies. Note immature conelets and open cone of the serotinous tree (USDA Forest Service photo).

on either side of the right-of-way where it passed through much of the Public Domain. From this checkerboard pattern of ownership, timbers were harvested with which to tie the rails together. Many of the ties were lodgepole pine.

Lodgepole pine is not always straight and tall, nor is it always serotinous. In California, where its dwarfed and crooked form gave rise to its Latin name, *Pinus contorta*, cones open as soon as they mature. It is from the serotinous form of the northern Rockies, seeding in after fires in dense stands of tall, slim stems, that its English name derives. These were the stands from which the buffalo-hunting Indians selected poles for the framework to support the scraped hides of their portable lodges, long before white settlers used somewhat larger sizes for log cabin homesteads, barns, corrals, and fences.

Prolific seeders from early youth, lodgepole pines have both serotinous and prompt-opening cones in the same stand, even on the same tree. But the seeds hoarded in closed cones are perhaps more useful than those from any other serotinous pine because a higher percentage of them stays viable a long time. A few seeds germinated from an encased cone that was more than 150 years old. The age was determined by a count of growth rings laid down over the cone, now buried deep within the tree. Germination of 50- and 60-year-old seed is not uncommon.

So much seed is released after a fire or after a harvest when the sun's heat opens many cones that the resulting stands are overcrowded. As many as 300,000 seedlings have been found per acre, with 175,000 remaining 8 years later. No wonder no species on the American continent is so prone to stagnation. While effective in protecting watersheds, such stands are a problem to the forester responsible for wood production. With so many stems competing for limited space and moisture, little growth takes place and there is no market for the small sticks that must be removed to allow a selected few to develop.

This ecological history of vegetative competition may be witnessed throughout the Rockies, for there lodgepole pine is one of the most widely ranging trees. From sea level to elevations of 11,000 feet, the smooth velvet green of young pine forest can be found with lodgepole as the pioneer species following last year's fire. In another block, whole mountainsides of stands of poles originate from, and mark, the holocausts of 1910 when drought and lightning overwhelmed the feeble efforts of an infant Forest Service with one of the most destructive fires ever recorded. The notorious Yellowstone National Park fires of 1988 consumed lodgepole pine stands regenerated periodically from earlier conflagrations. New forests of the species promptly arise. But even in these situations, one finds mature veterans 300 years old that have escaped the blazes now ready to relinquish their positions in the stand to encroaching Douglas-fir or other species destined to be closer to the climax forest cover type.

Trees for Many Lands

South, East, North, and West, pines save up seeds in persistent cones against a day of emergency. On sites where that emergency is periodic devastating fire, serotinous species become dominant, occupying the land in even-aged pure stands. Intolerant of shade and rarely able to persist among other trees, this is their normal way of growth. Yet some of them, like the lodgepole pine of the west, show an amazing ability to seed where other species have been burned out. Somewhere in or around these burns there have been trees of the serotinous species, surviving more or less by accident among alien stands— perhaps holdovers from ancient burns—to provide the seed for a new forest. Their secret is not in numbers, but in holding ever ready that surplus of seeds in cones that open only after fire or when the parent tree is dead.

The name *phoenix* has been given another tree, the aspen of the Lake States, but it even better describes these pines that come up from the ashes. The phoenix, in mythology, was a sacred bird that at the end of its life set its nest afire, fanning the flame with its golden wings to burn itself to death. From the ashes would emerge a worm that turned into another phoenix. Seeds of pines, although winged, cannot blow in like aspen seeds from miles away, but, rather, survive fire and afterward sprout. So, too, from death by fire comes new life to serotinous trees.

   Projects for the Amateur Naturalist

1. Locate micro-sites, like rock crevasses or cracks in concrete, where trees grow. Now observe growth there in contrast to trees of the same age and species in normal sites. You may wish to chart diameters and heights of the compared trees.

2. Dissect a pine cone and draw its parts. Use a dendrology textbook for identifying the parts (see Figure 9–1).

3. Sample the atmosphere for fungi spores. To do this, put rubber cement on paper. The spores will adhere to the sticky paper. Test out the collection sheet by placing it near the fruiting body (head) of a mushroom fungus, shake or blow on the head, and see what happens. Toadstools are, of course, mushroom heads.

FIGURE 9–1. Conelets of a southern pine (USDA Forest Service photo).

10

Mountain Heights To Low Bogs

Spruce and Fir Trees

*L*ong years past, my wife and I with two diaper-clothed infants (before the days of Pampers) made our home in a log house in the northern woods. The diapers were washed in a tub by the spring and hung to dry on a line beneath the spruce and the fir trees. How fragrant those cotton clothes were at eventide, the oily droplets of resin permeating the air! And in their blanketing of all that lay beneath the branches of the trees, the diapers too were saturated. No synthetic aerosol dispersant could match the aroma of the terpenes that exuded from the foliage of the evergreens. The pleasant smell of the Adirondack Mountain woods captured by the diapers made the otherwise unpleasant task of washing them a joy to long remember.

Terpenes dripping from spruce and fir, on the other hand, cause air pollution. Air testers call the liquid droplets particulates. The sun's rays reflecting and refracting on and through the minute droplets, accompanied by temperature inversions, give the air the haze that led early explorers to name the summits of Virginia "Blue Ridge" and the span of high hills that serves as the dividing line between North Carolina and Tennessee the "Great Smoky Mountains." Perhaps it is more accurate to say that the opaque and transparent droplets in the air caused a temperature inversion, just as particulates of solid and liquid effluents pouring from industrial and residential chimneys cause the smog that results in upside down climate: it's warmer on the hilltops than in the valleys.

These natural air polluters, especially the firs, are also sensitive to air pollution. Ozone, sulphur dioxide, and oxides of nitrogen affect their vigor. The chemicals are the principal constituents of "acid rain."

Virgin red spruce and the understory of ferns and the seedlings and saplings of the parent trees (USDA Forest Service photo).

Second-growth red spruce about 50 years old at the end of a railroad tram high in the West Virginia mountains (USDA Forest Service photo).

Alike, Yet Different

Spruce trees, of the genus *Picea*, and fir trees, the *Abies*, have much in common. Aesthetically pleasing are (for most species) the tall deltaic spires of the trees of both genera, the branches often hugging the ground. One wonders why the New England poet Longfellow didn't include these trees when he wrote of "the forest primeval, the murmuring pines and the hemlock." For aesthetics some choose the spruce and the fir, others white pines that often precede in ecological succession or hemlocks that encroach to join the spruce and fir to form climax stands in the northern woods and southern mountain forests.

The two genera are look-alikes in their pyramidal forms, suggesting similar growth habits. They both have short needles, exude oil, develop small cones in which are winged seeds, and put out whorls of branches at seemingly regulated intervals. Distinguishing the genera and species by tree characteristics becomes a problem for amateurs. To add to the confusion, species of both genera hybridize. Anatomical features then take on the appearance of neither or of both of the parents.

But there are differences. Spruce trees of the eastern woods bear square needles; those of the fir are flat. The four-sided spruce leaves can be rolled between the fingers; the two-sided ones of the fir cannot. (I remember the difference in a juvenile way: *s* for spruce and square; *f* for fir and flat.)

Spruce needles when pulled from a twig leave a peg behind, giving stems a rough appearance and a sandpaper-like feeling to the touch. When a fir needle is pulled, the whole of it comes loose, exhibiting a round scar on a smooth twig. Spruce needles have rounded ends; for fir there is a notch.

The bark of spruce trees has no blisters; for fir it does. In these blisters are oleoresins. To early observers they appeared as minute mammary glands and functioned accordingly in the release of resin when squeezed. Pioneers called the fir she-balsam; while the spruce, without the little bumps, they named he-balsam.

Another distinction is in the cones. For spruce they are pendulant, hanging like ornaments and remaining intact even when falling from great heights to the ground. In contrast, erect fir cones, a bit stouter for their length, break into pieces when they hit the ground.

White spruce is often confused with balsam fir. Spruce cones are slightly shorter: 1½ inches (2 to 4 inches for fir).

Distinct growth rings of spruce wood make age-counting easy. Late-wood, that laid down in the summer, contrasts readily with the much wider ring of early-wood. This spring-wood is also lighter in color. For fir, the transition from early-wood to lavender-tinged late-wood occurs more gradually. Therefore, growth rings are not quite so distinct as for the spruce trees.

Distinctions Between the Spruces

White spruce is distinguished from black spruce by hair on the branchlets of the latter species and by its smaller cones. Red spruce is distinguished from black spruce by the latter's persistent cones. Red spruce cones fall at the end of the year, while black spruce cones may hang on for 30 seasons. Red spruce cones, too, have smooth scales, in contrast to the wavy edges of those of black spruce. Where the ranges of red and black spruces overlap, red is identified by its smaller, duller, cones that curve downward on short stalks. The conspicuous layering habit of black spruce, discussed later, sets this species apart.

Flowers and Seeds

All of these species are monoecious. That's Greek for "one house." One tree produces flowers or strobili of both sexes, though the two kinds of flowers are usually borne on separate branches. At first the female conelets appear cylindrical, growing in one season into maturity. Pollen sacs arranged spirally behind the scales of male cones develop into catkins at pollen-dispersal time.

For the spruces, the male flowers are attached to the sides of branches; the female, globe-shaped and purplish, at branch ends. Just inside the thin scale at its wide base, observers find two ovules, each containing an egg to be fertilized by the sperm carried in the pollen grains. So two small, winged seeds fall from each scale in autumn. In a normal forest with no fire, this occurs every 2 to 5 years.

Seed crops of balsam fir often don't amount to much until trees are 30 years old. Yet seeds of old trees of this species lose viability. Then heavy seed crops of winged, wedge-shaped seeds, falling at 2- to 4-year intervals, tend to compensate for this reduced germinative capacity.

Spruce—Fir and Wildlife

Spruce grouse, conveniently, have the same range as the genus *Picea*. Whether there is a symbiotic relationship—that spruce trees require the assistance of the bird as well as the other way around—is unknown. This bird is also known as the "fool hen." So foolish is it that the bird allows a person to come within striking distance before it flies. Because it can easily be knocked down and killed with a stick, the spruce grouse is credited with saving the lives of people lost and starving in the far north woods. The meat is tough and gamy in contrast to that of the ruffed grouse. The bird, however, is now protected by law in much of its range.

The blue grouse, the other of the three American woods' grouse, to some degree also depends upon stands of these species for food and cover.

Moose, deer, and rabbits browse trees, and bears strip the bark of black spruce to eat the sweet sapwood. Porcupines also strip the bark from trunks and branches of coniferous trees. While hemlock is favored by the spiny "pigs," every spruce tree in an area of an acre or more may be killed. So damaging are porcupines that some states have had a bounty on them and open seasons on hunting them.

Birds eat seeds of these trees, while rodents, like squirrels and chipmunks, cache them for winter food. Multiple stems of trees coming from a single hole in the ground attest to the vigor of the seeds stored by animals. Stomach records show the importance of fir seeds for rodent food.

Rodents also feed on the bark of fir trees, while beavers are fond of black spruce, not for food, but for construction material for their numerous lodges in the low-lying north woods. *Castor's* activity also raises water tables which, in turn, kills trees.

Insect and Disease Attack

People think of the spruce budworm when they think of bugs that attack *Picea*. They are partly correct. Spruce budworms are most damaging to fir trees. Only when a lot of spruce trees are in the fir stand do the former serve as hosts for infestation, the insects hollowing out the growing tips, defoliating trees, and causing death.

A beetle also plays havoc with red spruce, and a minute aphid leaves its tell-tale "wool" on balsam fir twigs. That bug, regrettably an introduction from abroad, causes abnormal growth due to contamination by a substance in the insect's saliva. The chemical-biological reaction turns wood dark and brittle: called redwood, it bears no resemblance to the western tree by that name. In the North Carolina mountains, this balsam wooly aphid has destroyed mature Fraser fir over most of that species' range.

Hemlock loopers, the famous inch-bug, take long journeys on fir trees. So also does a blackheaded bugworm.

Heart-rot fungi seriously disturb these trees, especially the balsam fir. Stands disintegrate at an early age when infected by the decay-causing pathogens. Dwarf mistletoe, a green plant parasite, forms degrading witches' brooms, especially on black spruce.

Uses of the Wood

Early uses for these species of wood included cordage from the pliable roots of white spruce. Indians laced their birch-bark canoes with this twine. (Those who like to work with their hands can weave baskets from the roots. If the fiber is too dry and stiff, simply soften it in hot water.) Fish barrels, vessel spars, and top-masts were hewn from the boles of black spruce. Large roots and the lower parts of its stems were also selected for knees, a structural timber of ships. From balsam fir came the stuffings for pillows, the aromatic foliage so important as a deodorant.

Great volumes of spruce and fir now feed the pulp mills of the United States' Northeast, the Lake States, and Canada. Each American annually consumes roughly the equivalent of the growth of ⅔ acre of these forests for paper products. From cellulose fibers, mills make all kinds of paper, including finest writing sheets and newsprint.

Wood of spruce, being odorless, comes in handy for butter boxes. So too does the wood of balsam fir. White spruce finds its way to the marketplace for crates and rough lumber. The yellowish, lightweight, and strong wood of black spruce—because the trees are usually small—seems limited in its markets to pulp and fuel. Red spruce, on the other hand, a resilient and straight-grained wood, is the raw material of stringed instruments. Millmen plane good-quality spruce into attractive trim, called millwork, and into ladder rails, paddles, and even industrial refrigerators.

The light-colored, easily worked soft wood of the firs of the eastern forest has never been important in the lumber marketplace, although sawmills cut its boles into boards for local use. Many trees make good utility poles.

The wood of all of these species is nonporous. Lustrous spruce wood, indistinguishable among the species, has resin canals visible with the naked eye or with a hand lens. In a section of sapwood cut along the radius of the bole of a tree, these tubes appear as white flecks that run between the cells of cellulose and lignin. Other cells sheathe or enclose them, controlling the secretion of resin. Neither balsam nor Fraser fir wood has resin canals, hence their use for cooperage (barrels). Otherwise, leaching of gum could degrade the produce stored or shipped therein.

We should mention here that sometimes white and red spruce and often balsam fir make good Christmas trees. I say "sometimes" because the spruces tend to drop their needles in warm, dry rooms and the white spruce develops an unpleasant odor after being in the house a little while. Folks especially like holiday wreaths of balsam fir.

Chemical Uses

As have other plants, the balsam fir of the eastern North American forest has been called the balm of Gilead, a reference to the biblical aromatic plant (named for the region in ancient Palestine) that, with its fragrant yellow oleoresin, served as a salve for wounds. (The biblical balm of Gilead today is purchased as Mecca balsam.) Poetically Christ is referred to as the Balm of Gilead, healing the wounds of the people of a broken world.

Here the oleoresin is the exudate of the trunk of the she-balsam mentioned earlier. The balm of the balsam fir was used at least through the American Civil War as an external application to the injuries of combat.

Microscopists, those who work with microscope slides, are familiar with the resin as Canada balsam. The transparent gum holds slide mounts in place. Pharmacists mix medicines with this material. Europeans call Canada balsam Strasburg turpentine.

Resins, nonvolatile mixtures, are insoluble in water but soluble in organic solvents like acetone. From resin comes rosin after steam distillation removes turpentine from the exudate of the tree. Oil of spruce, boiled from young branches of "black spruce" in the Allegheny Mountains in pioneer times, may actually have been from balsam resin. The "concoction," after boiling and evaporation to obtain the oil, was reported to have had a "bitter, astringent, acidulous taste."

From the spruce, particularly red and black spruces, came spruce beer, usually the nonfermented type. Young, leafy twigs were boiled and flavor and sugar added to produce the forerunner of soda water, a "grand old beverage of backwoods" America.

Spruce gum, a child's delight before the entrance of chewing gum, also came from black and red spruce resin bled from tree trunks. Burgundy pitch, an old-world ingredient in varnish and medicine, likely found use in colonial times. In fact, all of the oleoresins of these conifers, because they are oils or fats that hold resin in solution, are useful ingredients of oil-based paints.

Ecological Trends

Canadian foresters learning of spruce and fir forest fires in the north woods of that nation choose not to ignore them, but to let them run their course. New, naturally regenerated forests that follow a holocaust likely will be ripe for harvest in 80 to 100 years. At that time economists expect demand for wood to make commercial harvests feasible, in spite of distances of the timber from the centers of commerce and the mills at those centers. The inaccessible trees aren't needed now; if they were protected from fire until needed, they would by then be over-mature and full of rot, and the stands sparsely stocked. Natural mortality would have taken its toll. Foresters know that a single fire, though out of control, leaves enough trees alive to supply seeds that soon germinate when they fall to the ground. Sometimes heat encourages cones to open and thus hastens seed dispersal. Regeneration then takes place under the stark-naked stalks of a fire-scarred forest.

These species also seed-in on fields abandoned by agriculture, where storms have laid bare the land, and following clearcutting. In the first case, white spruce is referred to as old-field spruce. In any case, the trees usually do not remain long as pure stands. Aspen, pin cherry, gray birch, paper birch and red maple—all weed trees—soon appear along with eastern hemlock, jack pine, yellow-poplar, and other, more desirable competitors.

In time, the less tolerant species pass out of the stand, leaving the site to spruce and fir and perhaps hemlock. Then maybe at an age of 80 years, stands should be ready for a pulpwood harvest. But by that time, 70 percent of the trees in a stand of fir probably will have heart-rot. Red spruce lives much longer.

Of course, all of these spruce and fir species are not equally destined for all sites, though generally we note their occurence on shallow soils. Such may be at the ridge top or in swampy lowlands. The peat and muck of the swamp may be deep, perhaps 20 feet down to bedrock. Yet it is physiologically shallow, as the roots extend downward but a few inches if the water table is permanently high. So we find red spruce from sea level bogs in the North to 6,000-foot elevations in the South, white spruce from about 300 to 2,800 feet in the North, and fir from sea level to 5,000 feet. Black spruce grows to the northern limits of tree-growth, shown on National Geographic Society maps by the little trees parading across the page near the Arctic Circle. At that locale, growth is immeasurably slow: no rings can be discerned. Trees perhaps 50 years old are a foot tall, growing prostrate and shrubby, and each year extending skyward only about as much as is the accumulation of organic matter on the surface of the cold, moist tundra. Trees 2 inches dbh and a hundred years old are not uncommon.

Red spruce may behave similarly. When boring these trees for age determination in the Maine woods, foresters add 40 years to the breast-high ring count. That's how long, on average, it takes them to grow 4½ feet tall. And to further confuse, a 14-inch and a 2-inch tree growing 20 feet apart may both be 150 years old. Or they both may be 60. Age differences are attributed to site quality and the history of the stand—for instance, fire, harvest, and insect predation, as well as micro-site distinctions for individual stems.

One observes floating mats of this pioneer tree extending out from the shores of frigid ponds. Those mats in time become the north woods' bogs and muskegs.

On mountaintop and low bog, shallow soils encourage windthrow. So too does the absence of taproots. Perhaps if taproots were part of their nature, these species would not be found in the thin mantles of soil.

Balsam fir, though less tolerant than the spruces, endures well the shade of its own or that of other trees. However, balsam fir tolerance diminishes after trees of the species reach 10 to 15 feet in height. Openings, made by dying trees or cutting, release stagnated ones. Then the residual stems grow rapidly, seeming to compete in a race to reach the sky.

Balsam fir grows on low swampy ground as well as on well-drained hillsides. Stands of this species begin to fall apart at an age of about 70 years and have pretty well disintegrated by the time they reach 90. Windthrow and fire that damage the thin bark destroy many trees and stands.

All of the species covered in this chapter appear both as pure stands or mixed with each other and other trees.

Locales

Three species of spruce point their spires skyward in the eastern forest, though all three extend westward to the Pacific slopes. These are white (*Picea glauca*), red (*P. rubens*), and black (*P. mariana*). [Important spruce trees limited to the West—and therefore not a concern of this chapter—include the Engelmann (*P. engelmanii*), Sitka (*P. sitkensis*), blue (*P. pungens*), and weeping (*P. breweriana*).] White and black spruces are trans-Canadian, found in Alaska as well as on the northeastern seaboard of Canada and the United States. Red spruce dips southward into the Great Smoky Mountains of North Carolina and Tennessee where virgin stands yet display the beauty of these forests.

The true fir of the eastern forest is balsam (*Abies balsamea*) in the North and a close kin, Fraser fir (*A. fraserii*), in the Great Smoky Mountains. Here, as with red spruce, virgin forests till recently filled the air with terpenes, hydrocarbons exuded from the foliage of conifers. Alas, the balsam wooly aphid has taken its toll so severely that while technically "virgin," the stands no longer appear primeval. Fraser fir, while found as far south as the Georgia border with North Carolina, extends to the top of Mt. Mitchell, the East's highest peak, almost 6,900 feet in elevation.

Fraser and balsam firs do not overlap in their ranges. Fraser occurs with ferns, mosses, and viburnums like witch hobble (a shrub). As site quality improves for balsam fir, more hardwoods enter the stand. These first may at times appear subclimax to spruce and hemlock, though generally considered very shade-tolerant in relation to red spruce.

In the north woods, the spruce—fir forest cover type captures much of the land in the Hudsonian and Canadian life zones. Balsam fir, a short tree, seldom grows taller than 75 feet. Sixty feet is typical. In peat bogs on which it is commonly found, a pH of 4, quite acidic, is normal. On such sites, from the Lake States to Labrador, high surface temperatures of the dark-colored, heat-absorbing soil, droughty conditions in those spongy lands, and frost heaving that kicks seedlings out of the ground take their toll. On such lands the ground is frozen much of the year to a depth of 2 feet. This species, like some spruce trees, grows in permafrost (which does not occur in the "lower 48" states), the surface several inches thawing enough in summer to sustain tree growth. A rule of thumb for muskeg temperature in the arctic permafrost is that it is 10°F lower than adjacent soils.

Scandinavia's Presentation to North America

We note here the presence of Norway spruce (*P. abies*) throughout much of the northern three-fourths of the United States and into Canada. An important timber tree in the higher latitudes of Europe, early timbermen and landscapers brought it to America. In its native habitat, resin from its veins is used as raw material for Burgundy pitch, and its bark is used for tanning leather. There, too, spruce beer, derived from boiled twigs, has been a favored drink, and its wood continues to serve the paper and lumber industries. West of the Atlantic, Norway spruce's highest use is for landscaping. However "escapes" from early-day plantings—beginning not long after the turn of the century—intrude into forests of other conifers and of deciduous trees. Shelterbelts and windbreaks of the American prairies and plains often include rows of Norway spruce. Its appearance as a fir no doubt encouraged a taxonomist to assign *abies* as its species name.

Names and Their Derivations

By now the reader recognizes the writer's fascination with tree names. Black spruce looks black. Standing a hundred yards from the edge of a stand, one might readily surmise the trees are dead, the bark appearing charred. Especially is this apparent in Alaska's *taiga*, a Russian word adopted by Native Americans of the Yukon country for their "land of little sticks." Short, brown hairs on new growth seem to blanket the whole tree, suggesting an eerie profile of desolation. In Maine, folks call the lowland forests of this species "black growth." Foresters' type maps even designate them that way.

Sometimes black spruce is called bog spruce, for its habitat. Miller, the botanical classifier, called it *mariana*. Here seems to be his reasoning, though a bit circular: it's a New World species. Perhaps he considered other North American spruces the same species as those of his native land. Though black spruce lives on moist flats, along lake shores, and in bogs of sphagnum moss, its name does not relate to "marine." To Miller, *mariana* meant Maryland, but black spruce doesn't grow in the state with that name. To him, Maryland meant the whole of the New World. He was a Scot, his loyalty was to Mary the Queen. Had he his way, maybe this land would be the United States of Maryland.

As for *white* spruce, the glaucus bloom on new needles radiates a faint *bluish* tinge. The species bears two other common names: cat and skunk. The "cat" name connotes nothing about the feline variety. Here it is the polecat, the skunk, the odor of which the tree mimics with the bruising of its needles.

Abies, the genus to which dendrologists assign the true firs (in contrast to Douglas-fir) simply refers, in classical Latin, to an evergreen tree. The *balsamea* name for the northern species is obvious; *fraserii*, the species in the southern mountains, honors the tree's discoverer, a Scot plant explorer of the late 16th Century. A ground-hugging dwarf form of *fraserii*, variety *prostrata* (naturally!) is found in matted stands on exposed wind-swept summits in the Southern Highlands.

Big Trees Among Them

On many sites, trees of these species may be economically mature for pulpwood before reaching the century mark. Sometimes it takes 200 years for sawtimbers to be 24 inches dbh, the size desirable for lumber. Large trees occur among them. The National Tree Register of Big Trees, maintained by the American Forestry Association, records these data for the largest individual of each species:

Species	Date	Circumference (feet)	Height (feet)	Location
Black spruce	1972	5	83	Minnesota
Red spruce	1973	14	110	North Carolina
White spruce	1975	10	128	Minnesota
Norway spruce	1976	16	108	New Hampshire
Balsam fir	1962	7	116	Michigan
Fraser fir	1972	9	87	North Carolina

The Muskeg Bog

The likelihood that many readers never have journeyed into a bog, there to sink abruptly to the knees, suggests a few lines to describe these sites where trees grow on partially decayed wood. Organic debris 60 feet deep is not unusual, though 3 to 8 feet is normal, the upper 6 inches consisting of raw sphagnum. Chunks of charcoal in the peat are common, telling of past fires that destroyed the forest; yet it started anew. Black water oozes beneath the sedge peats of black spruce stands. At the base of the organic zone lies bedrock, often of limestone which counteracts the acid exuded by the peat and raises the pH from the typical 4 to 6 or 7. Sand and clay may also underlie peat. Raw woody material resting just above the mineral layer and at the base of the peat indicates that forests once arose from the mineral soil. Organic matter and water in time filled the sunken zone to cause the death of the earlier stand of trees.

Some foresters believe that pH and peat depth are guides to the quality of the land for tree growth. The best guide, however, is the plant material from which the peat is derived—heath, mountain laurel, blueberries, or alder. Each provides a clue to the vigor of the stands of timber growing in these organic residues.

Adventitious roots sprout on black spruce stems growing in bogs. As the organic horizons fill in, burying trunks and cutting off air to roots, new layers of roots arise from buds hidden just beneath the tree's bark. Some folks think of these as advantageous. They are, but the word is adventitious: to arise, to appear. Four or five layers of new roots, to a depth of twenty feet, may emerge as bog depth increases.

Another phenomenon in the bog is layering. Here's how it works for black spruce. A branch hangs near the ground, its weight eventually bending it to the soil surface. As needles fall from above, the litter layer deepens. In the absence of fire in a cold climate, organic debris collects more rapidly than decomposition occurs. Eventually a part of the branch is buried in the ground. It takes root. New air-layered trees replenish the forest as older stems succumb. Other new trees sprout from roots growing just beneath the surface of the land.

Neither red nor white spruce layer in nature. The latter, however, can be rooted in greenhouses by partially simulating nature and then applying a bit of green-thumb technology.

Appalachian Balds

Ecologists continue to be fascinated by the treeless, dome-shaped summits of Southern mountains. No one can account for the development of those balds. From a distance they appear like the shaven head of a caricatured monk. Closer, it can be seen that grass and heath shrubs, like rhododendron and mountain laurel, cover the ground.

Did Native Americans cause the disturbance to the vegetation? Are the balds their ancient burial or ritual grounds? Or could fire, browsing wildlife, or ice and windstorm permanently disturb the land? One ecologist suggests that these openings on the hilltops within the forests of spruce and fir may be attributed to post-glacial climatic fluctuations. The deep soils have no chemicals known to be toxic to trees. The balds, though above 4,000 feet, lie below tree line. (Nature draws no such line in the eastern United States).

From the slough to the summit, woodlands of spruce and fir add immeasurably to man's aesthetic pleasure. These trees, once the subject of cut-out-and-get-out abuse, return in new forests to supply his physical needs as well.

🌲 🌲 🌲 Projects for the Amateur Naturalist

1. Shape Christmas trees. Nicely formed Christmas trees seldom occur naturally, though, from a distance, it may appear otherwise. Try your hand at

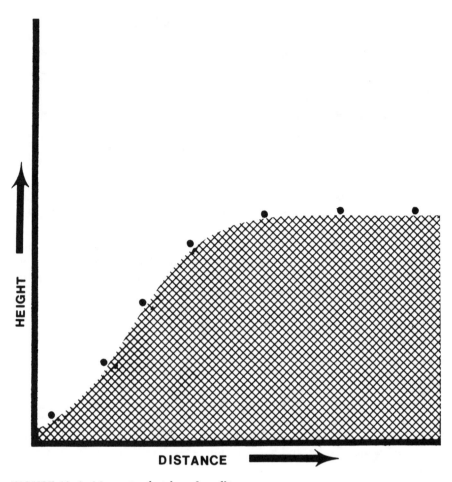

FIGURE 10–1. Measuring heights of seedlings.

shaping several (pines, spruces, firs). It takes patience and an artist's perception of conical symmetry. Several shearings a year should do the job.

2. Measure heights of seedlings that germinated from seeds that were disseminated by wind into an open field (see Figure 10–1). How tall are those 5 feet away from the wall of trees, 10 feet away, 20 feet, 30 feet, and so forth? Graph the variation.

3. Find a stream that flows below a forest, a recently harvested forest, a replanted forest, a farmer's field, or a construction site. Sample the water, using a quart jar, below at least two of these situations, being careful not to stir up sediment. Let the water evaporate and measure, perhaps by weight, the silt and clay that remain.

11

Trees on the Range
Junipers and Pinyon Pine

Other chapters deal with the giants—coast redwoods, Douglas-fir, and sequoias of the Sierras—big trees that pierce the sky. These pages, in contrast, treat the other extreme—the open forests of small pinyon and juniper trees that cover a vast landscape in high range country of the western one-third of the United States. For short trees, even when 250 to 350 years old, 30 feet is typical of their greatest height, though an occasional stem twice that tall may develop. The many species—or varieties, depending upon the system of classification—of trees in these forests persist on dry, shallow, gravelly, or rocky soil on the mesas, slopes, and canyon walls. Elevations range from 2,000 to 9,000 feet, depending upon latitude, aspect, and local rainfall.

For details of taxonomy, the reader should consult a reliable dendrology text. Suffice to record here three species of pinyon pines: *Pinus cembroides* (Mexican pinyon), *P. monophylla* (singleleaf pinyon), and *P. edulis* (the nut pinyon, most common of the three). Earlier botanists called *monophylla* and *edulis* varieties of *cembroides*. Some dispute takes place about a fourth species: perhaps *P. quadrifolia* (Parry pinyon) is really a variety of *P. cembroides*. And, while on the subject, foresters spell it pinyon, Webster uses pinon, the Spanish say piñon, and the reader can see the author's preference.

Junipers in mixture with the soft pinyon pines are many, including the one-seeded *Juniperus monosperma*, the alligator bark of *J. deppeana* (once called *pachyphloea*, a fitting title from the Greek), the Utah juniper *J. osteosperma*, and at higher elevations, the Rocky Mountain juniper *J. scopulorum*. And don't overlook ground or common juniper (*J. communis*), common throughout Europe, Asia, and most of the United States, as well as in the land of the forests of dwarf-like trees.

Pinyon pine and its juniper associates on the lower slopes of the arid West (USDA Forest Service photo).

"A Worthy Purpose"

The principal purpose of these forests in nature, at first glance, must be to hold the world together. Yet, Indians have used them for perhaps 20,000 years, and neither they nor the white man's ax have much affected them. Indians, birds (particularly turkey and the always present pinyon jay), and mammals feed upon the nuts, especially rich in vitamins and proteins, of the pinyon pine. People in places like New York now eat most of the "commercial" harvest. Easy opening of the cones in times other than the brief period of natural seed dispersion is facilitated by piling the cones and heating them slowly. When eaten whole, the brown seeds are consumed raw or, preferably, roasted overnight in large outdoor ovens. About a million pounds per year go to market.

The nuts, claimed to be better than those the Spaniards found at home, were pounded into flour by the colonists as well as by the natives who for so long had lived off of the land. Pinyon pine was used by Indians for house timbers, posts, and firewood, the resinous wood giving off a pungent aroma when burned. It is also easily worked by crude hand tools, utensils having been found by archaeologists in ancient dwellings. From the cones an incense is derived.

The chemical nature of the wood of the nut pines is unique and complex. From no other tree has a turpentine been extracted containing ethyl caprylate, the compound that gives an exquisite fragrance to the liquid. This organic chemical, an amyl alcohol, has been isolated as the acrid oily liquid also occurring in insufficiently distilled grape brandy and as an ingredient of the orange. Not only is the pygmy tree a conifer for food and flavor, resin from the wood makes good caulking for boats.

Junipers, too, have some primitive uses carried over to modern times. Generally the heartwood, resistant to rot, makes good posts; the berry-like edible fruit also gives gin its characteristic taste; oil from the wood and leaves is used in perfumes; and leaf abstracts find favor as a pharmaceutical diuretic. (And for that reason the cowboy steers his stock so as to avoid the "cedars," as members of the *Juniperus* genus are most often called.) Juniper bark was also employed by aborigines for sandals, for cradles, and for torches. The sugar-rich berries contain oxalic acid, the taste of which may have influenced the writing of the ancient Galen who considered the fruit effective in combating the bite of the viper and adder and the miseries of the plague. Another oldtimer, Dioscorides, reported that the wood smoke drives away serpents and insects. These early observations are probably best understood in the light of Linnaeus' comment that Swedes make beer and Laplanders distill "tea" (?) from the berries, an able "remedy" for the bite of the viper. No doubt, that most cosmopolitan of plants, *J. communis*, was the relative of which they wrote.

"Be It Ever So Humble"

Pinyon—juniper woodland is ubiquitous throughout the upper austral lifezone on the mid-slopes of the Rocky Mountains and the eastern face of the Sierra Nevada. This upper austral (meaning south) zone, one of about seven (depending upon whose classification) such ecological strata, is synonomous with upper sonoran, a name derived from the arid Mexican state of Sonora. The 1-mile-plus elevation range, over a 75-million-acre area, typifies much of interior North America and consequently gives significance to the forest cover type both economically and ecologically. In a sense, this vegetation almost wholly inhabits the low ranges of all the southwestern mountains.

Precipitation varies in the upper austral from 12 to 18 inches per year. On the low side, the woodlands are open; where precipitation approaches the upper limit, canopies may nearly close. Below the pinyon—juniper lies the desert shrub biome where rainfall tallies as little as 6 to 8 inches annually. Above, in a rain belt of up to 25 inches a year, one ordinarily finds the forests of ponderosa pine.

Temperatures in the pinyon—juniper type generally read about 5°F lower than in the shrub zone below and 6°F greater than in the tall ponderosa pine forests at higher elevations.

"The Company One Keeps"

Although few other tree species occur in the pinyon—juniper mixture, limber pine (*P. flexilis*), named because the branches are so flexible they can be tied in overhand knots, frequently joins with pinyon—juniper at higher elevations. Natural grasses are important components of the pinyon—juniper desert country. (This is not chaparral, for that's a "Mexican" word for scrubby evergreen hardwoods, usually oaks.) Prominent and much-grazed grasses include grama (*Bouteloua*), needlegrass (*Stipa*), wheatgrass (*Agropyron*), and bluegrass (*Poa*). Pinyon—juniper woodlands often are ecological extensions of the grassy lands beyond the forest in the long rain shadows on the east side of the Rockies. Herbs and shrubs, like *Ceanothus*, that encroach prolifically may, in contrast, be extensions of the Great Basin shrub that lies in the rain shadow to the east of the Sierra Nevada Mountains.

Maintaining the coniferous woodland in the foothills of the Continent's highest divide depends on the exclusion of fire and the control of grazing. Wildfire and overgrazing result in at least a temporary dominance by shrubs over the pines and junipers. Decades may be required for the slowly growing trees to regain their climax positions in the canopy. Overgrazing, however, results in the expansion of the acreage in pinyon—juniper because cattle and sheep prefer grass and forbs to these pungent conifers. They may denude the land between the trees. Consequently, grazing both prepares the site for conifer seed and reduces competition for soil moisture for the newly germinated seedlings. But the large, heavy seeds of both groups of trees fall close to the bases of seed trees, so, without assistance, the forest type spreads slowly.

Extending the Range

Extension of the species into adjoining areas is usually by animal transport of seeds. Rodents and birds ingest and excrete some of the seeds without destroying them. Birds are especially effective in spreading the bony, wingless, berry-like juniper fruit. (They ofttimes get drunk on fermented ones.) Softened by digestive acidic juices and scarified in the gizzard, the hard, waterproof juniper seed coat can readily absorb moisture when it reaches the ground in the bird's droppings. Only then can the embryo enlarge and emerge as a tree seedling. This explains the precise line of juniper trees along fences and under utility lines!

Lest the reader be concerned as to why junipers with "berries" are classed as conifers, a word of explanation. These fruit *appear* as berries, but really are covered with cone scales that have thickened and grown together. One or two seeds are inside the hardened cover.

Viability of pine seeds is short, making prompt germination upon dissemination important for regeneration. All the more so the need to have immediate sprouting from seeds, since they develop, on the average, only every 2 to 5 years. Cones house about 30 seeds, but in good years about 300 pounds (over a half-million seeds) per acre may be available for man, bird, rodent, and reforestation. Harvests for man's or nature's needs occur over a brief 10- to 20-day period in the fall of the year.

Holding the Line

Seedlings of pinyon pines tolerate competition, but lose that ability to endure close neighbors after reaching the sapling stage. Such tolerance is related to site quality: in loamy-textured soils, the moderately deep and wide-spreading root system effectively absorbs adequate water supplies, while fine-textured clays hold moisture more tightly, and the trees grow more slowly. The taproot provides needed anchorage for these open-grown trees exposed to high winds, even though their short stature would not indicate the need for such special protection.

The nut pines as a group, when found in open, sparse stands, show scrubby, contorted, and sprawling form. Indeed, they appear equally as picturesque for their lack of stature as do Douglas-fir trees for their noble erectness. Yet, on the more moist sites at higher elevations where pinyons may grow in relatively crowded and protected conditions, they will be straight. Here, too, diameters may reach 2 feet and heights attain 60 feet.

Although nutrient levels have not been found to affect the growth rate of these species, it does appear that Rocky Mountain juniper prefers soil derived from limestone. In the Edwards' plateau cedar brakes in Texas, too, junipers influence soil pH—the relative alkalinity or acidity—in a way similar to that of eastern redcedar in the Northeast (Chapter 7).

On calcareous and sandy sites, soil immediately under the junipers will be slightly more basic (higher pH) than in the adjacent openings, indicating their ability to "forage" for calcium beyond the crown's drip line and to concentrate the nutrient in needles. From them it is released to the soil as foliage decomposes following needlefall.

Junipers have another intriguing adaptation: the ability to suppress competing understory plants. This may be associated with an extract of decaying foliage that decreases germination of some range species, much as juglone, exuded by the roots of black walnut trees, injures other plants (Chapter 23).

A Nature Note

Before we leave these hardy dwellers of the near-desert, it is necessary to consider one more point basic to much of ecology. Junipers and pinyons grow on these xeric sites not because they thrive only here. On the contrary, they, like nearly all trees, grow faster and larger on better-watered, fertile soil, especially if competing plants are controlled. Why, then, do we rarely find them on such mesic sites? Because on those sites other trees grow even faster, these dry-land species losing out in the battle for space in the sun. But where the going is rough and rainfall sparse, these scrubby but hardy conifers survive with less water than any other tree. Whether by sending roots deeper to hidden moisture, by an ability to transpire less moisture from their small leaves, or by a power to extract moisture from soil too dry for other plants, the junipers and pinyons continue to dominate the landscape of the xeric western foothills.

There, then, is a miracle in nature. That under the skies of turquoise blue, growing in the earth of red and yellow hues, and in the shadows of the silver-tipped mountains, should stand, as a climax woodland, trees so modest in their requirements for sustenance. Or is it rather that in this environment one sees "men as trees walking" and hence more fully recognizes that objects of nature—whether trees or men—serve best when tested by the elements. It may not be just to hold the world together that these stalwarts serve. Perhaps philosophy's end is their greater usefulness. But that is "a matter of a pinyon."

🌲 🌲 🌲 Projects for the Amateur Naturalist

1. If you live in an area where cattle, sheep, or pigs graze, see if you can see over time the effect of grazing by the various kinds of animals: how much soil is left exposed, how the infiltration rates differ (see Chapter 7), what kinds of vegetation are eaten and left, how close to the soil the plants are cropped, and how high the animals reached.

2. See the forest from the air (see Figure 11–1). Order aerial photographs of a forest or park from your county Agricultural Stabilization and Conservation Service. They are not expensive. You can order them enlarged to various scales. With two photos of the same scale you can see the lay of the land in three dimension through a simple stereoscope. It's fun to watch the tall trees pop off the page to poke you in the eye. ASCS will help you locate on their master maps the land you want to view and assist you in placing the order with their photo office. With those photos, look for the number of trees per acre (density), erosion patterns, and species (needleleaf or broadleaf trees). What else can you see?

3. Choose several plots of forest land and determine the stocking density (number of trees per acre). It will probably vary by tree age. Do this on a sunny day near noon. If more than 70 percent of the ground is shaded, the stand is well stocked. If leaves hide the sun from less than 40 percent of the ground, the stand is poorly stocked.

FIGURE 11–1. An aerial photograph. Note the forest stands of various sizes or ages. With a magnifying glass you may be able to also distinguish between broadleaf and needle-leaf trees. Note, too, cultivated fields by the contour plowing, a clearcutting in a forest that has been windrowed, farm ponds, and buildings (USDA Soil Conservation Service photo).

12

Swamp Dweller

Baldcypress

*H*ow do you get a tree to grow in a foot of water when its seed requires exposed mineral soil for germination? That's the question foresters ask about southern baldcypress. Watching nature hasn't been too beneficial on this score, for since we began observing forests and studying the habits of particular trees, *Taxodium distichum* hasn't been noted for its abundant regeneration. Except for chestnut (Chapter 19), this species probably has had the greatest reduction in volume over the past century of any American tree.

Dendrologists, not given to poetic exhibition, have described the species as unique among southern conifers: "In the dim light of an old-growth bald-cypress forest, the massive, often ashy-gray columnar trunks with their peculiarly swollen, fluted bases, and branches bearded with Spanish moss, produce an unforgettably dismal, even sepulchral effect." The reason, perhaps, for the handle "the Dismal Swamp" in coastal Virginia-Carolina! From there to the Rio Grande Valley of Texas, stalwarts stand, one tree reputed to be 3,000 years old.

Don't be fooled by accounts of ancient baldcypress forests if those accounts are based on ring counts. Increment cores from opposite sides of the same tree may vary by 10 percent. False rings, put down as a result of short spurts of growth following periods of drought in otherwise wet areas, enable cypress stems to fudge their age. Hence, three or more growth rings—rather than a single ring—may occur in a year. Ages of 500 years or more are reported, but I doubt their accuracy, even for this tree of rot- and insect-resistance. However, because of the immunities, it not only lives beyond a "ripe old age," but was once in great demand for shingles, shakes, and posts—anywhere wood is used in contact with the soil and exposed to the weather.

A lot of what we see today is not the offspring of the virgin timbers, but a variety commonly known as pondcypress. Many of the southern coastal plain swamps where baldcypress was most widely distributed have undergone this transition. The pond variety, usually called *ascendens* (sometimes called *nutans*) because of its slender ascending appearance, dominates the "black water" river overflows where dark-colored lignin from decaying wood is suspended in the water. Smaller trees with smaller leaves characterize pondcypress. The following statements apply to both kinds of cypress trees.

Unique among southern conifers, baldcypress is deciduous, shedding its leaves each fall like the broad-leaved hardwoods. The naked crowns in winter put "bald" in the common name. In fact, lateral branchlets fall with the scale-

Southern baldcypress and an understory of swamp hardwoods in the South. Note the buttressed base and the conical knees (USDA Forest Service photo).

like leaves. Note that semantically precise woodsmen run the words together since baldcypress is not a true cypress—such belong to the family *Cupressaceae*—but is a member of the redwood or *Taxodiaceae* family, along with the sequoias.

About the Old Forest

Although baldcypress stands are common in the muck swamps and sloughs and along the "red water" rivers carrying silt and clay from the Southern Appalachians and the Piedmont province, best growth really occurs in mesic sites. Mesic conditions—neither too wet nor too dry—are the deep, moist loamy soils which never flood. Why, then, don't we find this swamp dweller there? Because it cannot compete with other vegetation on mesic lands, but on wet sites, it is king and is adapted to survive—or so we thought.

Failure to survive as a forest cover type has been attributed to fire (yes, even in the swamp), drowning (yes, even a baldcypress can get too much water when it's a young, struggling seedling), and failure to retain adequate numbers of seed trees. The high cost of building elevated tramways into the swamps in the late 1800s and the years that followed forced lumbermen to harvest every merchantable tree. Often they were girdled a year in advance of felling; for then the dried tree, when felled into the swamp water by "flatheads" working from a rowed skiff, could be floated to the wooden stilt-supported rails.

Nature is cyclic, and the weather is in nature's realm. Every so often—perhaps once in 5 years or once in 500—surface water in any swamp disappears. That's the time for baldcypress and its pondcypress variety, both ecological pioneers, to become established. But the seeds must be available and they must come to rest on a saturated but not inundated seedbed. And there's the rub, for although produced about every third year, the sticky seeds are scattered only by water, never by wind or animals. To make matters worse, they are often washed from the site of initial deposition by suddenly rising waters that, simultaneously, destroy a potential forest or create one on another site.

About the New Forest

Suppose now that the seed has been "cast upon the waters" and evenly distributed. Suppose, too, that just at this time—while those seeds are still viable—a drought comes, and the pond almost (but not quite) dries up. Suppose also that the soil which is still a little moist remains just so for three months in the spring and into early summer. If the suppositions hold, we've probably got a crop of germinated baldcypress seedlings. But one thing yet is needed: the seedlings must not be inundated for more than three weeks during their first year. If the water is warm, reducing the level of free oxygen, or if there are silt and clay sediments in the water to precipitate to the bottom and clog the soil pores, death will likely follow.

How to imitate nature without diking, ditching, irrigating, and draining hasn't been figured out. Some foresters grow seedlings in nurseries for a year (trees are by then 30 inches tall and ½ inch in diameter), then thread the stiff long taproots into holes poked into the ground with a sharpened broomstick. Healthy trees on the best sites may grow a foot or more that first year, but if the soil is covered with water, the woods laborer may nurse a swollen foot from an alligator entanglement. The possibility of threading a cottonmouth moccasin's tail into that planting hole deserves consideration too.

As those young trees grow, swamp rabbits may clip as many as 75 percent of them—but only on nonflooded sites. Nutria also, the oversized rodent pest introduced from South America in the 1930s, pull seedlings out of the ground to eat the roots. Damage is greatest on flooded sites, for this creature prefers to feed in the safety of the water.

How to economically regenerate new stands of this valuable softwood is a matter awaiting the wit and wisdom of researcher and practitioner. Any tree that can produce freakish appendages like knees and buttresses ought to be able to handle its own "sustained yield" problems. The solutions to those problems have thus far eluded foresters.

Woodland Cathedral

Graceful gothic arches formed by interlacing branches of cypress trees tower above the algae-green bayou. Rising from the mixture of silt and peat that carpets the floor are groups of cypress knees, standing erect, resembling monks in the Woodland Cathedral's sanctuary.

The wood thrush sings a solo, while a choir of prothonotary warblers and American redstarts keeps cadence with the wind. The tones rise to a crescendo a half-hour after daylight, then gradually die to a hush as though all the creatures of the wild are at rest. The morning sun beams through crowns of delicate green and gold hues, like a stained-glass window. As the sun moves, its light is radiated and reflected from leaf to leaf and to the ground.

The Woodland Cathedral is a small island in a 175-acre forest beside an East Texas river.

The "columns" in this Cathedral are southern baldcypress, measuring at least 38 inches in diameter, breast height, and 30 inches above the butt swell. The height of these columns exceeds 120 feet. Among the cypress are thousands of overcup oak seedlings coming to life from seed that fell in a dried-up swamp. This is a combination of factors—proper seedbed, dried-up swamp, and seed abundance—that occurs rarely. Should these oak seedlings endure high water, certain to follow, they will be a significant component of the forest. Foresters call the oak the climax of ecological succession; the cypress is a pioneer.

In times past, the river carved out the vale and later filled it with silts and clays to form an alluvial plain. Throughout the area, natural levees and oxbows formed from the cutting and mounding of old meanders that bear no relation to the river's present course. Some natural levees of recent origin are deep sands deposited at the river's edge. This new soil, washing down from banks cut upstream, is an ideal seedbed for willows and cottonwoods. In time and with ecological succession, sweetgums and blackgums intrude. Later still, oaks and hickories, more tolerant of shade, will become established under the crowns of the more light-demanding trees. A few loblolly pines also may occur on higher, drier land where openings in canopies and exposure of the mineral soil provide the requirements for seed germination and seedling survival. But no *Taxodium*!

No doubt the probably extinct ivory-billed woodpecker nested in the Woodland Cathedral in past decades. A hole in a windthrown, yet well-preserved, baldcypress could have been the entrance to a former nest. The bird has not been seen in the area since shortly after commercial logging began at the turn of the century.

In the Woodland Cathedral tract is a one-half acre area where the trees have been killed by the excretions of perching birds. A putrid odor permeates the air. Nitrogen toxicity, one might say. Currently, the land is home for a rookery of blue herons, but these fishing birds should not necessarily be blamed for the death of the stand of trees. The site once could have been a buzzard's roost.

As the tract never has been cleared for farming or shows evidence of wildfire, there are no stands of pine. Rather, the forest is a complex community of about 50 broadleaf tree species and another 25 woody shrubs and vines typical of those found on early cutover East Texas lands. The baldcypress cathedral forms the centerpiece.

The stand is, of course, not virgin. Its river accessibility probably is responsible for its being selected for harvest soon after white men encroached on the Indian's territory.

Blue Elbow

Texas, the land of bigness, has its petite treasures too. Blue Elbow Swamp, a forested natural area, is a micro-wilderness in a land of vast expanse, a primeval jungle of modest proportions, by Texas standards, at the edge of industrial urbanization.

In the southeastern corner of the state is a 4-square-mile swamp. Had John Bunyan journeyed here, it might have inspired his description of the Slough of Despond, the almost impenetrable boggy terrain through which his pilgrim had to travel en route to the Celestial City. Here occur a stand of baldcypress and a mixture of hardwoods, once of commercial value.

One observer described the locale this way: "Tie up to a cypress root and walk a hundred yards inland (from the river) along a piney ridge, and the human signs are gone. Deeper still, except for an occasional fisherman along the lush canals, the swamp seems as elemental as it must have been when the first logger set his saw against his chosen tree."

The words ring true, but there is more. Here is a place where salt water may intrude with fresh, where salt spray during Gulf coastal storms alters vegetative composition, and where new land forms at the urging of the river. Here, too, the odors of the manufacture of paper, petroleum, and cement may permeate the air, yet one may witness primitive wilderness conditions. Man intrudes, but, with few exceptions, only to the swamp's edge.

How Blue Elbow Swamp, the name now popularly used by fishermen, got its title is partly conjecture. Perhaps the color alluded to the black water, laden with lignin from decaying forest vegetation that accumulates in this pond as overflow from the usually quiet Sabine River near where it empties into the Gulf of Mexico. The Elbow no doubt refers to the sharp bend in the river at the northeast corner of the swamp.

Soils of Blue Elbow were delivered there in water suspensions of the sluggish river coming from faraway fertile calcareous blacklands and picking up silt along the way. While some organic soils in Blue Elbow border on the alkaline, the fibrous surface often has a sour smell, indicative of an acidic condition. On such poorly drained peaty sites, water stands even in periods of drought. Here among the baldcypress, I sank to my knees while making these notes.

Where water is deep, especially, the gracefully arching branches of the baldcypress trees are covered with Spanish moss. The deciduous conifers, on which the weeping tufts of grayish-green strands are rooted and from which they gain nutrients and water, grow well, although the presence of false rings makes age determination unreliable.

Knees and Swollen Butts

The reader may wish a discourse on cypress knees, those peculiar conical structures arising from the shallow, widespread root systems. He'll be disappointed, for their role and cause of origin remain unknown. We're convinced they're not needed for root aeration. The knees grow much faster than the roots and, therefore, demand and consume much oxygen. Yet, little gas exchange occurs between knees and roots. Removing the knees does not affect growth and survival of the tree. Maybe they are an adaptation for physical support in the peaty soils called "trembling earth." (That's English for the Indian *Okefenokee*, the swamp where, if you jump up and down on the ground, the vibration can be felt underfoot 50 yards away.)

An engineer's 10-foot pole won't remain erect on these lands, but the giant trees do. That has been attributed to the interwoven network of, and the anchorage afforded by, a deep root mass beneath the knees.

The reader will also be disappointed in the lack of an explanation for buttressing of trunks, the tapering in the lower part of the stem. This is not for support alone, as the swelling often abruptly terminates below the usual low-water level. Only when the swamp is drained will one discover this shape of the bole.

A Wood Worth Growing

Baldcypress is needed in the nation's wood economy. Resistant to rot, the heartwood makes good shingles, shakes, dock timbers, and pilings. Everyday uses include caskets, laundry tubs, boats, greenhouses, and stadium seats. It is a lightweight wood that may shrink appreciably upon drying. Hence, when used for interior panelling that may be polished to a furniture-like finish, special care should be exercised in predrying below the expected room humidity. Else, large gaps will show between the boards. And, too, only the heartwood is rot-resistant: the peripheral sapwood decays rapidly. Hopefully the swamp dweller will regain its rightful position in the economy as its ecology is better understood.

♣ ♣ ♣   Projects for the Amateur Naturalist

1. Observe insects in living trees, dead standing trees, and dead trees lying on the ground. Note the class to which each belongs: bark beetle, wood borer, leaf eater (defoliator), sap-sucker (aphids, scales), tip feeder, gall maker, or seed feeder. Listen closely—ear to the bark or decaying wood—for the sound of their activity.

2. Collect, identify, and mount twigs. Twigs—perhaps 10 inches long—must be cut during the dormant season to illustrate bud, leaf scar, and other characteristics. They are attached to heavy paper or coated cardboard with thin strips of tape.

3. Observe bird-nesting signs in standing live and dead trees. Is there a relationship that appears consistent between species of tree and bird?

13

Timber for a King

Eastern White Pine

*T*he royal reigning duo, William and Mary, in the colonial period, commanded that white pines above 24 inches diameter should be preserved for the Crown. It seems their majesties were afraid that timbers for ship masts were getting scarce. And indeed they were. The islands of Britain could no longer supply their Highnesses' naval need. But the majestic stems appropriated by the Crown were not in Britain. They were, rather, in New England. There, large broad arrows were blazed on the trunks to warn off would-be loggers. But alas, it all the more frustrated the royal pair. Lumberjacking colonists were not about to preserve the best timber for barging to England where ships would be built to later use against the colonies. The Crown's trees were promptly cropped.

Following the American Revolution, landsmen and loggers had a change of heart. Now a new navy, busily protecting the fledgling nation's boats from North African pirates, needed great trees. The broad arrow policy was again invoked. And for decades those giants of the northeastern forests were saved for the building of boats.

Gifford Pinchot, father of American forestry, called the management of eastern white pine plantations on the Biltmore Estate in the Appalachian Mountains of North Carolina "the first practical application of forest management in the United States." Plantings as early as 1890 by Pinchot (later to be the first chief of the U.S. Forest Service and Governor of Pennsylvania), Henry Graves (also, later, to be Chief Forester and Dean of Yale's School of Forestry), and Carl Schenck (the now-and-then immigrant from Germany who set up the first forestry school in America on the lands of the Vanderbilts in the Pink Beds of the Great Smoky Mountains) are even today the principal source of information on the long-term management of this species throughout much of its range.

A large eastern white pine believed to have been selected and blazed with a broad arrow as a "mast" tree for "H.M.S." in Colonial days (USDA Forest Service photo).

Where It Grows

White pines grow naturally along the Appalachian Trail from Maine to Georgia. They've also been successfully planted on the Florida border of Georgia. Natural sites involve all kinds of soils and underlying rocks. Generally podzols, the Russian term for ash-white, are preferred. These soils are derived from granites, schists, and gneisses at elevations of 2,000 to 4,000 feet. Here, the acidic nature of the humus, coupled with abundant rainfall, causes the iron and aluminum oxides to leach from the surface horizon, leaving the light-colored insoluble silicates behind. Dark reddish-brown mineral pigments then coat the particles in the lower illuvial layer of soil.

Some white pines persist in locally dry sites because of intra-specific grafting of roots. These unions enable movement of moisture from adjacent moist soils to trees on xeric spots. Thus, trees some distance from streams may be sustained during periods of moisture stress by water supplied through root unions.

Sites like these were once covered with American chestnut (see Chapter 19), but the occurrence of a blight wiped out that broadleaved tree. In the openings caused by the disease, as well as those caused by fire, hurricane, and timber harvests, *Pinus strobus* entered.

Large openings and exposed mineral soil encourage the reestablishment of white pine forests. Then the species usually occurs in pure, even-aged stands. Later, from 1 to 20 years, other species encroach and eventually replace white pine in the forests. Beech—birch—maple and spruce—fir forest cover types exemplify those that may take over the land if left unmanaged and if no natural catastrophe occurs. Eastern hemlock is another shade-tolerant tree that enters the forest and later excludes the regeneration of pine.

A Southern Highland Situation

An example, not unique, of hemlock invasion in the Southern Appalachians illustrates an ecological complexity. There, in a fertile cove, Forest Service timber markers had selected certain trees to remove in a harvest. A college professor, finding timber-marking paint on trees in his favorite "virgin" forest where he often brought students to study plant ecology, became highly indignant. A controversy ensued in which Sunday magazine supplements and preservationists drew swords with federal foresters over the management of government lands. The author, invited as a neutral observer to analyze the situation, indeed found large white pines, many over 30 inches dbh and many under 10 inches. Mixed with the stands of pines were eastern hemlocks, also ranging in sizes from over 20 to under 10 inches. All of those pines, regardless of their size, were the same age. This typical even-aged nature of white pine was borne out by increment borings. True, a 10-inch increment borer can only enter two-thirds of the way into the center of a 30-inch diameter tree; but wood cores so removed may be matched with those of smaller trees. Wide rings are matched to wide rings and narrow to narrow, all relative of course, but enabling

This "lone" white pine, overshadowing its progeny, was long a famous landmark in the "cut-out-and-get-out" lands of the Northeast (USDA Forest Service photo).

the forester to ascertain ages of larger stems, making unnecessary the cutting of trees to count their rings.

How It Grows

Now, we know that white pine cannot come in under hemlock canopies. The former is too shade-intolerant and requires bare mineral soil for seed germination. The opposite, however, is the case for hemlock. It is shade tolerant, and its seed may germinate in the duff of the pine forest floor. All ages of *Tsuga canadensis* trees will be represented. Hence, sampling a small tree won't give the age of large ones nearby. But the hemlocks must be younger than the pines.

Oh, we neglected to tell you the age of those "virgin" white pines above 30 inches dbh. Barely 60 years! And the hemlocks from 50 years down. How come these large trees at so early an age? In rich, fertile, moist coves, white pines grow rapidly—3 to 5 feet in height each year in the early years and nearly an inch in diameter each year.

Look now at the soil of this site: deep loam made up of colluvial silts and clays washed from the slopes of the cove—all the way to the ridges—and the residual sands released in the weathering of the crystalline rocks. The land is rich in organic matter, too, from accumulated leaf litter in the cool climate of the mountains. Here the average dominant and codominant trees may well exceed a hundred feet in 50 years, a land-productivity–tree-growth relationship the forester refers to as site index.

Look further at the soil and use a spade. The washed-in colluvium is 6 inches deep. Below it is an old surface soil. Dig deeper with the spade. The old surface layer is really a plow zone; for 6 to 8 inches under what was once the surface is a plow sole, the line left in the ground from perennially plowing this fertile cove. But wait, you say, why would the mountain people of the Appalachian Highlands put their "hands to the plough" in these small coves? The rest of the story is in the Court House records. They did because they were a staunchly independent people. This was their soil, their land to farm. But finally fortitude was not enough, and we find the tragic account of land abandonment and mass migration from the hills to the towns below. By oxcart and on foot, they left the land they loved in the agricultural depression of the 1890s. When the farmers left the land—warm, freshly plowed, and ready for seeding—white pine seeded in to begin anew the ecological cycle. (Later the U.S. Forest Service acquired the land under the Weeks Law of 1911.) We note the warmth of the seedbed, for, in contrast, soil under a dense forest canopy is cool because little solar radiation reaches the woodland floor. Root growth and, hence, tree vigor are consequently reduced in shaded sites.

A Northern Highland Situation

The sensitivity of white pine to soil nutrient levels is well documented. Growth reduction may be accompanied by foliage chlorosis, shortening and death of needles, and a decrease in the number of years that needles persist before falling from the twig to the ground. This, due to potassium deficiency, is notable on deep sand terraces of glacial outwash in the Adirondack Mountains. There, too, a bright-yellow discoloration of current season's needle tips, appearing in the fall and affecting most strongly the upper parts of trees, is symptomatic of magnesium deficiency.

Deep sandy soils occur rather extensively in the Adirondack Mountains of New York State. These level "sand-plains," as they are locally called, were formed from glacial river deposits as lake terraces during the late Pleistocene Ice Age. As the glacier receded and the lakes were drained by nature, expanses of easily tilled soil were uncovered. Virgin spruce, pine, and hemlock forests followed in the course of history. Then, because of the favorable topography of the flatlands and the absence of loose stones, farmers broke new ground early in the nineteenth century. One hundred years of extensive agriculture followed. During that time little, if any, fertilizer was applied or soil-improving crops used, and the farm lands, depleted of their natural fertility, were finally abandoned. Chunks of charcoal, still found in the surface horizon of the soil, attest to the effort to apply nutrients—as wood ash—to these impoverished sites. "The raising of field crops or animals was no longer profitable," said one historian.

Even the quality of native vegetation continued to experience a declining transformation. After abandonment for cultivated crops and hayfields, poverty grass took over, and then *Polytrichum* moss encroached. Other less demanding mosses and lichens next invaded the areas, and finally there was no vegetation. Erosion followed and presented a despairing scene.

Then, around 1930, foresters decided to put these lands back to work. Pines, spruces, and other conifers were planted on the old-fields; and, once again, the prehistoric lake terraces supported trees. But after a few years it became evident that these plantations weren't growing satisfactorily. Symptoms of a nutrient deficiency appeared.

Professors S. O. Heiberg and D. P. White of the College of Forestry at Syracuse, New York, attributed these malformations—slow growth and small chlorotic needles that drop off prematurely—to a deficiency of potash in the soil. Subsequently, the symptoms of low potassium availability were noted in native white pines of the region. Dr. E. L. Stone of Cornell has also found this potassium deficiency to accompany shortages of magnesium in sandy soils.

White Birch Nurse Trees

I describe one observation here to demonstrate the ability of white birch (*Betula papyrifera*) to restore available potassium to the surface soil. Because of this soil-enriching influence, native white pines appear healthy and normal.

In the eastern Adirondacks, vigorous white birch trees about 40 feet high occur rather sparsely in old-fields. Under these trees one finds many white pine seedlings and saplings. These pines thrive under the crowns and on all sides of the birches, but only to the crown edge. They manifest none of the characteristics of potassium deficiency. However, isolated white pines scattered throughout the same field but not growing under birch crowns exhibit symptoms of malnutrition.

Chemical analyses of the soil showed the amount of "exchangeable" potassium to be much greater in the plow horizon under the birch—pine groups than in the open. Other chemical differences were also obvious from the analyses.

Below the plow horizon, the soils do not seem to differ appreciably. From samples taken at several depths in soil profiles, it was learned that, both in the open and under birches, a rapid decrease in potassium occurs with increasing depth. Only traces of exchangeable potassium are present in the upper subsoils and the amount of the nutrient is relatively constant to a depth of 4 feet. This emphasizes the importance of the surface soil to the nutrition of plants—even for forest trees that often have deep root systems.

The ameliorating effect of white birch on white pine nutrition, judging from foliar analyses, shows that birch trees have the ability to "forage" for scarce potash in lower horizons and return this nutrient to the surface soil through decomposition of fallen leaves. The element then becomes available to understory pines. As might be expected, these pines have about twice as much foliar potassium as those grown in the open. All open-grown white pine needles analyzed well below the critical potassium limit for this species.

One important factor remains unknown! What was the condition of the site under the birches prior to their germination? Did the birches, for instance, come in on decayed brush or ash piles? If so, the foregoing discussion would need modification, for the soil, and thus the trees, would have been supplied vital nutrients released from the organic debris following decomposition. As a result, a condition favorable for establishment and growth of birch, and subsequently pine, would have followed. However, no peculiarities, such as charred wood or darkened organic leachates, were found in the soil.

A more plausible explanation is that birch, by its strong nutrient cycle, supplies organic matter that enriches the soil directly under its crown. This continual return of nutrients to the soil through deposition of leaf litter on the surface, followed by decay and leaching, is not unusual. It is an important factor influencing soil fertility. Plow-zone calcium concentrations, for instance, are significantly greater under redcedar crowns than under neighboring red pines on abandoned field soils in Connecticut (see Chapter 7). And when only the logging slash (tops and branches) of maples and pines or the humus from natural woodlands of pines and hemlocks is applied to potash-deficient soils, substantial improvement in the vigor of pine and spruce follows. These applications also result in higher potassium concentrations in needles. Thus, one might say the nutrients were restored to the surface soil by the "pumping action" of the birch.

A Nutritional Malady

Since the total amount of potash present is quite sufficient, it seems apparent that basic nutrients, like potash, are leached about as rapidly as released by mineral and organic matter of the surface soil. The slow rate of silicate soil breakdown and the great loss to drainage water certainly contribute to the potash deficiency problem. Some potash is, of course, absorbed from lower soil horizons by plant roots before the nutrient is lost to streams or percolated past the root zone. Translocated to above-ground tissues, it is again released in soluble form in the surface soil following decomposition of these tissues.

Considering organic matter as largely colloidal in nature, it seems apparent why the relationship between the content of that material and available potash exists. Exchangeable potash is absorbed in ionic form on the minute colloidal particles in the soil. The amount of mineral colloidal matter in coarse sandy soils is too small to have much effect on the supply of potash in ionic form. Hence, most of the element in available form is held on the organic colloids. So in light soils, organic matter is the "frugal custodian" of the potash supply.

A Barren Land Reclaimed

One will no doubt wonder what earthly value such barren lands as these Adirondack Mountain sand-plains can be. Fertilization for cultivated crops continues to be economically prohibitive, and cattle starve if dependent upon grass and forbs growing in the sand-plains.

How about tree crops? Spruces and some pines—white and red—as noted earlier, won't grow well, but Scotch pine does. Scotch pine, quite in demand for Christmas trees in the New York City area, brings a premium price when magnesium-deficient. Then it is marketed as "golden Scotch," its yellow needles caused by chlorosis still prominent on trees planted a generation earlier.

But even the potash-demanding spruce and pines may make nice Christmas trees if fertilized. Commercial muriate of potash is easily broadcast in plantations of trees less than 10 feet tall.

Chemical Tests as a Tool

Can laboratory tests of leaves tell us in what soils to plant Scotch pine and where not to plant white spruce? Can potash-deficient, abandoned agricultural land be so readily recognized?

To learn the answer, we sampled thousands of leaves of many species of native plants. Trees, shrubs, grasses, herbs, and even moss were tested. In the leaves of six species, potassium was found related to exchangeable potash in the soil plow horizons. From these relationships we obtained an index of site potential simply by analyzing the foliage.

White pine was the most useful species found. Analyses showed a high consistency between soil and leaf potash for both early July and late August leaf sampling. Also of special interest was the consistently lower amount of potash in needles as the growing season progressed.

Choke cherry (*Prunus virginiana*), American beech (*Fagus grandifolia*), trembling aspen (*Populus tremuloides*), bunchgrass (*Andropogon gerardi*), and wild strawberry (*Fragaria virginiana*) leaves likewise showed a potash relationship in plow-zone soil.

When exchangeable potash concentrations in plow zones analyze less than 20 parts per million, deficient-appearing white pines usually result. Based upon this observation and the soil-leaf potash relationship, foresters can know the critical foliage values below which planting sites have too little of the nutrient for satisfactorily sustaining the growth of economically important trees.

Foliage Symptoms for Diagnosing Ailments

Discolorations in leaves of native trees also serve to indicate soils too potash-deficient for the more desirable conifers, such as white and red pines and the spruces. This seems especially true for wild black cherry (*Prunus serotina*). About the middle of August, bright red leaf margins appear. They extend almost to leaf tips and one-half the distance to the midrib in the center of the leaf.

The line of demarcation between pigmentation is well defined. By late September, the colored margins widen and extend to the leaf tip. Red color intensity also increases, and blue and violet hues result. Autumn coloration is distinctly different. Trees so affected occurred only on low-potash soils. Other malformations indicative of low-potash levels were subsequently noted for gray birch, blackberries, red maple, and several herbs.

In contrast, jack pine and Scotch pine show no potash deficiency symptoms and apparently do not demand much of this nutrient from the soil. These latter species, however, exhibit signs of magnesium starvation: the needles have golden tips.

An Insect Malady

Fortunately throughout its range, this species seeds-in in dense stands—5,000 or more seedlings germinating in a typical acre. That is good because white pine weevils and white pine blister rust take their toll. The former, a pest that attacks terminal buds, results in crooked stems. A lateral branch then takes over to grow skyward as a substitute for the dead terminal stalk. The trees are not killed, only deformed. As the weevil doesn't fly higher than 20 feet, any damage done will be in the first few years of the life of the stand. Because, too, all the trees in the new forest are never attacked, a dense stand assures a satisfactory number of straight, healthy trees to be carried toward maturity. Once the terminal shoot grows beyond the insect's range, the forester may direct the harvest, perhaps for fence posts or pulpwood, of the insect-deformed

These gray birch leaves exhibit potassium deficiency. They serve as deficiency indicators for other trees like white pine. Can you find unusual coloration in foliage of nearby trees which could suggest nutritional problems?

individuals. He thus frees residual stems from competition and so encourages optimum growth.

Sunshine, a Malady

Sunscald injures southern and western sides of white pine trees, particularly young saplings with smooth bark less than ⅓ inch thick. It is not necessarily due to high summer temperatures, but may be caused either by late afternoon summer temperatures high enough to kill cambial cells or by rapid dropping of the temperature after sunset in winter. North and east sides of trees are less susceptible, as temperatures do not fluctuate as much on these faces. Injury occurs after late-wood growth (the radial increment of summer-wood) is complete and before early-wood (that laid down in the spring) is produced the following spring.

Whether topography and direction of slope influence the occurrence of sunscald is not known. If they do, regeneration harvests on southern and western exposures, especially, should be by the partial-harvest shelterwood method, as gradually opening the forest in several cuttings permits early development of deep, corky bark layers that, when complete exposure occurs, should be fairly immune to sunscald.

Shelterwood harvests maintain openings with diameters less than the heights of residual stems, as holes in the canopy small enough to permit shading from the south greatly reduce injury. Yet, such openings must be large enough for good seed distribution. If widths of openings have to be wider than heights of residual stems, foresters suggest harvesting strips that run in a northeast to southwest direction to minimize exposure to the late afternoon sun. Screens of sunscald-resistant species, where available, are left on the south and western boundaries of forests. If they are not present, white pines with low branches may be retained on stand borders.

Many seedlings die of heat (if released too soon), drought, pales weevil attacks, and logging damage. Scattered low-lying slash on the forest floor reduces solar radiation, retards moisture evaporation, and encourages the growth of *Polytrichum moss* that, in turn, favors establishment of white pine. However, dense moss may be detrimental to early growth of seedlings of this species.

A Pathological Malady

Fomes annosus, a root and butt rot fungus that spreads from infected dead to living roots, increases epidemically with frequent thinnings of plantations. The disease seldom occurs in unthinned plantations, possibly because of the relative scarcity of such stands for observation or because the disease does not build to epidemic and noticeable proportions until stands are more than 20 years of age. By that time, thinning is usually done. Trees dying through natural thinning use up soluble carbohydrate reserves in roots, leaving dead tissues—a poor medium for growth of this fungus in contrast to healthy roots left following a harvest of living trees. However, annosus root rot does occur in natural stands where previous cutting has taken place. Living trees are probably infected through root grafts or contact with infected stump roots. The disease is even more serious in slash pine (see Chapter 18).

An Environmental Malady

In these times of environmental talk, emergence tipburn, a needle blight of white pine of unknown origin, concerns foresters. First described in 1908 and recently most obvious, death follows reduced growth. Symptoms include browning of current year's needles from their tips, usually in midsummer. The dying terminal halves of the needles first appear reddish-brown, and later the dead portions wither and break off. Sometimes the entire crowns of small trees are affected, but not necessarily those of large trees. In 1961, the disease symptoms became evident throughout the Southeast within several days.

Foliar dwarfing, chlorosis, and stunted shoots follow dieback of the needles for several years. This is accompanied by shriveled or wrinkled bark and raised pockets of pitch on the bole. Extensive dying of feeder roots also occurs. The malady does not seem to have soil or tree-age preferences. Plantations and naturally occurring stands are affected. Varying degrees of tipburn among susceptible trees and the absence of symptoms on neighboring stems indicate that resistance may be attributed to genetic factors. There is evidence that the malady is caused by atmospheric conditions, perhaps excessive ozone—the gas liberated by the operation of electric motors, sulphur dioxide given off where coal is burned, or the chlorine gas of industrial manufacturing.

And White Pine Blister Rust

The infamous fungus that causes white pine blister rust does its mischief. Where it does, gooseberries, currants, and other plants of the genus *Ribes* must be present, for *Cronartium ribicola* spends part of its life cycle on these low-lying understory plants of the woods. Forestry crews once pulled up the little bushes to later burn but, alas, *Ribes* seeds remain viable in the soil for years and, following a fire, may germinate. Some people call for the eradication program to begin again. But it would probably meet with little success.

The rust may spread hundreds of miles from pines to *Ribes*, but not more than a few hundred feet from *Ribes* to pines. Eradicating pines would likely eliminate the disease more readily than eradicating gooseberries, but that would end this chapter here, and I have one thing more to say.

You recall that the official Charter of the Massachusetts Bay Colony in New England required the stockpiling of white pine trees on the stump for the Royal Navy. In the three hundred years since, kings and empires have fallen, several generations of these conifers have been harvested, and softwoods find little employment in merchant ship construction. Yet, for a thousand other uses, *P. strobus* remains, even where royalty is not appreciated, timber for a king.

🌲 🌲 🌲 Projects for the Amateur Naturalist

1. Pines generally consistently have a certain number of needles in a bundle (fascicle) as they hang on a branch. (White pines usually have five.) Now with several hundred samples, determine the reliability of the number given in various tree-identification books for a particular species.

2. White and red pines, among others, ordinarily add one whorl of branches each year. Find the age of trees by counting the whorls on several such trees. Whorl-counting, with experience, can be used in multi-whorl species like the southern pines. There, the longest internode of each group begins the season's elongation in the spring.

3. Map a forest soil profile. Either a hole several feet deep may be dug (be sure to refill it) or a road-cut cleaned with a spade. Show the soil horizons (litter layer—fresh leaves; fermentation layer—partially decomposed organic matter but the origin still identifiable; humus layer—wholly amorphous and material of unidentifiable origin; A_1 layer—some organic matter mixed with mineral soil; A_2 layer—mineral soil above a stiff subsoil; B layer—stiff, compact soil, usually clayey in contrast to the A layer; C layer—parent material from which the surface soil is derived; and D layer—bedrock. All horizons need not be present. Show, too, plant roots and stones in the profile. Cross-section paper is useful for charting, using a scale of 1 inch = 1 foot.

14

From Monterey to the World

Monterey Pine

*I*f the biblical observation that "A prophet is not without honor except in his home country" could be said of trees, Monterey pine would be the most likely candidate for honor.

At Home and Abroad

Found in nature at several isolated locales along the California coast and on the Guadalupe Island off Mexico's Pacific coast, most *Pinus radiata* stands in North America are but a few thousand acres. Only one exceeds 8,000 acres. Efforts to extend the limited range adjacent to the existing stands have been only partially successful. Yet seeds carried to Australia and New Zealand more than a hundred years ago by the pioneers of the land "down under" were successfully planted. And from those seeds extensive forests developed. A century later North American industrialists, observing the notable growth in those vast plantations, directed company foresters to again try to produce this warm-winter tree beyond its original territory. If it could be used for lumber and pulpwood—and fresh fruit baskets—in Australia, why not so in the U.S.A.?

Efforts in Florida—where thousands of acres were planted by the administrative edict of well-travelled and observant industry chiefs—as well as in lands far beyond its natural range in California failed, but the species was found hardy in the rainforest climate of the Puget Sound locale. Yet the growth of trees in the island continent continued to gain worldwide attention. Introductions in Chile and Uruguay in South America, in South Africa, and in Spain also have been productive. Some South American plantings failed, poor drainage and high water seemingly the cause.

The unique southern Pacific situation, at first note, could logically be

Monterey pine, the California signal tree, and its offspring (USDA Forest Service photo).

An early-day introduction into South Africa of Monterey pine. This stand averaged 88 feet tall and 9 inches dbh when about 10 years old (source unknown).

attributed to the absence of natural "predators" where the species has been introduced. There, insects and disease-causing fungi are not likely to have appetites for *P. radiata*. But this, on further study, appears not to be the case. For it is the climate among the factors of site that is most responsible for controlling the natural range. Why then, when removed from its normal locale and with the immigration of microbes and insects to attack the trees, should stand establishment and growth still be good? In spite of the differing climates, this is not understood.

Climate Preference

At home, Monterey pine grows on coastal and island forests, from sea level to thousand-foot elevations, where average rainfall for any particular locale ranges from 15 to 35 inches a year. While the mean is more than 30 inches, minimum and maximum recorded annual precipitation within the zone amount to 5 and 50 inches. In this relatively maritime climate of high humidity, summer fogs prevail and winters are mild. The most adverse climatic factors are abnormal summer rains (that favor disease-causing fungi), frost, hail, and wind.

Soil Preferences

Next to climate, soil is the factor most limiting to the survival and growth of Monterey pine; hence, the species is sometimes called an edaphic climax cover type in the language of the forester. Monterey pine does best on calcareous sandy loams high in organic matter. It also grows in sandy soils lacking in fertility and even in sand dunes where its ability to endure is accompanied by tolerance to salt, both in the soil and as ocean spray on foliage.

The species prefers deep organic matter mixed with the mineral soil, while its presence encourages the deepening of that soil humus horizon. Humus (H) layers develop under 3 to 6 inches of needle litter on good sites only. This H layer is the work of microflora and microfauna as well as larger soil animals and plants that decompose the needles. Because the H layer is homogeneous, one cannot tell from what material it is derived. Just above the H is the F layer, indicating fermentation and evidenced by the partial breakdown of needles, twigs, and other organic material, the origins of which are yet identifiable. On the surface, and added to it each year, is the litter or L layer. Depending on the vigor of the trees and the density of the stand, annual supplements of needles may amount to ½ inch or so. Equilibrium is maintained between needle-fall and decay on better sites with an L layer depth of 6 inches. Decomposition is more rapid on better sites because of the higher nutrient levels in the foliage on which the lower forms of life feed and which stimulate their vigor and reproduction. Greater volumes of foliage, of course, also are produced and fall to the forest floor on productive lands.

In Australia's forests, zinc and phosphorus have been found to be inadequate to support the rapid growth of planted trees. Fertilizer applications of these nutrient elements correct disorders, especially a dieback caused by zinc deficiency.

Site quality and site index, measures of the productivity of lands for the growth of trees, are useful tools for *P. radiata* management. While tree heights often and generally reach 70 feet in 50 years (SI) on high-quality sites where the soil is 4 feet deep, stems may top out at 120 feet. Site index will likely be highest on northern and eastern aspects (in the northern hemisphere) where favorable moisture supplies are apt to be conserved for tree growth rather than evaporated as on the warmer southern and western slopes facing the afternoon sun.

Discriminating Preferences

An intriguing ecological characteristic involves the botanical tree associates of Monterey pine. Monterey cypress accompanies the pine in low areas in its home base, while Bishop pine is the principal associate at higher elevations. For both altitudes and in between, California live oak is the most abundant understory component. Further north, redwood mixes with Monterey pine along the coast, Douglas-fir on the middle slopes, and knobcone pine at the upper reaches. Ground covers of grass, ferns, vines, poison oak, the infamous manzanita bush that seems to capture the country, and coyote brush compete for soil moisture and nutrients.

Also interesting is the apparent confusion as to the tolerance of *P. radiata* to shade. Rated from very tolerant to intolerant by silviculturists on the tolerance scale, the species has the ability to survive and grow in the understory and in competition for the light of the sun. No doubt, genetic variation and site factors play a role in variously calculating tolerance.

Chromosomal Preferences

A tree of such high commercial value "down under," though of little use for lumber or paper at home, is bound to have its genes thoroughly scrutinized. Differences among racial strains include growth rates, immunity to insect and disease attack, physical properties of the wood, and the time at which trees flower. Less dramatic differences now known between races, indicating the enthusiasm of the chromosome sleuth to know this species, include branching habits (do twigs turn up or down?), number of whorls (are there one, two, three, or four flushes of height growth each year?), and individual dominance (in an even-aged stand, do some stems stand head and shoulders above their neighbors?). "Phenotypes," those trees showing particular characteristics in certain environments, are tested in experimental plantings to ascertain the genuineness of these appearances. Until now, most such trees appearing to be elite fail to materialize as superior "genotypes" when progeny arising from them have been observed.

Crosses between species, however, exhibit hybrid vigor. When Monterey pine is crossed with knobcone pine (*P. attenuata*), an associate in the forest, the hybrid exhibits favorable characteristics of both species. The resulting cross has the rapid juvenile growth of its Monterey parent and the drought and frost resistance of knobcone pine. The hybrid is especially appreciated as a Christmas tree, although Monterey pine itself is often aesthetically bushy and well-formed for the purpose when young.

Geneticists also examine the capacity of the tree for vegetative propagation. Needles cultivated in sand flats in growth chambers with controlled environment can be made to root. So, too, small branches take root and become trees. On such asexually reproduced trees from parents known to be prolific and early seed producers, flowers have formed on stems only 2 years old. Cones produced on the young trees a year later have viable seeds.

Flowers and Seeds

Sometimes a tree has flowers of a single sex only. It is then called dioecious. Most cone-bearing ones, including Monterey pine, are monoecious, with both male and female flowers on the same tree, but separated in different organs. As with other species of trees with imperfect flowers, male flowers are borne on the side branches, a natural provision to reduce the chance for selfing and, hence, nonviable seed. Wind carries pollen upward and outward to the female flowers (technically *strobili* for pines) high in the vertical terminal branch of neighboring stems. Otherwise gravity would likely cause much pollen from the top of a tree to fall to the flowers on the branches below the same tree. No birds or bees are involved here: just wind.

Cones of this species are often serotinous—that is, heat is required to open them and so the "delay" or serotinous condition. Closed cones have been retained on trees for years, during which time viability of encapsulated seed slowly diminishes—perhaps by 50 percent in a decade. In addition to heat, nature stimulates cone opening by a unique technique for drying them out. Secretions of resin in the vascular cells of the peduncle, or cone stem, block the movement of water from the branch to the organ.

To get Monterey pine seeds to germinate doesn't require stratification as for many other members of the *Pinaceae* family. No acids, no cold temperatures, and no scarifying of seeds are necessary. Germination seems to depend on air temperature following seed-fall in autumn.

The serotinous nature of the cone, the often intolerant nature of seedlings, and the requirement of mineral soil for seed germination suggest clearcutting as an appropriate regeneration harvest method. As dense slash reduces reproduction, it should be scattered; and felling might best occur just after seed-fall. However, "repro" can be too abundant, especially when the harvest is accompanied by a slash-disposal fire, resulting in a million seedlings per acre. Such abundant reproduction may call for precommercial thinning of little trees in order for an adequate number to attain sufficient vigor and growth. Partial cutting, as with a modified shelterwood method, can be used to control density of the new forest.

We noted earlier the erratic behavior of the species in respect to shade tolerance. This is also evidenced by the high stand densities in a clearcut-regenerated forest. Following commercial harvest, "weed" live oaks in the understory of the former stand serve as nurse trees, providing shade for young seedlings. Too much light and heat, especially on exposures to the sun, and serious desiccation result.

Mineral soils for seedbeds, as said before, are preferred. Regeneration occurs in and among annual grasses, but not among the perennials. Apparently seeds reach the soil after annuals die in the autumn.

When seeds germinate, perhaps a dozen cotyledons or seed leaves form. These delicate needles unroll from the seed. As the seedling grows, primary needles appear on the stem. They are borne singly. Later, secondary needles, bright green and flexible and grouped together in bundles of three in a sheath, are the only kind produced for the balance of the life of the tree.

Mycorrhizae—The Good-Guy Fungi

Because there are no pines native to Australia, and because members of the family *Pinaceae* require mycorrhizal fungi for survival, a real stumbling block to success could have occurred in Monterey pine introductions there. These soil microflora, of which perhaps a dozen species participate symbiotically with various pine species, occur naturally in California soils, growing on and infecting the roots of pines and aiding conifer growth by behaving like root hairs. The reader may know of slime balls, one of the stages in the life history of the *Rhyzopogon* genus of mycorrhizae, a root-infecting fungus. Water and nutrients move into the living tissues of tree roots as they pass through the pathogen's microscopic strands growing into and between the plant cells.

The absence of mycorrhizae was for a long time the missing link in the chain of knowledge necessary for introducing slash pines into the Atlantic isle of Puerto Rico. When seeds were planted, nothing happened. When seedlings were brought from Florida nurseries, they grew, having brought in attached to their roots adequate populations of the fungi for inoculating island soils.

The Australia-New Zealand situation was different. Mycorrhizae were found even on sterilized seed. In fact, spores of some fungi have been collected at altitudes of 30,000 feet and brought to earth to germinate. How, then, had they earlier found their way to the South Pacific isles, like those hearty souls who went to the remote Outback? Even without the pines for a symbiotic relationship, they were present when the Aussie pioneers migrating from the Monterey peninsula carried the pines to that land.

Some Pros and Cons

Fast growth (giraffe-like internodes are as much as 16 feet long) and its monopoly of the softwood market in the land down under (few other softwoods grow there) have influenced the introduction of Monterey pine until now it is the most widely planted tree. Many other species have been tried, but without success.

Yet Monterey pine does have defects: the wood is ofttimes weak and brittle, thus trees break in the wind. Considerable lateral movement (not necessarily circular) of the stem—especially in the upper crown—not related to the force of wind causes some trunks to lean and, consequently, develop compression wood. Ordinarily this malformation of cambial cells, stimulated by compression stresses or gravity on the side of the tree in the direction of lean, is not serious. A birds-eye grain, also not a disturbing defect, occurs as a result of heavy epicormic needle development on the trunk. These needles pop out from hidden dormant buds in the inner-bark when trunks are exposed to light and, thus, heat, as when stands are thinned. Nor do Monterey pines self-prune: branches remain for years, hanging on long after they die.

On the plus side is the species' effectiveness in erosion control and improvement in the rate at which rain water infiltrates the soil. Both result from the favorable humus buildup noted earlier. As for that good growth, stems grow 150 feet tall and 18 inches in diameter in 35 years.

A new set of environmental factors comes into play when an exotic is introduced. Insects that elsewhere may be secondary become primary under certain silvicultural and climatic factors; and diseases of stem, root, and foliage are often ineffective on nonindigenous plants. This may be why "down under" Monterey pine stands are known to contain 550 square feet per acre of basal area (BA/A) in contrast to maxima of 180 square feet for many North American conifers. (Cutting off all trees on an acre at breast height—4½ feet above the ground—and adding together the areas of all these stump tops gives the BA/A. It's an important stand description device for the forester.)

A couple of unusual botanical innovations call for citation here. One is the "bracket" formed at the base of trees. It is a reinforcing development of wood between the horizontal roots and the stem, believed to be stimulated by wind action. Another is the inverted umbrella branching habit, in contrast to the water-shedding umbrella of Douglas-fir. With the inverted style, water runs down the trunk to saturate the ground adjacent to the main stem, leaving dry ground at the usual drip line of the crown. Also notable is the ability to root graft with other trees of the species and to interlock with roots of trees of other species. (While intra-specific root grafting is not uncommon, no interspecific truly grafted roots for any trees are known to have developed.)

Certain diseases, as well as natural hormones and synthetic silvicides, translocate through grafts and interlocking roots. The latter behave as grafts, although they can be separated physically by breaking the roots apart without destroying tissues.

To the World

We made it this far in our discussion of Monterey pine without talking about semantics. The tree was named *P. radiata* in Paris, at the botanical garden there, from a cone sent in 1787 and from a seed planted in 1812. Named in English for the old Spanish community on the California coast, also known by the early navigators as the Bay of Pines, the relatively tall stems stand out as a useful landmark for men of the sea. Douglas, the British botanist, called it *P. insignis* for the ensign or signal he could see while sailing along the coast. Races or varieties have been given various species titles.

Though the French taxonomist could hardly have known, the name he gave this tree seems prophetic, for *radiata* means to branch out from a hub like the spokes of a wheel. In migrating to the distant points of the globe, *Pinus radiata* has done this.

🌲 🌲 🌲 Projects for the Amateur Naturalist

1. Determine the volume of wood in 20 standing trees, using tools suggested in Chapter 4, Projects 1 and 2, and Table 14–1 below. For trees between 6 and 10 inches dbh, count the number of 4-foot "bolts" at least 5 inches in diameter in a tree. As a "rule of thumb," 80 bolts equal a cord.

TABLE 14–1. Volume Table (giving board feet ÷ 10 for standing trees) (Multiply figure in body of table by 10 to get board feet)

Tree diameter inches	Number of 16-foot logs		
	1	2	3
10	3	4	5
12	5	8	10
14	7	11	15
16	10	16	21
18	12	21	28

2. Now convert the volume in board feet or cords to an acre basis. This will, of course, depend on the area in which the 20 trees grew. If they were in a plot ⅒ of an acre (66 × 66 feet), then simply multiply by 10.

3. Look for small fungus "hair" on the small feeding roots of pine trees of all ages and sizes. A hand lens may be necessary. Distinguish between the mycorrhizae (good-guy fungi) and real root hairs.

15

Woods of Longevity
White-Cedars and Junipers

Atlantic and northern white-cedars, not truly cedars, and the junipers, including eastern redcedar, are evergreens of diversely different sites that produce wood recognized for its durability. Among the trees closely related to eastern redcedar is Ashe juniper. We find it in once commercial stands in the hill country of central Texas, the western extremity in this discussion of these trees. There it occurs with scrub oaks and mesquite on the expanse of land called the cedar brakes.

On sites not too greatly differing from the wet bogs of the habitat of Atlantic white-cedar grows another rot resisting tree, the southern baldcypress—again misnamed, for it's not properly catalogued as a cypress. Its range overlaps with Atlantic white-cedar to the north and east, but extends south to the Gulf and westward into Texas (see Chapter 12).

ATLANTIC WHITE-CEDAR

Atlantic white-cedar (*Chamaecyparis thyoides*) is a tree pioneer on open peaty soil. On these sites, it's likely the first tree to reinvade following fire, hurricane storms, or clearcutting. Always within a hundred miles or so of the coast and within a hundred feet of sea level, the stands of dense slender stems with interlocking crowns lend an eerie stillness to the dark, dank swamps. The trees, seldom in mixtures with other species, mature at about 80 years of age.

The durability of the heartwood is illustrated by the examples of trees windblown in the last century that were more recently "mined" from under the many years' accretions of peat that buried them. Even under serotinous pond pine stands, one finds cedar logs in the debris, illustrating both the once greater extent of white-cedar forest and the ecological succession of the pioneer

A dense stand of Atlantic white-cedar along the eastern coast (USDA Forest Service photo).

species by the wet-site pine. And sometime past I recall the story of the replacing of Philadelphia's sewer pipes: from the excavated trenches workers raised the original pipes, fashioned from white-cedar heartwood, laid down in colonial days. The high value of the wood for its durability strongly suggests intensive management of the species for use by man.

Acid Swamps

The generally acidic Atlantic white-cedar swamps, called glades (although Webster says glades are "open spaces surrounded by woods") often have a sour smell.

A pH of 3.5 is not unusual. Sometimes water lies above the ground, standing in these organic soils because of the saturation of the sandy subsoil. Thus, the white-cedar endures the chemically reduced soil conditions to the exclusion of pines. Beyond the swamps, where the amount of finer soil particles (silt and clay) increases, hardwoods and baldcypress replace white-cedar. Stagnant water swamps, too, are more likely to be covered with hardwoods; the white-cedar habitat is likely to be a freshwater bog.

Mineral soils may be buried some 20 feet beneath the debris collected over centuries in the absence of drought-induced fire. When fire occurs, it often crowns, moving rapidly in tree tops and killing stems standing in isolated ponds. Ground fires occur simultaneously, once the peat is ignited, burning under the surface of the land, even through winter snows, until the organic matter is again saturated with water.

Viable seeds are safely stored throughout the profile of peat. There they wait for subsidence of water, extinguished fires, and the clearing of land to induce germination. New forests develop in peat, sphagnum moss, or even on mineral soil if moisture is adequate. Seeds sometimes germinate in the crevices of old logs, long buried in the litter and now exposed; but pine needles and broadleaf foliage are improbable germination beds. Only because of its temporary or subclimax position in ecological succession is white-cedar not more common, considering the vast acreages of peaty seedbeds within the species' range.

Already noted is the fact that these trees mature at a young age. When mature, long, clear, straight boles with little taper provide high-quality lumber. Height growth remains steady from seedling time until mid-age, then declines gradually. Diameter growth, however, continues longer. Stand volumes, long before reaching maturity, tally as much as 30,000 board feet per acre. That's a high volume stand for any forest east of the Pacific Northwest and the northern Rocky Mountains.

As many as 1,700 stems per acre are found in stands 60 years old. Such stand density—trees spaced at 5-foot average intervals in each direction—is rare among forests of that age for most species.

Seeds and Seedlings

In time, the value of white-cedar wood will be recognized and efforts made to regenerate these forests along the Atlantic seaboard. Nature will provide some able assistance. For instance, more than 2 million dormant seeds per acre may be stored in the upper few inches of the forest floor. Some will have lost their germinative capacity, but not many, for delayed germination is common with this species. Half the crop of seeds ordinarily remains dormant for a year after seed-fall.

The number of seeds stored in the organic duff has encouraged the use of the upper part of the forest floor for artificial regeneration. Workers simply shovel the fibrous materials into baskets, one bushel taking care of 20 planting spots. Sowing the duff is done between growing seasons. Some light, probably providing heat, is considered necessary, though seed germination does occur in completely shaded sites.

Once the seeds are sown, successful establishment requires adequate moisture within reach of the short taproots arising from the small seeds. As such minute seeds have little stored starch for seedling food in the cotyledonous stage, successful stand establishment demands favorable light as well as moisture.

To supply good moisture often requires drainage, the ditches having devices that control water levels. Uncontrolled drainage in peat soils may lower water to a critical level, especially if air pockets form around roots when water subsides.

Regeneration

Foresters clearcut white-cedar in blocks or strips of 5 to 10 acres in order to obtain natural regeneration. They give two reasons: partial cutting, as with the selection system, results in serious windthrow of residual stems because the trees have shallow roots in the fibrous soils; and where light reaches the ground through openings in the crowns, weed encroachment makes expensive weed-tree control necessary. Even when an area is clearcut, shrubs, vines, and an assortment of broadleaf weed trees capture the area. Control of the jungle of brush is greatly simplified in large openings where chemicals can be used.

When the overstory is removed, as many as 2½ million seedlings on an acre arise from upwards of 8 million seeds typically falling over a 2-year period. These seeds drop in the fall and winter from cones that, like a homemade barometer, open when dry and close again when wetted by rains of a half inch or more. One tree may produce a crop of more than 4,000 cones.

Wind, of course, aids distribution. Seeds from a 50-foot tree growing in the open can be carried 600 feet when the wind moves at 5 miles per hour. Most seeds, on the other hand, likely land not 50 feet from the tree that produced them. Water in a swamp also aids dissemination.

While the shade-intolerant white-cedar competes reasonably well with broadleaf encroachers like paper birch, species of greater tolerance, such as black gum and sweet bay, may form a climax forest on swampy sites. The hardwood trees that get an early start in white-cedar stands increase in vigor with time, so with declining vigor of the conifer and the thinning of its canopy, the timber type abruptly changes. Dense shrub growth does overtop the younger conifer; in that event, the white-cedar stems are as slender as grass.

When labor was cheap, trees in white-cedar stands were pruned to provide high quality lumber. While lower branches die early, they persist—especially in closed stands—for many years. No doubt rot resistance of the durable wood is responsible. Valuable trees with long, clear, straight boles and little taper below the crown result after branches fall.

Wildlife in These Woods

Among the severest competitors of young and mid-aged Atlantic white-cedar trees are the black bears that roam these remote and inaccessible (to man) woods. They have hearty appetites. Birds, along with the bears, also damage these forests. Here's how: seeds of greenbriar, a thorny vine growing in clumps in its initial stages, are transported in the bellies and passed in the droppings of both bears and birds. Great masses of the aggravating vine that later arise from the fecal-deposited seeds weigh down tree tops and break trunks, deforming the boles. Eradication by herbicides seems essential in managing these forests.

Browsing by white-tailed deer in winter, nibbling of seedlings by cottontail rabbits, and girdling of little trees by meadow mice are evidences of wildlife abundance in these wet woods. To manage deer, fencing newly established stands may be necessary to temporarily exclude the offenders. Glade thickets, with their excellent cover, are prime areas for integrating timber and game management.

Problems for Atlantic White-Cedar

Fires play havoc with Atlantic white-cedar, readily destroying forests of all ages. A second fire following close after a first, before there is time for a new stand to replenish the supply of seeds stored in the duff, usually eliminates the species from an area. If the fire is sufficiently hot to consume other woody growth, the stage of ecological succession may be set back to a quaking bog or even to open water. If protected from fire beyond the commercial rotational age, the type is followed by a bog climax of an assortment of wet-site deciduous species.

Light fire can be helpful silviculturally, seeds germinating in the duff shortly thereafter producing a pure, dense stand. Caution here, for prescribed fire techniques cannot yet be recommended. Charcoal in the upper layers of peat and of charred peat on the surface of the ground give observers some idea of how long it has been since a fire, often disastrously, last passed over the land.

Near the coast, stands are killed occasionally by salt water brought on by storm tides. But white-cedar may replace stands of other species, especially hardwoods, killed by salt sprays. When that occurs, the conifer is likely to be free of competition until past middle age. Then sweet bay and holly trees begin to capture the site.

We have already alluded to the durability of the wood of the species and thus its resistance, due to natural fungicidal chemicals, to rot. Living trees, too, are notably free of fungi and insect attack. Two pathogens infect foliage, but without serious consequences. Another causes spherical swelling of the bole or branch, a broom-like growth of foliage arising from dormant buds beneath the bark near the globe-shaped canker.

NORTHERN WHITE-CEDAR

Indians called it Os-soo-ha-tah, feather-leaf, but a 16th century king of France assured the perpetuation of the Gallic name when, as though by an order from the throne, the crown's botanists called it arborvitae from *l'arbre de vie*, meaning tree of life. Medicine boiled from the branches and foliage seemed to give new life to St. Lawrence River explorers who, until Indians introduced them to the concoction, sickened and died of scurvy. So enthused were the royal druggists that they introduced eastern arborvitae to European pharmaceutical gardens. Some say (or argue) that the tree was the first New World species to be introduced to Europe. Even now, chemists distill oil from its leaves to treat the common cold.

The tree has other common names, like thuja (sometimes spelled thuya),

Northern white-cedar of the Lake States (USDA Forest Service photo).

which is simply the genus name, meaning, also simply, tree. Eastern arborvitae is *Thuja occidentalis*, the latter word translating "Western." This is the name for the New World species in a genus that has oriental, or Eastern World, types as well.

Of all these names, I prefer northern white-cedar. Though not a true cedar, it bears a characteristic cedar-oil odor all its own. And like cedars, both true *Cedrus* and its juniper imitators, the heartwood is durable.

Northern White-Cedar Wood

As we've noted, it's the tree's medicinal value and not its durability that gave reason for naming northern white-cedar the tree of life. But durable it is, having the ability to withstand insect and fungal attack. For this as for most woods, resistance to decay organisms depends on the amount and toxicity of its extractive oils. (For redwood, tannins rather than oils provide decay resistance.)

The wood of the tree is among the lightest of American woods, so light that from it fishermen whittle decoy minnows. Railroaders like white-cedar for crossties because of its durability; steel plates between the rail and the wood compensate for its weakness. The tender wood readily crumbles when cutting across the grain with a knife. Checking occurs along the growth ring, separating the wood into thin flexible slats that make good canoe ribs. For this reason, too, northern white-cedar finds a ready market for fabricators of pails, tubs, boats, and water tanks (in spite of a faint bitter taste). Once an important component of Lake States' commercial forests, its market potential today is limited. Though structurally similar to Atlantic white-cedar, the distinctive oily odors for each species separate the two kinds of wood. Unlike other "cedars," thuja wood feels especially dry to the touch.

Campers may be glad to know that the tree's fibrous inner-bark makes good pillow stuffing (it has been used in upholstered furniture), while the outer-bark serves as thatch for an emergency woods lean-to.

From Seed to Harvest

Both male and female urn-shaped cones, ½ inch long, develop at the ends of branches. From the female, at the end of the season, fall the minute (⅛ inch long) winged seeds. They take hold on soils derived from limestone outcrops, best sites for the tree, or in glaciated basins covered with sphagnum moss or decaying reeds, sedges, and woody plants. Upon germination the seeds produce two cotyledons or seed-leaves. That's unusual, for most conifers are polycots, displaying many needles that encompass the seed as they unfold. As good seed crops occur only at 10-year intervals, foresters must take advantage of the infrequent opportunities to regenerate stands of these steeple-shaped trees. Red squirrels steal their share of the cones, hoarding them in caches in the northern forest.

While seeds germinate on the moist, decayed litter of these sites, seedlings become established as well on burned-over land and where skidding has laid bare the soil or trampled the ground cover of moss. In time the trees reach heights of 40 to 60 feet with 2- to 3-foot diameters. Short stems of such girth, of course, exhibit much taper. Diameter cores of virgin stands of the slow growing thuja typically show 20 rings to an inch of radius; the trees seem to stand still in the cold, wet bogs of moss. Well-managed second-growth stems grow twice as fast, while properly thinned old-growth forests exhibit fair increment some 10 years after releasing residual white-cedars from stagnation-causing competition.

The American Forestry Association's champion is a Michigan thuja 18 feet in circumference and 113 feet tall in 1972. In contrast to an earlier statement, heartrots, common to the species, hollow out interiors to make ring counting to ascertain age impossible. When no conks show on the bole, woodpecker workings tip the forester that the tree has heartrot; apparently for this species, only trees with the infection are tapped by these birds.

Site quality relates to the depth of peat—the more or less decomposed plants in a swamp—and the internal drainage of the site. Growth rate improves as peat deepens and with more rapid draining of water from the organic deposits that make up the forest soil.

Many northern white-cedar stands, especially in low-lying areas, are pure; this shade-tolerant tree at other times shares the site with eastern hemlock, eastern white pine, black spruce, and a few hardwoods. In high elevations of the Southern Appalachian Mountains, where the species occurs in many islands, its often shrubby character encourages overtopping by more domineering kinds of trees. Where occurring in pure stands, the species forms the climax forest.

Ground fires, a bane of the bog forests in the natural range of white-cedar in the North—from the Lake States to Nova Scotia—destroy considerable acreages as they creep beneath the surface of the soil and deep snow throughout the winter months. In the spring, the long smoldering fire crops out some distance away, in many directions, from the fire's last observed position. Surface fires, those running above the ground, also take their toll on the oily, fibrous-bark trees.

Other than the heartrot already mentioned, few diseases or insects—and none of significance—damage these trees. Red squirrels do eat buds, deer and moose browse twigs, and porcupines girdle the shaggy, thin-barked stems.

Foresters recommend harvesting the species in narrow clearcut strips about 75 feet wide. This is partly because of the short flight possible for the small, winged seeds that begin their journey from stubby trees. Few seeds fly more than a 100 feet. Another reason is the windthrow so prevalent in larger openings, even though root grafts, common among trees of this species, encourage wind-firmness.

These trees also layer—a low branch that touches the soil puts down roots; from this branch a new tree develops. Often these young "seedlings" serve as advance regeneration in a harvested forest.

Ironically, the leaves are acidic, thereby increasing acidity of the soil as they fall and become incorporated therein. Yet the trees grow best in alkaline soils: indeed, they exhibit more vigor where soil pH nears its maximum—above 8 on the scale.

Landscapers' Choice

Landscapers like to plant the natural and many horticultural forms of northern white-cedar. The tree propagates readily from cuttings to assure clones of the desired variety. It shapes well when clipped. For windbreak planting, too, the tree finds use, effectively blocking the wind to shelter the soil.

Two kinds of short needles, flat and keeled, alternate in pairs on the twigs to give the tree a graceful appearance. Its twigs form fan-like sprays, the yellow-green scale-like needles shedding with the twigs after several years on the tree. Northern white-cedars are trees to enjoy.

Cedars of the Brakes, the Glades, and the Basin

We earlier wrote of eastern redcedar (Chapter 7) and the junipers of the western range (Chapter 11), and in the context of durable woods alluded to the Ashe junipers of the Texas hill country's cedar brakes. The brakes harbor a lot of scrub oaks along with these fence post producing junipers that never acquire a size of higher value. As recently as the 1950s these trees were harvested, hauled to courthouse squares in rural counties, and sold from trucks to farmers. As the old trees contained adequate heartwood, the posts were serviceable for years. Unfortunately the same procedure is now used, but the second-growth is almost all sapwood, little more durable than a pine post without preservative treatment. But the post buyers, to their regret, rely on the reputation of the species.

Cedar glades of the Arkansas Ozarks once produced on the alkaline soils there a fairly high quality eastern redcedar for furniture and posts. With silvicultural treatment of these rocky outcrop lands of limestone-derived soils, they may do so again. But for the Nashville Basin of Tennessee, where once valuable stems were cut for chests and closet panelling, the future of the tree is not so bright. The high pH soils there are too fertile for growing trees. The Basin is farm-crop land.

For the heartwood of these trees—the white-cedars and the assortment of junipers—durability is a prized characteristic. Natural decay resistance gives long life to these timbers in a variety of uses.

🌲 🌲 🌲 Projects for the Amateur Naturalist

1. Collect, identify, and mount tree seeds. Seeds are placed in transparent bags, and the bags are stapled to a thin board or heavy cardboard. Most seeds ripen in the fall of the year. Some fruit, like drupes and cones, may need to be opened to obtain the seed.

2. How does a forest affect fish? Dip that fly in a trout stream that is open to the sun and then put it in upstream or downstream where the creek is fully shaded. Note the difference in fish tales to be told. A thermometer will suggest why.

3. Using the curves shown here, determine the site index (SI) for a tract of land (see Figure 15–1). Measure the diameters and total heights of at least five trees (using tools made in Chapter 4, Projects 1 and 2). These SI figures are then averaged. Remember that SI is the average total height of all the dominant and codominant trees in a stand at 50 years of age. It is for even-aged, relatively pure, natural, second-growth forests. You can't use the method in plantations, virgin forests, or complex mixtures of many species and ages. The curves shown here are for loblolly pine. Each species has its own set. However, for practice you may use this series.

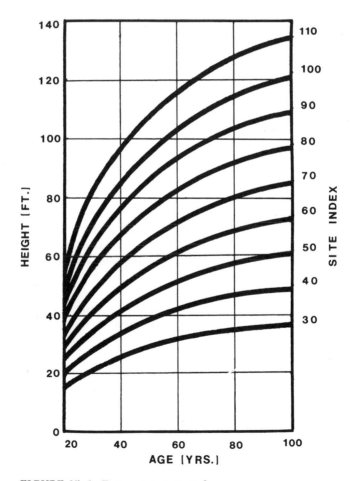

FIGURE 15–1. Determining site index.

16

Pioneer Plant for Paper Pulp

Virginia Pine

*B*oy Scouts in the natural range of Virginia pine (*Pinus virginiana*) know this species well. The two-match requirement for starting a fire is easily met when the little tepee in the ring of rocks is built of the twigs of Virginia pine.

Ready ignition also results in wild fires that clear the land, but the shallow-rooted Virginia pine needs no serotinous cones for natural regeneration (see Chapter 9). Virginia Pine is a prolific sprouter from tree bases, and the land is soon a forest of little "seedlings." The clumps of coppice reproduction may grow two feet in height the first year.

While seeds seldom fly with the wind more than a hundred feet, prolific seed production and dissemination from walls of trees beside the openings and from individual trees within a burned-over area also assure a dense stand of seedlings. Winged seeds are released from cones when parent trees are as young as five years. The abundant seeds produce "thickets" of as many as 40,000 stems per acre. Empty "burrs" persist on tree branches for years, suggesting individual stems that are good seed producers and that a forester might therefore save for future seed-tree harvests.

Where They Grow

Virginia pine, until early in this century called Jersey or scrub pine, has been confused with pitch pine, especially in the barrens of South Jersey. While its principal range extends from New Jersey and Pennsylvania southward to Alabama, a few small islands of these trees occur in Mississippi and along the Ohio River in Indiana. Indeed, the species' best growth has been charted at the edge of its range in southern Indiana. Plantations of Virginia pine survive and grow well, too, in Iowa and Texas, far beyond the tree's natural occurrence.

Most pure stands occur in the Appalachian Mountains and the Piedmont province.

Virginia pine is famous for invading old fields abandoned by agriculture. This occurs especially on sites underlain by shale and on other poor and eroded soils too infertile to support loblolly and shortleaf pines. Reclamation foresters recommend planting the species on lands surface-mined for coal and minerals.

Vast stands occur as second growth in the high-elevation tabletop land of the Cumberland Plateau in Tennessee. When a foreign investor recognized the species' value for paper pulp, management of stands of trees in the Cumberland Plateau by foresters intensified. They now needed to maximize growth. Domestic entrepreneurs had ignored the tree until then.

How They Grow

Short-lived Virginia pine deserves its "scrub pine" name. It seldom exceeds 50 years in age and is typically less than 12 inches in diameter at maturity. Fully grown stems less than 40 feet tall are not unusual.

Young seedlings, like most southern pines, have a degree of tolerance to shade. And like other hard, yellow pines of the region, tolerance diminishes with age. Thus, these trees respond to release from their neighbors that compete for light (and water and nutrients). So, too, controlling undesirable weed trees with herbicides spurs residual stems to reach maturity at an earlier age. Grapevines and the thorny greenbriar vines (*Smilax*) join dozens of weed-tree species as competitors.

Foresters use heavy equipment for precommercial thinning of dense stands, those with 10,000 or more rather evenly spaced seedlings on an acre. Dozers pushing sharp blades at 10-foot intervals through a tract of 10-foot tall seedlings and saplings free residual trees to grow faster. It is not the best way to thin, but it is the cheapest: by this method, well-formed trees are destroyed and inferior stems retained.

Intolerance to shade has been demonstrated in greenhouses. Potted seedlings exposed to abnormally long days under incandescent light quadruple their rate of growth.

Virginia pine stands, as ecological pioneers, give way to climax oaks and hickories. Fire or catastrophic storms may delay or set back plant succession to the initial pine sprout or seedling woodland. Clearcutting harvests do the same.

Ground-cover indicators tell something of site preferences for the species. Better lands support flowering dogwood trees, while club moss covers the soil. Bear oak trees and reindeer moss denote poor sites for Virginia pine.

Christmas Trees

Those who know the forests of Virginia pine become used to the species' disheveled appearance. The ragged view is caused by the random dispersal of needles on twigs that, in turn, diffuse background light rather unevenly. Thus,

Virginia pines began to be planted across the South for Christmas trees in the 1970s. Carefully nurtured and periodically sheared, these will be marketed as "choose-and-cut" (often involving a family outing) or wholesaled to big-city chain stores (Gerald and Nancy Lowery, Spring Valley Farms, photos).

many observers were surprised when the species began to be prominently planted for Christmas trees throughout the South and even into Texas—well beyond its natural range.

Christmas tree producers plant the trees at wide spacing, enabling workers to conveniently shear the foliage several times a year for the life of the trees. Depending on the market, Yule trees may be grown for three to six years, to heights of 5 to 15 feet. Growers use fertilizers to improve nutrition, herbicides to control competing weeds, insecticides to eliminate budworms, fungicides to cure fusiform rust fungus infections, and irrigation water to overcome the effects of droughty seasons. Finally, at harvest time, the trees are sprayed with green paint to enhance appearance. The paint acts like glue, enabling longer needle retention on decorated trees in warm buildings. Thus, the once low-value and unattractive tree attains economic and aesthetic prominence.

🌲 🌲 🌲 Projects for the Amateur Naturalist

1. Distinguishing true seedlings from sprouts. Locate a forest of Virginia pines (or another sprout-producing species, such as trembling aspen). On a 1/10-acre plot (66 × 66 feet), determine by digging into the soil and observing the rooting habits the number of "seedlings" originating from seeds and those originating as sprouts. Trace the "seedling" root, if a sprout, to the parent tree.

2. Determining tree litter pH. After leaching with distilled water for 24 hours, use litmus paper or a pH kit to measure the acidity/alkalinity of freshly fallen and older pine needles and of broadleaf foliage undergoing decomposition. Lower than 7 is acidic (sometimes called sour); higher is alkaline (sometimes called sweet or basic).

3. Value of a forest for watershed protection. Ascertain the annual precipitation and the cost of a gallon of water where you live. Assume that 90 percent of that cost is for purification treatment and delivery. Rainfall in feet × 43,560 square feet (the area of an acre) = cubic feet of water per acre. A cubic foot = 7½ gallons. Assume, too, that 50 percent of the precipitation is retained in the soil under a forest and only 10 percent in nonforested land. (The rest runs off the land or is transpired from vegetation foliage.) How much should a municipality pay a landowner to retain trees on the land?

17

Krummholz and Elfinwood

Subalpine Fir

Near timberline and around the rocky outcrops in isolated patches above the usual tree line grow the subalpine firs (*Abies lasiocarpa*). Early taxonomists called the high-altitude conifers of the Rocky and Cascade mountains "alpine" fir, but, in truth, no trees grow in alpine heights. Even foresters confuse subalpine fir with corkbark fir (*A. arizonica*), but the latter, some say, is a variety of subalpine fir. Though the wood from these trees is insignificant in the lumber market, commercial buyers and sellers mistakenly call subalpine fir white fir (*A. concolor*).

Associates Among the Trees

A climax species, the shade-tolerant subalpine fir follows the more light-demanding lodgepole pine (*Pinus contorta*), Douglas-fir (*Pseudotsuga menziesii*), and western white pine (*P. monticola*) in ecological succession. Lightning-set fires in the range of the species encourage the establishment of the serotinous lodgepole pine. As these forests mature, the slightly less light-demanding Douglas-fir gains a foothold. In time—perhaps two hundred years—the white pine of higher commercial value attains dominance. Under the canopies of any of these trees, seeds of subalpine fir germinate and, as the even-aged stands of the others fall to the elements of nature, the species eventually becomes established as a pure forest-cover type. Able to develop under their own shade, subalpine fir trees in time form an uneven-aged forest.

Limber pine (*Pinus flexilis*) and bristlecone pine (*P. aristata*) sometimes interrupt the woodlands of otherwise pure subalpine fir. Nearby these stands likely will be found glades of quaking aspens (*Populus tremuloides*) growing in clumps that originate as sprouts in zones slightly more moist than where the fir trees grow.

Perhaps the fir's closest associate is Engelmann spruce (*Picea engelmannii*). The two species grow together in the tundra as well as in the stands of upright trees at lower elevations. In the Middle Rocky Mountains, spruce typically makes up 60 percent of a stand of the mixture. When the two species grow together, it is the fir that succumbs until equilibrium for growth potential is reached for a particular site. Thus, in time, the subalpine fir—Engelmann spruce mixed-species forest, in the absence of fire or tree-toppling storm, becomes a pure spruce forest.

Engelmann spruce also outruns subalpine fir in natural regeneration. The former has smaller seeds with more aerodynamic wings, carrying them far from the parent bole. Near a seed-bearing subalpine fir tree, however, regeneration may be exceptional. Fifty thousand seeds to a pound, they readily germinate in the deep duff and thick moss under an old stand.

Associates Among the Lesser Plants

Fields of pinkish purple flowers on long spikes announce the location of a recently burned-over area that earlier sustained subalpine fir. Fireweed, a genus in the primrose family, invades promptly to hold the soil together and to provide cover for wildlife. Some of the finest honey comes from the combs of bees that have gleaned nectar from these flowers.

Bighorn sheep and other grazers range the fields of crested wheatgrass. Its abundance in the spring rescues many mammals and birds from starvation in the harsh winters occurring near the summits. Elk feed on the sedge *Kobresia myosuroides*. Wildlife of many kinds sometimes depend on the red buffalo berries growing along streambanks, while mushrooms, toadstools, Indian paint, and other fungi provide autumn food for avian and mammalian species.

In the tundra, where isolated trees of subalpine fir sometimes grow, snowball saxifrage's leaf pattern allows each of the leaves in the ground-hugging rosette—lying below the level of the cold, drying winds—to absorb full sunlight. As the short growing season requires efficient utilization of the sun in summer, the overlapping pattern permits each leaf to absorb maximum light.

Perennial ground plants in this arctic-like climate may be more than 250 years old. The snow willow, though a tree of the *Salix* genus, appears as a shrub in miniature, only a few inches tall. Yet, the flowering big-rooted spring beauty extends its roots as much as three feet into the soil, there to be protected from deep freezes.

In the subalpine woods, lichens cling to rocks, the acid they exude decomposing the minerals and thereby playing a role in soil genesis. Indeed, even at high elevations, soil may be many feet deep, and tree roots may fully utilize the mantle that rests upon the stony parent material.

Associates Among the Animals

Rabbits, sheep, goats, and birds directly affect the life of a stand of subalpine fir. Jackrabbits repeatedly nip seedlings in winter until the little trees have grown above the level of snow upon which the hares feed. In doing so, they restrict tree development. Bighorn sheep and mountain goats also browse seedlings. The goats break trails through snow in winter to find salt licks. Then, in the thaw of spring breakup, these big game animals feed upon many species of delicate wildflowers found among the firs. The Clark nutcracker, named for Lewis' colleague of the famous westward trek, extracts seeds from the cones of the fir. (It was on this famous expedition of 1805 that subalpine fir was first observed and described, though called a "pine.")

Other animals seem to play no direct role in the life of trees of the forest, but the reverse may not be so. In this life zone the caribou live, gathering in herds on blankets of snow during spring thaws to avoid noxious insects anxious for the blood of any mammal. The mountain pika, a small mammal living in rocky crevices near and above tree line, is a haymaker. Not a hibernator, it harvests grasses and forbs all summer, storing the fodder for winter consumption in its "caves" in the rocky glaciated rubble. Hoary marmots, their coats in winter etched in silver as a camouflage, also make these highlands their home, while ptarmigans, their plumage changing with the seasons, find security among the islands of fir trees above the general timberline. In summer they blend in with the lichens growing on the rocks; in winter their white feathers hide them in the snow. So, too, we find the little golden-mantled ground squirrel that sometimes riddles whole mountainsides with its tunnels. Pocket gophers and voles here find abundant food and a safe habitat.

Quiet ponds receiving the waters of snow melt become the habitat of dragonflies, darting this way and that upon the surface of the cold effluent. Streams of blue-green water, colored by reflection on the glacial flour that has washed in over the ages as icefields retreated, and ponds and lakes support several kinds of trout. The fish feed upon the flies that arise from mucous-like eggs glued to the rocks in the water. Because of over-fishing by flatlanders enjoying the high-country sport, anglers are encouraged to return to the lake or stream the success of their casts.

Spire-Shaped and Prostrate Habit

Rugged weather, so tough that few can endure it, excludes many men from a mountain home. Those who can endure have a special countenance, a peculiar character. So do the subalpine fir trees.

A thousand feet below the timberline on the slopes, the crowns of trees of this species, in dense stands, appear spirelike, reminding a viewer of the steeples of gothic cathedrals. Occasionally these stems rise to 100 feet and exhibit a girth of 2 feet. In open subalpine meadows, taper increases. Here growth is slow—trees 200 years old do not exceed 5 inches in diameter. At timberline, "banner" trees occur, looking like the flags carried by guidonbearers at the head of the squad in the line of march. Wind and weather have pruned the branches on one side of the banner stem, while allowing their retention on the other side.

Above the general timberline, wind, snow, cold, ice, hail, and lightning sculpt unusual treescapes. Heavy ice and snow weigh down trees, pointing them to the lee. Strong winds of hurricane force for weeks upon weeks bend them, and phototropism is unable to counteract that force. Fierce hailstorms do likewise, and the electrical discharges of sudden lightning storms strike trees that do not die but, in recovery, exhibit odd shapes. Meanwhile blasts of wind-carried ice polish the exposed wood of dead trees. These phenomena also contribute to subalpine fir's prostrate habit—trees growing horizontally for 30 or 40 feet as they hug the ground. Both from above and in profile, the island groups of trees have triangular shapes. Main stems of these bent-to-the-lee trees may be several hundred years old, but at the root collar they are a mere few inches in diameter. Seldom will their height exceed 5 feet.

Measurement is difficult, for the main stem cannot be isolated from its lateral neighbors. In this horizontal position, "layering" also takes place. When branches layer, organic duff and mineral matter slowly bury a bent-over stem lying upon the ground. Subsequently the branch takes root, forming a new tree, but the new tree remains attached to the old parent.

At these high elevations, clumps of subalpine fir trees sometimes take on the appearance of giant ribbons. Growing in rows perpendicular to the wind for perhaps hundreds of years, these contiguous bands serve as windbreaks. Deep snow in the lanes between the rows prevents establishment of new fir trees there; meanwhile the ribbons with large skirts protect existing stands from winter blows of hurricane force. In contrast, tree islands in the upper portion of the ecotome often grow parallel to the wind.

Other ribbons look like garlands draped upon the land. Running for a hundred feet, these creeping *solifluction lobes* of dwarfed subalpine firs connect with one another as they gradually (perhaps over centuries) move, mostly by gravity, in waves down a slope.

European alpinists call the isolated subalpine fir trees or groups of trees in the windswept barrens *krummholz*, meaning crooked wood. Because of their dwarfish appearance, these trees also take the name *elfinwood*. North Americans adopted the terms to describe forests of subalpine fir and its Engelmann spruce kin near the summits of the western mountain ranges.

In summary, as the observer progresses up an alpine mountain slope, he or she passes through groves or groups of (a) upright spire trees in a dense forest, (b) smaller but still spire-like trees as one nears timberline, (c) banner trees standing out among other stems in a grove, (d) smaller banner trees in conifer islands, (f) the ribbon and layering forests, (g) small islands of prostrate trees and solifluction forms, and then (h) to the treeless tundra.

(a)

Subalpine fir trees east of the Continental Divide in Colorado's India Peaks
Wilderness exhibit the (a) dwarfed "elfinwood," (b) wind-sheared "banner" trees, and
(c) crooked wood of the "krummholz" (© S. Laurence Walker photos).

(b)

(c)

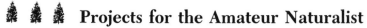 **Projects for the Amateur Naturalist**

1. Effects of streams running through a forest. From the bank of a stream, chart "riparian" changes that occur as you move upward. Does surface soil depth differ? Tree species? Depth of leaf litter? Small plant species? Depth to groundwater?

2. Water pH. Sample water from various sources (lakes, streams, faucets) and test for pH, using litmus paper or a pH kit. Compare these readings with bottled water, Coca Cola, and distilled water. (Note: freshly distilled water will be on the acid side of 7. Determine why.) Ascertain the influence of the water source (i.e., well water from a sandy aquifer, runoff into a lake from a conifer forest, spring, or streamside runoff in a deciduous woodland). Faucet water has a source!

3. Water retention by trees. How much rain water do tree leaves retain, thereby reducing soil compaction by the impact of rain drops? Place a container, perhaps a large tub lined with waterproof plastic, under a tree. Place another of the same size in an adjacent open area. Compare the volume of water collected during and after rains of various intensities.

18

Sandhills and Flatwoods

Slash Pine

At one or another time and place a species of southern yellow pine has been called swamp pine, Cuban pine, Caribbean pine, and rock pine. Why its permanent name is slash pine is unknown to this writer. Slash pine (*Pinus elliottii*) is its "permanent" name for the present and only north of a line that crosses the peninsula of central Florida. Below that line, South Florida slash pine (*P. elliottii* var. *densa*) predominates.

Forestry professors in the 1940s and earlier taught that slash pine is *P. caribaea*. Later dendrologists separated trees that grow on West Indian islands and in Central America from those found in North America. *P. caribaea* remained the scientific name for the maritime and more southerly species, while those of the mainland took the name of a forest botanist, S.B. Elliot (*P. elliottii*). Still later, in the 1950s, foresters cataloged the South Florida variety *densa*, noted above.

The natural range of slash pine runs from South Carolina to southeastern Louisiana (east of the Mississippi River), at elevations from sea level to 300 feet.

South Florida slash pine's natural range follows down two forks of a Y on either side of the flower state's finger until they converge at Lake Okeechobee. From there variety *densa* extends to the Florida Keys. These trees have heavier wood (hence *densa*), due to wider summer-wood growth rings, than that of the typical species. They also have a seedling grass stage similar to that of longleaf pine: needles crowd at the bud just above the ground line. Like longleaf pine, too, the young taproot is thick and quite carrot-like. Later, the crowns appear broader than do those of the more northern trees of the species. Under the microscope South Florida slash pines of North America's subtropical forest region often exhibit abnormal morphology: seedlings have polyploid genetic characteristics. They bear genes with several atypical chromosome numbers.

Sandhills Sites

Slash pines grow well in the sandhills of the Carolina Fall Line, the zone that separates the Piedmont Province from the Coastal Plain and that was once the Atlantic Ocean's coastline. They also do well in the deep, sandy, geologic-aged dunes of West Florida. Successful seedling survival and growth in both areas can be attributed to the lack of competition by other plants for the limited water available in these coarse and sterile soils. So droughty are they that, before planting, bulldozers must first prepare the site by pushing into windrows the potential competitors for soil moisture, the scrub oaks and brush that cover the land. Prescribed fires also accomplish the task, for the roots of weed trees or lesser vegetation sprout to consume scarce water and nutrients and later to block sunlight; thus they hinder survival and retard the growth of seedlings. Consequently, foresters use clearcutting, site preparation, and planting as the regeneration method of choice.

Flatwoods Forests

At the other moisture extreme, slash pines grow well in moderately drained "crawfish flats." Industrial foresters, especially, intensively manage blocks of hundreds of acres of table-level land to produce raw material for pulp and paper mills. Here natural regeneration following clearcutting or seed-tree harvests may be appropriate, because a single tree often produces over 15,000 seeds in a typical seed year. Afforestation on old-fields, like those abandoned after King Cotton migrated to the High Plains of Texas and the valleys of California, are especially desirable. On these recently cultivated lands, weed trees and other perennial plants that compete with pine seedlings are absent for a while.

Both permanent and intermittent streams flow through slightly higher land within the range of slash pine. Along these watercourses slash pines persist for generation upon generation; on slightly higher lands adjacent to the water courses, longleaf pines predominate. This rather abrupt ecological transition is a matter of fire history: the moist coves exclude fire, protecting the slash pines, while on higher, drier lands, periodic fires kill seedling pines of this species. On the other hand, longleaf pines in the grass stage growing above the moist streamsides endure and require fire. In the damp drainages, however, the more rapidly growing slash pines overtop the longleaf seedlings, eventually causing their death by excluding sunlight. And, again, longleaf pine seedlings require fire, not likely to occur in the damp drainages, for overcoming brown-spot needle blight (see Chapter 3).

Extending the Range

Because of the ease of plantation establishment and the species' rapid growth, foresters were encouraged to introduce slash pine to the north and far to the west of its normal occurrence, into Texas. That the tree self-prunes, thus enhancing its use for lumber and utility poles, and produces a copious flow of resin desirable for the gum naval stores market furthered interest in extending its range. Wherever the species is planted, it escapes, the wind carrying seeds of the abundant and annual crops to create new forests. Improved fire protection, beginning in the 1940s, also encouraged the establishment of new stands of slash pine across the South, both within and beyond its natural range.

Problems do occur. Annosus root rot kills many trees planted on abandoned agricultural land. The disease enters the stand following thinning harvests. Spores in the air of the fungus *Fomes annosus* come to rest and germinate on freshly cut stumps. Fungus mycelia then grow down the stump into the root and, through root grafts, infect and kill residual standing trees.

There are lesser problems. The weight of ice in winter storms bends stems of all ages to the ground, for the species is not adapted to weather conditions north of its natural range. Crooks in boles and forked branching habits turn out to be genetically inherited characteristics (as are limbiness, limb size, and the angle of branching), introduced with seedling stock to a new area.

Grazing cattle rub saplings "raw" of their bark, distorting their form, while the resinous quality of the wood limits its use to certain pulping processes. And the southern pine beetle, the adult's rear end appearing as though kicked in by an angry forester, makes its distinctively *s*-shaped tunnels beneath the bark, thereby girdling and killing trees.

Scientific Exploration

The potential for slash pine to be the South's most important timber resource, so considered in the 1950s, led industries, governments, and forestry schools to intensify research on the species. Geneticists worked to improve its seed production, its quality for pulp and paper, its density for lumber, and its production of oleoresins for munitions and paint industries.

They learned that cones ripe for seed extraction float in SAE 20 oil, indicating specific gravity of 0.90 or less. Heavier cones are too green, the seeds when extracted in driers not yet viable. They also found that streaking trees for gum naval stores stimulated flower/cone/seed production, probably because the carbon:nitrogen ratio in the growing tissues—in this case the cambium—had been affected. Researchers noted, too, how sulphuric acid and the herbicide Paraquat, when applied to wounds, stimulates and extends the flow of gum. By grafting, they showed that seed production can be handily improved, and how needles can be air layered to produce new trees—clones of the parent.

Silviculturists determined how much the depth of the surface soil and the depth to mottling colors (indicative of changes in moisture) in the soil influence tree growth, and that under optimum soil moisture and nutrient conditions, trees may never become dormant, producing seven growth flushes a year, each with a whorl of new branches. Other foresters ascertained optimum nutrient levels for maximizing growth and showed that wood production may be stimulated by applications of nitrogen and phosphorus fertilizers. Thus, slash pines are expected to play an important role in the "South's Fourth Forest," a vast woodland of intensively managed and genetically improved stands of high-quality trees.

Projects for the Amateur Naturalist

1. Effect of thinning on growth. In a box of soil, plant seeds of a rapidly germinating plant (marigolds, wheat grass, or rice grass will do) at precise intervals of 1 inch in rows and between rows. After germination, periodically remove every other plant in predetermined portions of the box. Note differences in growth of the residual plants.

Typical of the widely spaced plantations of slash pine in the Southeast, these trees respond to release by thinning and by fertilizing with nitrogen and phosphorus.

Prescribed burning in May and "chopping" with heavy equipment in July was carried out on this sandhill area covered with wiregrass and scrub oaks. Planting will follow in the coming winter.

Gum naval stores operators streak and cup planted slash pine stands like this one for oleoresin production. The gummy substance from which turpentine is distilled and rosin solidified also comes from longleaf pines and trees in natural stands (USDA Forest Service photo).

2. Monetary value of an acre of trees. A typical second-growth unmanaged forest contains at 40 years of age about 5,000 board feet (100 board feet in 50 trees). If the stumpage value (trees standing in the woods) is $150 per 1,000 board feet, calculate the average value added as growth each year for the life of the stand. Now, if interest rates at the bank are 6 percent, compounded annually, would the landowner be better off not growing trees if it cost $100 to replant the land? Use the formula $(V_n) = V_o (1.0p)^n$, where (V_n) is value at 40 years; V_o is value or cost to reforest the tract (100); p = interest rate (6); and n = number of years (40).

3. Grazing value of a forest. Clip and weigh the grass and forbs (broadleaf grazing plants) in milacre (6.6 × 6.6 feet) sample plots under several kinds of forests and in the open. From the sample, convert (by multiplying by 1,000) to an acre basis. Ask a cattle farmer what he pays for hay. Is it worthwhile to graze these forests?

THE BROADLEAF TREES

*Also called deciduous trees (though some—like live oak and holly—
are evergreens) and dicotyledonous—meaning two seed-leaves
(though bamboo is a monocot and some dicots have from one to eight
seed-leaves). Commercially, these are the hardwoods (though aspen is
a soft wood), and botanically the clothed-seeded angiosperms (though
ginkgo is a naked-seeded gymnosperm).*

19

Lost Bonanza

American Chestnut

*O*riginating in the mainland of China, it spread across the northern hemisphere to western Europe. From there it entered the United States through a northeastern port, probably New York, and marched north, south, and west, devastating and conquering the land in its path. Within 20 years, scenes of desolation pocked the mountains—from the ridges to the valleys. Forests, farmlands, and cities were affected.

It wasn't a brand of communism or a Mongolian horde, this intruder into America, but, rather, *Endothia parasitica*, the fungus that causes chestnut blight. It appeared about 1904, supposedly in a shipment of nursery stock. Spreading throughout the range of the American chestnut, that oriental disease wiped out, perhaps forever, a tree species' unique capacity for serving the American people.

The Tree That Had Everything

Before the blight, American chestnut (*Castanea dentata*) was a prized feature of forests in southern New England and the Middle Atlantic States, west to Indiana. Majestic stems grew southward through the Carolinas to northern Georgia, Alabama, and Mississippi. In the Appalachian mountain region it is said that one of every four trees was a chestnut. From this straight-grained versatile cousin of the oaks, industrious pioneers peeled bark to roof buildings. From its straight logs, clear of knots and other defects, later generations cut boards for framing, siding, and interior woodwork, while veneer cores were sawed for furniture stock. The hard and lightweight wood, taking a high polish, was easily worked by tools. Boards glued, nailed, and seasoned well. They did not warp, check, or shrink. Because of its resistance to decay, industries sprang

Blight-killed American chestnut snags in the Blue Ridge Mountains of the Appalachian chain. Note the young sprouts. These are about as large as the coppice get before the blight hits them too (USDA Forest Service photo).

up throughout the region to use chestnut for posts, poles, piling, and railroad ties. Its delicious nuts were highly prized, almost a staple food for many rural people and a major food for wildlife. Of graceful form, it was a favorite shade tree on the courthouse square and on the rural homestead. Poets, like Longfellow, photographed the tree in words: "Under the spreading chestnut tree, . . ."

Yet these were not all of the chestnut's values. Tannic acid in its bark and wood, serving as a fungicide to ward off native pathogens, became the basis for a great tannin extract industry. Essential to production of heavy leather, this organic chemical can be tasted in the wood. More than half of the vegetable tannin used by the American leather industry at the turn of the century came from chestnut. And as competition forced elimination of usable wood wastes, the "spent" chips, after the tannic acid had been boiled out, were converted to pulp to be used in the manufacture of fine papers and linerboard for boxes. So important was chestnut in the Southern mountains that some major timber operations became subsidiaries of leather companies, organized to harvest other species for lumber on lands bought to insure supplies of chestnut tannin extract. At least one contemporary giant of the southern pulp and paper industry was an extract company in the early 1900s.

Industries great and small were founded on these abundant and versatile trees. And in the days of Theodore Roosevelt and other early conservationists, when those new professional men called foresters talked of sustained yield, managed forests and permanent industries, chestnut—more than any other species—seemed to have what such a program would require. In addition to the great demand for its many products, it grew more rapidly, perhaps, than any other tree. And chestnut did well on a variety of soils, from poor mountain ridges to rich fertile valleys. American chestnut reproduced prolifically, both by seed and by sprouts, and competed effectively for soil moisture and nutrients with neighboring trees of other species in the forest. The wood was salable in small sizes, providing markets for thinnings and early income to pay expenses while waiting for larger timbers to grow to sawlog size. Even the cost conscious industrialist saw possibilities for a bonanza in longterm management of chestnut when the clock tolled the twentieth century. Neither insect nor fungus attacked this stalwart of the woods until that fatal shipment arrived in the American port.

A Threat That Became a Catastrophe

Such was the situation in 1904, when Herman W. Merkel, a forester at the Bronx Park, found something wrong with chestnut trees on the grounds of the New York Zoological Garden—the famed Bronx Zoo. Swollen or sunken cankers were forming on limbs and trunks of the trees. They spread, encircled the stem, and killed the tree above the point of infection. Recognizing these as extremely serious symptoms, Merkel called in W. A. Murrill, mycologist on the staff of the New York Botanical Garden. He and other mycologists identified the disease as one caused by a fungus new to science, gave it a Latin name, and showed that it kills the inner-bark of living tissues and sometimes rots the sapwood. They found, also, that it produced two types of spores: one a dry, relatively large, and windblown disc; the other much smaller, sticky, and dispersed by rain.

Meanwhile, as the chestnuts at the zoo were killed back to the ground, the pestilence was beginning to spread. Northward into Connecticut and Massachusetts and across the Hudson into New Jersey, the same blight appeared. Chestnuts in forests, as well as shade trees on lawns, were rapidly dying. Gradually it dawned on forest scientists that this was not just another interesting tree disease, to be studied, catalogued, and talked about. Scientific and, eventually, political leaders soon realized that here was a threat to the very existence of this much loved tree and the industries it supported.

But all this took time—far too much time, as it turned out. No special funds were appropriated to study or combat the disease until 1911, when magnificent shade trees were dying as far south as Philadelphia. The U.S. Congress appropriated $5,000 in 1911 and $80,000 in 1912 and again in 1913 to enable the young forestry profession to control the menace. Pennsylvania's legislature appropriated $240,000 for the 1913–1914 biennium and appointed a Chestnut Tree Blight Commission to study the matter. But what could have been exterminated with better knowledge and minor costs in 1904 had spread in seven years to unmanageable proportions. Evidence that *Endothia parasitica* could have been controlled early at little cost is best illustrated by an independent infection in North Carolina that was stamped out in 1908.

To guide control efforts, federal and state agencies stepped up research. Scientists of the Pennsylvania Commission soon proved that the disease could not be controlled by tree surgery, by chemical sprays, or by injection of fungicides. Researchers in Europe, finding related fungi that attacked only dead wood, could not find the lethal organism on European chestnuts. Then, in 1913, Frank N. Meyer, one of the famed Dr. David Fairchild's far wandering plant hunters, found the disease on chestnuts in China, "9 days by bullock cart northeast of Peking," hence circumstantially proving its oriental origin.

Back in Pennsylvania—Penn's Woods—scientists cooperating with the Commission learned how the disease spread so fast. Large spores, carried by wind, could obviously spread some distance—perhaps half a mile or so from an infected tree on a dry blustery day. But the tiny, thin-walled spores, extending from their pustules in sticky gelatinous threads, proved to be the real culprits. Not only were they washed by rain down the tree trunk and into minute breaks in the outer-bark, thus contacting the vulnerable inner cambial layers, but by the thousands they stuck to the feet of birds. Here was a mechanism of nature that could account for spot infections miles away from known sources: on one downy woodpecker were counted nearly 7,000 spores. Migrating birds might well be capable of spreading the disease across whole states at a single jump. Now no chestnut stands in the nation could be considered safe.

The spores, when deposited on the bark of trees, produce spore horns that exude from bark pustules. When dissolved by rainwater, the minute particles wash into bark wounds. Other spores are "shot" from pustules into the air and carried great distances by wind. Upon contact with the inner-bark of the host tree, microscopic, hair-like fungal mycelium spreads throughout the living cambial tissues and, occasionally, in the sapwood. The parasite soon is lethal to the tree.

As it turned out, the worst fears materialized. The Pennsylvania Commission planned a heroic holding action; within a mile-wide swath, cut across the breadth of the state, all chestnuts were to be eliminated. But even before that work got underway the plan had to be abandoned—bird-borne killers had already jumped the planned defense zone. Stands to the west which the barrier was to protect had been attacked. A similar plan to cut an isolation strip across the Appalachian Mountains in North Carolina had to be discarded. Not until the disease was discovered in Georgia did foresters give up on that effort to hold the quarantine line of battle. Penetration was as sinister as the proverbial fifth column, and as hard to pinpoint.

World War I, and perhaps the evident futility of control efforts, caused cuts in funds for chestnut blight work after 1914. Foresters, landowners, and scientists watched helplessly as the disease spread, sometimes in an inexorable crawl across counties, sometimes in mighty leaps into new regions. By the mid-1920s it was active in the southern mountains, the locale for most of the tannin extract industry. Within 40 years of its introduction into the New World, *E. parasitica* had reached the outer edge of the range of chestnut. The tree of many uses was doomed.

Salvage

Softening the economic impact was the native durability of chestnut wood. Unlike most species, which when killed deteriorate in weeks or in months, dead chestnut snags by the thousands stood for decades as tall white ghosts in the forests of mixed deciduous species. Only slowly did these stems lose the qualities that made them valuable. Dependent industries, faced with an end to their supply of raw material, had to be phased out, but often, because of the standing timbers, they had from 5 to 30 years in which to complete the changeover.

Nut crops, and the local economy they supported, were the first to go. Spreading early through the valleys, the disease killed the tops of accessible trees around homesteads and at the edges of fields, sites most convenient for the harvest of nuts. For a decade or so, nuts were still gathered from uninfected trees high in the southern mountains, but by the 1940s these had dwindled to ephemeral productions from sprouts and occasional seedlings. Loss of this game food, too, was an incalculable blow to wildlife.

Although standing dead chestnuts deteriorated slowly, checks, surface cracks that formed within a few years as the bark peeled away, reduced lumber values. Usually it was a relatively modest loss as the checks were mostly confined to the outer slabs and trimmings of the salvaged logs. Even poles made up of the whole trunk could still be sold 10 years after trees were killed. The standing snags often were infested with small borers, chewing pin-size holes that damaged wood for some purposes. More common, however, was the asset value for veneer stock of these "figure marks." Larger larvae of another insect gave the name "sound wormy chestnut" to a lumber grade frequently employed for interior trim, as attested by its use in thousands of homes in the 1920s and 1930s. Subsequently, as the material became scarce, wormy chestnut became popular for picture framing and other small articles. Hence, harvesting the dead trees could proceed at an orderly, even a leisurely, pace.

Scarcity causes demands in the marketplace for the most common of products. Chestnut wood makes excellent fence posts and split rails. "Makes," not "made," because these are still with us. The author literally stumbled on a fence in a 50-year-old forest in the Southern Appalachians, where in an earlier day it had fenced out cattle from the crop of corn. The fence was bartered, a truck was borrowed, and the posts and rails erected around an urban home. To the neighbors, the author was a wood fanatic, but he was outdone. Later he discovered that a millionaire in Arkansas had bought 5 miles of chestnut split rail fence and had brought it from the mountain farms of the Southeast to surround his ranch. Endurable nostalgia!

Salvage of chestnut for tannin extract followed a similar pattern. Some tannin was lost by leaching, but enough remained to justify harvest as long as accessible trees were available. Actually, occasional snags, cut by the boys of the Civilian Conservation Corps—the Tree Army—in the 1930s to reduce the hazard of lightning-caused forest fires and left lying on the ground, found their way to extract plants years later.

Though most sawlog stands of the species had been harvested by 1930, loggers were trucking occasional logs for lumber out of remote stands in the late 1940s. Now, too, the last extract plant is gone. And only now and then in the high Southern Appalachians does a sawmiller any longer harvest small pieces for table lamps, picture frames, and other specialties. The great chestnut salvage operation is over.

What After Chestnut?

Travelers in the chestnut country may still see an occasional dead snag, stark and gray against the sky, but if they look for vast clearings where chestnut trees once stood, they look in vain. Nature leaves no forest bare nor soil idle for long. Young trees replace old ones in the composition of the forests but, in the case of the American chestnut, other trees everywhere occupy the land vacated by its demise.

Just what trees have replaced chestnut and what determined the many successional patterns are complicated but fascinating ecological problems lacking adequate study. Soils and climate, composition of the stands, past fires, and logging history since the blight appear to be involved.

Chestnuts in mixtures with other trees were generally replaced by their associates unless logging or severe fire intervened. Single dying trees left spaces small enough to be occupied by the expanding branches of their neighbors. Larger openings made room for the sprouts and seedlings of those neighbors. Various oaks, the most common trees remaining in the deciduous forest, are the most frequent replacements, but, on better sites, a mixture of other valuable hardwoods has encroached.

Pure chestnut stands, and stands where clearcutting or conflagration followed the blight, had to be replaced by seed from distant sources—the light windblown seeds of pioneer species, such as aspen, birches, yellow-poplar, and some pines. In the mountain region, white pine and yellow-poplar have growth and potential timber values approaching those of the chestnut they often succeed, even though lacking the assets of the original species. By and large, chestnut has been replaced by other useful trees, but nowhere do its successors even approach it in versatility or overall utility.

The American chestnut is not likely to become extinct. New trees arise as sprouts from buds lying dormant in old, living roots. Others occur as seedlings from the seed produced by those sprouts, and both sprouts and seedlings live to produce crops of nuts before the blight infects and destroys them.

Toward a Future Chestnut

Once convinced the blight would be lethal to all American chestnuts, scientists saw but one possibility for restoring this doomed resource. Somewhere in the world they knew chestnuts must exist that could live when infected with the blight fungus, for the fungus could not have developed if it had always killed its host. If such trees, when found, had other qualities similar to *Castanea dentata*, they might be imported to replace it in America. To get on with the search, an exploring expedition to Japan and China was planned to search for promising chestnut trees in 1913. But this, like other major research and control programs, was a casualty of World War I. Only a few random importations of nuts were made during the following decade. It was not until 1927 that a chestnut expedition finally reached the Orient. By then a more far-reaching plan had been conceived—a bold idea indeed for those early days of forestry. Conceding that the American chestnut was probably unique—no other species would be likely to duplicate its many qualities—scientists decided to try to breed blight resistance into the American species. Thus, the search in Asia aimed primarily at blight resistance; species and varieties with good form and rapid growth were favored, but the import was to be sought principally for its gene, as indicated by its inherited resistance to the blight.

The prosaic statement in a report by the expedition leader—"We sent back over 250 bushels of the nuts"—tells us little of the magnitude and difficulties of this 3-year trek into the backwoods of Japan, Korea, and China. It carries no suggestion of the language barrier, the diplomatic obstacles to travel, and the primitive accommodations in those remote and sometimes hostile areas. Nor does it note the travel by foot, horseback, and bullock cart. And it fails to reveal the problems that stemmed from a lack of botanical knowledge of the areas to be searched or the species sought. Often these were wild-goose chases after reported "Chinese" chestnuts proved to be other species or identical to those already collected. Most of all, the report obscures the meticulous care taken under trying conditions to record the characteristics of trees from which nuts were obtained, the evidence of their resistance to the blight, their preferred habitat and climate, and the sterilizing, labeling, and packaging of the nuts for shipment to America.

All this was only a beginning, for from the broad selection of the strains of Asian chestnuts (and chinquapins) shipped to America, some 235,000 young trees were grown from the expedition's collections and field tested throughout the range of the native species. Tragedy overtook thousands as cows, deer, and rabbits found them appetizing, and weeds choked many to death. Others were winterkilled, for few of the imports proved as cold-hardy as the native species.

There were enough survivors, however, to show a great deal about the suitability of Asiatic chestnuts to American sites. While a few had the qualities of a timber tree, only one selection, of all the various imports, is now considered promising. Yet many were blight resistant, eventually producing flowers for the long dreamed of program of breeding.

Patiently, over the decades, a few devoted scientists have carried on the breeding work. Pollen from surviving American chestnuts is used to fertilize flowers on selected imports, or the import is used as the source of pollen. Nuts from successful crossings are germinated and seedlings nurtured over a 10- to 20-year period until they, in turn, bear seed. These will be used to grow seedlings for outplantings to learn if they have inherited the needed genes for blight resistance. During this time young trees demonstrate whether they have inherited good form, growth capacity, and climatic hardiness. Only by growing and observing progeny, however, can scientists determine how well trees transmit good characters to their descendents. Only then, too, can they proceed with the vital backcrossing and interbreeding needed to develop strains that retain both the hardiness and the qualities of Longfellow's majestic "spreading chestnut" along with the blight resistance of the imports.

So, for more than 50 years, the slow, persistent, and often disappointing effort has been maintained. Original hybrids have been back-crossed and interbred for three and four tree generations, while a new generation of scientists has replaced the pioneers in the program. Countless seedlings have shown early promise, only to succumb to the blight. Countless others have survived, but only as ragged, worthless scrub trees. Far out of the public eye and meagerly financed, the effort is still active to the credit of the chestnut geneticists.

Tangible results from half a century of breeding are meager—perhaps a dozen promising strains. Some show blight resistance, some good forest tree form and acceptable growth rates, but none is yet adequately tested or available for planting as the long-sought, blight-resistant tree.

One best sums up the hopes, the accomplishments, and some of the frustrations of the chestnut disease program with the story of the Clapper chestnut, an individual tree. A backcross of American chestnut on a Chinese X American hybrid, it is named for one of the pioneers in the breeding program. So promising was it in 1969 that it was featured in the press. With form and growth rate equal to its American ancestors, and for 20 years showing no blight damage in a region where *E. parasitica* spores are still abundant, here, perhaps, was the long-sought goal. Was this tree to become the progenitor of a new race of resistant American chestnut? But the returns were not all in, as so often occurs in scientific experimentation. Even before the article was in print, signs of blight damage had appeared. Now the crucial test is just ahead. Will it survive with minor damage like its Chinese ancestors? Hopefully it will. But if not, the project must go on. Other crosses will produce other promising candidates.

Eventually, the right genes will be combined. Then the lost bonanza that was American chestnut will be restored to the land.

🌲 🌲 🌲 Projects for the Amateur Naturalist

1. Collect, identify, and mount insects found in living trees, standing dead trees, and fallen trees. A convenient mounting box, where bugs are attached with straight pins, is a cigar box or firm cardboard tray-like box 2 inches deep. Note the species of the trees on/in which the insects are found.

2. Determine the suitability of a forest for the following species:
   a. deer (require a diversity of habitat types, from weedy, open fields to mature hardwood forests)
   b. rabbits (prefer a habitat in early stages of vegetative succession, from weed grasses to low brush)
   c. squirrels (most abundant in lands that have reached mid-succession— older conifers and hardwoods—to late climax—mature mast-producing hardwoods)
   d. quail (found in the early stages of plant succession—weed grasses to brush)
   e. grouse (similar to quail habitat, but also requires older mast-producing stands of trees)

3. Observe, record, and identify (if possible) injuries made to trees by wildlife (see Figure 19–1). Yellow-poplar replaced much American chestnut in the eastern forests. Standing, dead chestnut trees are riddled with worm holes.

FIGURE 19–1. Bird-peck on the surface of a yellow-poplar bole; picture made after felling (Tennessee Valley Authority photo).

20

Oranges That Are Apples

Osage-Orange

*B*efore barbed wire (or, if you prefer, bob wire) fenced cattle in and tres-
passers out, property owners considered Osage-orange trees ideal for hedges.
By the time of the Civil War, trees of this species, whose original range re-
sembled a narrow finger of land in Texas, protected faraway Bostonian lands
from intruders. One hedge there "planted by gentlemen of wealth" 10 or 12
years earlier rated a detailed description in a magazine of the period.

An Old Tale

An account by John Nance Garner, Vice President of the United States in the
1930s, tells how Osage-orange trees migrated to other parts of the country.
Garner was a son of Red River County, Texas, central to the limited 100-mile-
wide range of the species in the days before 1870. In those times steamships
plied the Red through Caddo Lake to the town of Jefferson lying by the river's
side. Jefferson was the last port of call. Farmers hauled their cotton to the
wharf there to be loaded on boats for destinations afar, especially for textile
mills in the Northeast and for cities like St. Louis on the Mississippi River.
Learning of the demand for the weighty, seed-laden fruits, cotton farmers
brought to the pier, in wooden wagons pulled by oxen and mules, not only
their bales of ginned bolls, but also the baseball-size spheres of Osage-"oranges."

Demand was especially great for the fruit in the Midwest, where landowners in the prairies sought the seeds for hedgerow vegetation. To the docks
came carts of horse-apples, colloquial lingo for the oranges. Shippers liked this
freight, too, for the heavy, hard-as-rock balls added ballast for the steamships.

The ballast was unloaded and sold at ports along the riverways where heavy machinery replaced cotton on bills of lading.

These fruits (the plural is correct for a single apple contains hundreds of tiny seeds arising from separate flowers) in time became impenetrable living fences, a ½-inch thorn hidden beneath each leaf on the tough-as-iron branches further discouraging intruders (see inset, Figure 20–1).

So important were these barriers through which even birds couldn't transgress that as early as 1855, in Illinois, contractors tended hedges for a dollar a mile until they were established. One historian found evidence that Ohio farmers early in the 1850s followed printed instructions, provided by the Office of Agriculture in the U.S. Patent Office, on caring for the living fences. Later,

FIGURE 20–1. Typical Osage-orange tree with "apple" in inset (USDA Forest Service photo).

he wrote, the fencerows made settlement possible as the counties furnished free trees as an inducement to plant hedges.

Oranges and Apples, the French and the Indians

And as these planted trees produced fruits, hedgeapple evolved as an appropriate, though local, name. Other names, too, described the tree or its uses. Every town in the original range of Osage-orange has a Bois d'Arc street; none has a lane describing the fruit. Those streets may have been so-named because many were paved with blocks of this wood. Contrary to the belief of some misinformed folks, this is not the wood of Noah's ark. Bois d'Arc is French for bow-wood, or literally wood-of-the-bow, probably called that by short-sojourning Arcadians from southern Louisiana parishes who witnessed the Osage Indians of the Texas post-oak belt fashion weapons from this flexible, tough wood. Bois d'Arc with anglicizing became bodark in tree books.

Some have called it mock orange for its similar outward appearance to the succulent citrus of that color. But, at least to me, the fruits look more like a mammal's brain. A lot of orange color appears on the tree, but not on the exterior of the organ of its seeds. Dark orange is the color in the deep furrows of the bark between the flat ridges; orange is the color of the thin papery scales of the inner-bark; bright orange is the hard, heavy, and toughest of all native woods; orange is the color of the twig pith; and orange are the lenticels on the bark of the twigs.

Shelterbelts and Windbreaks

Early, when success as a hedge became apparent, landowners and government agents introduced Osage-orange trees for holding the soil against the ravages of drying winds in shelterbelts and windbreaks of the Midwest. In Kansas alone, between 1865 and 1939, farmers planted over ninety-six thousand miles of these protective strips. Almost forty thousand miles consisted of single-row Osage-orange hedges. The Forest Reserve proclaimed by President Theodore Roosevelt from The Public Domain in southwestern Kansas in 1905 was, a year later, planted with trees of this species.

The years of the Great Dust Bowl saw many Osage-orange trees planted under the supervision of Federal foresters on farms of the plains and prairies. Windbreak and shelterbelt programs, pet projects of President Franklin D. Roosevelt, were ideal for encouraging the planting of this and other species on treeless lands for posts and fuel, as well as to protect the drought-plagued soil from wind erosion.

One journalist claims Osage-orange trees have been cultivated since 1818. Never mind the precision of the date: the shade-intolerant tree now grows throughout the United States, including the Pacific Northwest. Some lately published tree books show its natural occurrence extending far beyond the oft-argued original range to the northeastern seaboard. While, as noted, the original habitat was likely but a narrow zone just west of the pine-hardwood forests of

East Texas and extending slightly into Oklahoma, some maps show the species stretching into southwest Arkansas. In this natural zone, Osage-orange trees hug the moist river valleys where they survive even when inundated in times of growing-season floods.

Its wide distribution today must be attributed to man's industriousness. Trees with such heavy fruit and in which seeds are so tightly held do not likely escape to lands beyond the site of planting. These trees do sprout, and thereby may be reproduced conveniently by the technique foresters call coppice. However squirrels, deer, and birds eat the seeds after the apple has fallen to the ground and the hard coat has been softened by fermentation to make accessible to the animals the pulpy part. While deer consume the seeds, they much prefer to browse on the twigs. For wildlife, however, the species' highest use is likely to be for protective cover.

A Look at the Tree

In the winter when Osage-orange trees are unclothed of their foliage, the gnarled branches and crooked trunk become obvious. In summer, a low, rounded, ragged crown identifies at a distance trees of this species. It's an especially scraggly tree up close. The light-green color of the inconspicuous flowers appears after leaves are full size, any single tree housing blooms of only one sex. Foliage hides the strong stout spines. Thick, milky sap flows from injured trees.

Ordinarily, Osage-orange trees grow no more than 60 feet tall and 2 feet in diameter. Usually mature stems are smaller. The record tree, listed by the American Forestry Association, was 4 feet in diameter and 51 feet tall in 1972, spreading its crown over a 93-foot diameter circle. That tree is in Virginia, a thousand-plus miles from the species' original natural range.

A Drupe Fruit

Maclura pomifera, named for the American geologist William Maclure and the tree's conspicuous fruit (a pome), is the only species in the genus. *M. pomifera* joins mulberry and fig trees in the family *Moraceae*, all of which have joined-together, compound fruits.

The multiple fruit, the subject of much of this story, is a drupe or, rather, many small drupes compressed together, each at first displaying a silky strand of hair like that of the tassel of corn. These little drupes grow together to provide in one organ many brown nuts. Drupes turn pale-green to greenish-yellow as they ripen in the fall. Bruising the woody rough-surfaced "apples" causes a sticky, acidic, milky-white juice to exude. The bitter taste—along with the inaccessibility of the seed within the rock-hard sphere—suggests why wildlife and men refrain from eating them.

Pomes for seed extraction should be collected soon after they fall to the ground. Seeds sown in the spring are first soaked in water for 2 days. To get the seeds loose from the fruits, the apples are macerated in water, the pulpy fibers are then screened out, and some 12 thousand seeds per pound are collected. Instead, the apples may be stored to ferment in a cool, moist place for several months. Or, in the North, they can be piled outdoors over the winter. In the spring the organ is soft and mushy, and from the seeds a "fragrance" permeates the air.

Uses for the Wood

We've already mentioned Osage-orange wood serving to fashion Indian artillery pieces because the flexible material, not nearly so stiff as white oak, is hard. Hardness combined with durability when exposed to weather and soil also encourages its use for fence posts, crossties, insulator pins, and pulley blocks. In an earlier day, woodwrights fashioned wagon hubs, wheels, and rims from the wood.

Farmers staple wire to the posts while the wood is still green, the shrinking wood then gripping the staple tightly. So hard is the dried wood that it is almost impossible to drive staples into it. In that event, the barbed wire is attached to the post with hay-baling wire. With exposure to air, and hence the oxidation of chemicals in the wood, light-colored Osage-orange heartwood turns brown.

Textile workers boil a brown-yellow dye from the sapwood. An ingredient in khaki color also comes from this source. Root bark exudes a gold and yellow dye and a base ingredient for green pigment. Some fifty years ago, a dye-extracting plant in Pennsylvania bought Osage-orange cordwood in Texas. From the chipped wood came a brown pigment. And tannic acid, used in tanning leather, long has been extracted from the bark of the bole. Woodworkers in home shops should know that the wood does not glue well.

Wood stove enthusiasts will be happy to learn that Osage-orange is one of the best fuels for their furnaces. For this reason and because of its fast growth and an ability to regenerate by coppice, the species is a prime candidate for energy forests. These are lands set aside to grow wood repeatedly to heat homes and fuel industry.

A modern use for the oranges, though I cannot vouch for its validity, is to repel cockroaches. Readers of natural food magazines see ads recommending these fruits as a substitute for synthetic chemicals toxic to the insects. One friend, living a block from a tree that coated the ground with its balls, sent to Ohio for 2 dozen of the fruit at $1.50 each!

We've noted the modesty of this tree in size and in its contribution to society. Yet Osage-orange has played in our culture a peculiar role for which it is commemorated. Near Brazoria, by the southeast Texas Gulf Coast, stands a tree under which gathered an unusual assembly. The year: 1865. Purpose of the meeting: to announce the Emancipation Proclamation and to inform the newly freed slaves of their rights and responsibilities as citizens. Called the Freedmen's Bois d'Arc, this Osage-orange tree is a living monument to a noble event.

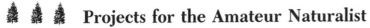 **Projects for the Amateur Naturalist**

1. Locate a windbreak of trees, perhaps a Plains States' shelterbelt, or a band of trees around a tennis court or farm home. Using a simple aerometer to determine wind speed, chart the wind speed and direction at 10-foot intervals on both sides of the windbreak. In cold weather, see if wind chill affects the temperature. (Leave the thermometer in the open and then shelter it from the wind to show the difference.)

2. Collect flowering plants (apart from trees), identify, and mount them. Note the proximity to woodland and determine the relationship. For instance, bluebonnets occur in openings adjacent to stands of trees, but not under the trees.

3. Observe fungi or the diseases caused by fungi on living trees, the fungi that attack the wood of standing dead trees, and the fungi that attack fallen trees. Note to which group they belong: butt rots, bole rots, cankers (swollen stems), blisters (on bark), misshapened or stunted leaves, leaf blights (spots on foliage), or leaf wilts. Conks, the fruiting bodies of certain fungi that cause butt and bole rots, may be apparent where no rotting wood is visible.

21

Cinderella Cellulose

Trembling Aspen

*F*rom the popples come pulp, and pulp is for people. Hence, the importance attached to aspen trees—commonly called popples—by the folks of the Lake States.

Populus tremuloides is so named in the Latin because of the quivering motion of its leaves in the slightest breeze. The petiole, the leaf's umbilical cord, is flattened so that it acts as a sail in the wind. Another has it that the flat petiole, being stiff, holds the leaf in a position that makes of it the sail that flutters in the wind.

Perhaps no tree has a greater range than trembling aspen. In North America it occurs from the icy tundra of northern Alaska to the Mexican Rockies and from California's Coast Range to the glacial outwash plains of Newfoundland. Its altitudinal spread is like its breadth of range—from sea level shorelines of either ocean coast, to the stream courses along lower slopes at 3,000 feet or so in the Rocky Mountains, and on to timberline at about 11,000 feet. Found on all sites, from the deep coarse sands to the wet clayey or peaty soils, aspen prefers mesic sites—neither too wet nor too dry, moist but well drained.

In the same genus with trembling aspen are cottonwoods and the balm of Gilead, the latter a small tree along streams in the "land o' lakes." Local folks simply call it "bam," ignoring the "l" and shortening the "a" for tongue economy. Its scientific handle, *P. balsamifera*, though apt, doesn't connote the biblical reference, and that of the old popular hymn:

> There is a balm in Gilead
> That sets the spirit free.

166

Gilead, the mountainous region west of the River Jordan, was especially noted for its balm, a product of a tree that now is impossible to identify with any certainty. Likely not an aspen!

Some intraspecific variation occurs among the aspens. On the west coast, for instance, is a variety *aurea*, the leaves of which turn bright yellow in autumn. This golden-leaf aspen is especially pleasant to see in Alaska when interspersed with the islands of dark-green conifers within the tundra.

A stand of trembling aspen, called a quakie, in the southern Rockies (USDA Forest Service photo).

Among families of suckers sprouting from the roots of a single root, called clones, one finds inherited characteristics such as fiber length. Foresters, when intensively managing forests, may select superior stems from these genetic strains.

When pioneers paddled the ponds of the Boundary Canoe Waters of Minnesota and adjacent lands, aspens occurred only as scattered stems, and usually along those watercourses or where tree cover, as on the prairies, was sparse. A short-lived tree of 60 to 70 years there (and 80 to 100 years further west in the Rocky Mountains), it gave way in the virgin forest to the white and red pines. Later spruces and balsam fir formed the climax forest. Only in the woodlands of the prairie provinces of Canada or in the Rockies—where invading trees grow slowly, too—is the aspen a more permanent cover type.

Bunyan's Toothpicks

It was in the late 1800s that lumbermen, having "cut-out-and-got-out" in the northeastern woods, migrated to the coniferous forests of the Lake States. Here the mythical Paul Bunyan and his blue ox, Babe, along with lesser men and beasts, logged the lands. Vast areas, clearcut without thought of regenerating the forest, reverted to county ownership because the taxes were not paid and likely would not be, so discouraging was the economic situation and the prospect that this acreage would ever again be of value!

Fire accompanied the logging, sometimes a little before or a little later. If before, the giant trees were like sparklers for a Paul Bunyan Independence Day celebration—a hundred miles to the south the northern sky would glow like an aurora borealis. Those fires would "crown," running for miles at speeds of several miles per hour in the tops of trees, while a few minutes later burning snags would fall to the ground to set afire the pine "straw," sticks, and forbs that had collected over decades on the forest floor.

If fire followed logging, it fed upon the logging slash, limbs and tops of trees left behind by lumberjacks. Sometimes these fires, particularly in the dry peat soils of dried-up swamps, would go underground, travelling for hundreds of feet before surfacing again. These ground fires, as they are called by forest pyrologists, consume the dry organic matter, obtaining adequate oxygen from the abundant pore space in the fibrous mat that is often 10 to 20 feet thick. Ground fire, usually a hot fire, crowns when it heads into uncut timber in extremely hot, dry, and windy weather. Flames then move swiftly in the tops of trees.

Other conflagrations accompanied logging, ignited perhaps by sparks from the puffing engines of steam donkeys and logging locomotives or the carelessly tossed roll-your-own. Whole towns, large mills, hundreds of miles of railroad tracks, and hundreds of thousands of acres of land lay scorched and worthless.

Coppice Reproduction

Worthless, or so men thought! From those ashes—and hence it's called the Phoenix tree—sprang millions of aspen trees. Not seedlings alone! There were suckers, too, vegetatively propagated stems arising from the roots of the occasional bole in the forest that, along with the pines and firs, had been killed by fire. The root systems, protected by the insulating capacity of the mineral soil, remained alive. Sunlight and, with it, heat reached the ground, to be absorbed by the black charred earth. That heat triggered the mechanism in the tree's physiology to cause a dormant bud, long idle and just under the bark of the root, to break dormancy and become a tree. As many as 110,000 such sprouts per acre have been recorded. Of those, one-fourth would be alive 5 years later.

The roots from which these sprouts arise are long laterals extending well over 60 feet, in one case tallying 83 feet. At various intervals those roots approach the surface of the soil, perhaps a built-in technique for just such events as coppice regeneration. (The silvicultural technique to obtain vegetative reproduction by simulating nature is called coppice.) At those locales, the suckers break through the ground. The associated pines and firs, unable to sprout, are not soon again to be found in the forest. The woods are now pure aspen.

The trees developed by vegetative propagation in turn produce new roots from which, should another fire inflame the site, other suckers will arise that may grow 8 feet tall the first year. More fires mean more suckers and more suckers mean more aspen, up to a point.

While most of the new aspen forests originated this way, some may develop through sexual reproduction, for the species is a prolific producer of small air-borne cottony seeds. So dense may be the seeds in the air at the time of dissemination that they cling together like clouds of cotton tufts; in the summertime snowstorms of seeds sail on the wind for a mile or more before their native parachutes lower the vessels gently to the ground. Once there, provided a mineral seedbed is too, dense clumps of several hundred little aspens will germinate on a square foot from the closely knit cottony tuft of seeds.

To get a new forest intentionally by encouraging sprouting is, to the silviculturist, to employ the coppice method. As a harvest technique, saws instead of fire are employed in the tree's removal, and the forest floor is exposed to sunlight and heat that, once more, triggers the mechanism that stimulates the buds to break dormancy.

Indeed, mature stands of aspen presently unneeded for fiber are sheared by bulldozers. From these stumps and the roots of the destroyed trees arise new trees, stems that will be ready for harvest when the market demands, perhaps three or four decades hence.

Single-Sex Trees

Most aspens are dioecious—male and female flowers produced on different trees. This reduces or virtually eliminates a degrading form of inbreeding, called "selfing," and hence assures sound seed with maximum germinative capacity.

Such seed-produced forests, however, occur infrequently because fires kill seed trees and seeds upon the trees. Indeed, the thin papery bark of this species is a poor insulator of the cambial growing tissues beneath the outer bark, so much so that modern prescribed burning techniques cannot be used in aspen stands except to clean up logging slash. Prescribed fires then are an insurance measure against wildfire and, perhaps, to encourage reproduction by sprouting.

Another silvical characteristic in aspen's favor of importance to the timber manager is a strong ability to express "dominance." Certain stems, because of some slight advantage that made them more vigorous, shoot out above their neighbors. It may be an inherited characteristic, a 3-day headstart in germination, or a micro-site—where the seed may have germinated in or near the dung of deer—of slightly superior quality. Hence, stagnation, even in dense stands of thousands of trees on an acre, is rare. While natural mortality removes those left behind in the struggle, the dominants make full use of light, water, and nutrients to grow more wood on fewer, bigger stems.

Fire Is Not Alone

Mortality, of course, has other causes. Sheep browse succulent sprouts, especially in the Rockies, while cattle break trees in nibbling grass underfoot. Tent caterpillars in the Lake States attack at 10-year intervals. While the loss of growth is serious, there is some argument as to whether they kill or just weaken trees so that secondary insects and diseases kill the trees.

Evidences of disease occur. As stands mature, heartrots—one type forming a tree-hugging conk shaped much like a horse's foot—decay the inner wood. Such weakened trees are broken readily in the wind. Target cankers expose concentric circles of wood, callous tissue results from the intermittent growth of the fungus and the formation of healing tissues. Still other fungi cause fast-growing warty tumors on stems, rough bark, and doty wood.

Sick trees also come about by off-site regeneration. Lands where aspens are not meant to grow include the sandy outwash plains of glacial origin. On those deep coarse soils of low fertility and low moisture, jack pines are nature's favored species. When aspens do come in on the jack pine plains following fire, deterioration of the soft hardwood trees begins at age 35; and 5 to 10 years later the aspen is gone. As even the roots are now killed, few suckers appear.

Foresters depend on plant indicators to provide clues to site productivity. The presence of sweet fern, for instance, means low-quality land for aspen, while the height of bracken fern can be directly related to the vigor of popples.

Porcupines have their fun and food in poplar groves. One group harvested 20 thousand cords of wood on a 7,500 acre tract in the north. But the porky is surpassed by the beaver in consistency of effort. Here he is, the eager beaver, handling (or mouthing) extensive logging operations in late summer. And this in spite of the bitter taste (at least to humans) of the bark. The sour astringent, they say, was used as a substitute for quinine by the early pioneers. Anopheles or not (judging from the size of those mosquitoes along our international boundary), a chemical that will shrink the tissues, driving the blood from them, would be quite useful if only to cheat some insects out of a man's blood. Come to mention it, the beaver's appreciation for the bark could have been why some imaginative zoologist called him "*Castor*" *canadensis*, except *Castor* is French and Latin for beaver.

Because beavers depend on aspen and Castor's fur is valuable, growing these semiaquatic mammals along with the popples may be legitimate multiple-use management. The paddle-tailed transient—moving with the timber supply like the cut-out-and-get-out loggers of old—harvests the trees within about a 100 yards of the water's edge. Where steep slopes make skidding easier, his logging chance may extend further from his pond, especially in late summer when food for the winter must be accumulated at the bottom of the water near the entrance to his lodge.

Serious browsers of aspen include moose, elk, and deer. In addition to consuming the nutritious foliage, these large herbivores chew off the bark during seasonal migrations or in the winter range. Bark removal, leaving dark patches of callous tissue over the xylem on the tree trunks, may girdle or provide infection entry points for fungi spores.

When the human loggers went through the forests of northern Michigan, Wisconsin, and Minnesota, they gladly skipped over the aspens, trees of little value for lumber. When retailed, however, they could have been marketed as cottonwood because of the similar characteristics of the grain.

Cinderella, Did We Say!

"Excelsior," cried Carl Schenck, the aged founder of the Biltmore Forest School, as he punctured the air with his voice, his finger pointing skyward during his lectures in the 1950s, a half century after the first American foresters were graduated from the little log college in the Southern Appalachian Mountains. Had one not known the erstwhile professor, he might have thought he was arguing for a continuing use of aspen wood: excelsior—curled wood shavings for packing valuable china and glass. But we listen more closely to the heavy Germanic accent, and discover it's "excelsior, the highest good," of which he speaks. And that, too, is aspen wood.

Now you've read the story of what happens to the tree following fire. And, as if by plan, new uses for aspens were developed. High-grade papers for books and magazines, made by the soda process, utilize much of the aspen produced by man and nature working together. More goes into disposable chopsticks for Japanese fast-food restaurants.

From worthless wood to finest fiber! That's why we call it "Cinderella cellulose."

🌲 🌲 🌲 Projects for the Amateur Naturalist

1. Illustrating nature. Tree bark, seldom an artist's choice, is prime material. Begin by reproducing this aspen trunk (see Figure 21–1) with pen and ink, then proceed to illustrate from living trees.

FIGURE 21–1. Trunk bark detail of quaking aspen (USDA Forest Service photo).

2. Observe a beaver lodge and dam. Measure the trees cut by beavers around their construction site and, with those data, compute the volume in merchantable trees utilized by *Castor*. (Use volume table in Chapter 14, Project 1.)

3. Leach chemicals from green, autumn-colored, or dead leaves of a particular tree with boiling water. When cooled, compare the colors of the leachate. Using a simple pH kit, obtained from a farm or garden supply store, compare the leached liquid for acidity or alkalinity. Compare the fluids with the water used for leaching for color and pH.

22

Living Riprap

Willows

*T*o engineers building roads, bridges, and levees, riprap is rock or concrete. It's the sustaining wall of stones thrown together, sometimes without order, to prevent undercutting of structures and roads by stream currents. Riprap reduces the ripsawing by the rough edge of rip-roaring water along a shoreline. The soil ripper is reduced to a ripple, at least in its effectiveness.

All the rivers and lakes of the world can't be lined with rock. Yet without riprap of some kind, erosion would have long ago leveled the land. Riprap there is, and it is alive: it is the roots of willow trees and shrubs.

Those interlacing roots form mats that bind together particles of soil, enabling banks of ponds and streams to withstand the forces of wave action or running water. Willows, of which there are more than 200 species, serve in this way. Included are the graceful drooping weeping willows of oriental origin (hence the species name *babylonica*); the arctic willow that, when mature, is all of an inch tall; the crack willow of Europe (that has "escaped" in the U.S.), so named because its brittle twigs break when blown by wind; and the shrublike pussywillow with the furry catkins that appear in the spring. Black willows are a cosmopolitan tree found from the Arctic Circle to the tropics. Its living riprap habit, notable in the icy climes, shows it to be dwarfed, creeping, or mat-like.

These trees are members of the *Salicaceae*, or willow, family. Of minor importance for timber production, except in the Mississippi River delta of the southern United States, they have major value for soil and water conservation. The natural mats formed by the roots are simulated by man in some parts of the world. In those lands, weavers weave the pliable stems, or osier, into "mattresses" for erosion control. Engineers did this in the lower Mississippi

An old stand of black willow in the Mississippi River Valley (Westvaco Corporation photo).

Valley until asphalt replaced willow as mattress material. But there this species forms living riprap on the kidney-shaped ox-bow lakes of abandoned river beds.

Black willow sites, its life history, and its silviculture are similar to those for cottonwood (see Chapter 24). However, in mixtures, cottonwood crowds out the slower growing black willow except on the wettest sites. Black willow matures earlier, stands then quickly degenerating as trees die.

Bare, moist, mineral soil—devoid of litter and ground cover—and full sunlight for the greater part of the day are essential for establishment of reproduction. Newly formed, low-lying land of fine sandy soil and old-fields that occasionally flood to depths of several feet usually satisfy these conditions. A pioneer species on frontland sloughs and low flats, it there becomes a timber tree maturing at 50 to 70 years. Since black willow produces abundant seed

Several species of willows and narrowleaf cottonwood serve as living riprap along creek banks in the dry western states (USDA Forest Service photo).

crops nearly every May or June, dense stands usually result after winter clear-cutting.

Black willow, most common of the *Salix* in eastern America in managed stands, should be thinned every 5 years, as the species stagnates early. Especially in pure stands where this tree does not assert dominance, stagnation and catastrophic mortality result if the forest is not skillfully thinned.

Kin to Cottonwood

Willows behave much as do cottonwoods in regard to submergence and its effects upon seed germination and regeneration. Good germination has occurred after seeds were under water a month or more. When several feet of silt and sand are deposited by high water on the surface of the ground, trees survive by developing a new root system just under the new soil surface. And, as with cottonwood, willow recovers quickly following extended periods of inundation during the growing season.

A sharp line of demarcation has been found between healthy and drought-stricken stands of black willow growing in stratified alluvial soils characterized by 2½ feet of heavy clay overlying deep fine sand. Tree roots extend only 3 inches into the normally saturated sand. Upon desiccation, such trees readily succumb, because the channels in the sand rapidly carry away water that would have been stored had the lower horizon been of more finely textured clay.

The soil of bottomland hardwood forests—typical of those for black willow and cottonwood—may lose 95 percent of its moisture within 5 days following light showers. The storage capacity, then, is about 0.1 inch of water. A 0.1-inch shower following a dry period of 2 weeks adds the equivalent of 12 percent of the total water-holding capacity. The same shower after only 5 days without rain provides a total moisture content of about one-half of the storage capacity. So sensitive are they to rainfall that trees of the genus *Salix* readily become dormant, even losing leaves, when the wilting point is reached for soil moisture; but they readily regain vigor and put out new foliage when the rains return.

Willow Wood

Characteristics of *Salix nigra* wood are similar to those of its cottonwood cousin, with a few exceptions. Willow, in contrast to *Populus*, is high in shock resistance and "works" well with tools. Notable uses are for artificial limbs, boxes, woodenware, novelties, and, as for cottonwood, veneer, excelsior, furniture parts, and pulp. A by-product of willow farming is especially sweet: honeybees feed on pollen nectar for nourishment in rearing early spring broods. Other uses are salicin, a medicine extracted from the bark for relieving pain, and perfume distilled from the flowers of an Egyptian species.

Some northern states once were important wickerwork centers. There osier culture—the growing of willows for this purpose—was practiced. Plastics, metals, and solid woods, however, forced that industry into oblivion in the United States. Nevertheless, we cannot endure without the stream-saving rip-rap of the willows.

🌲 🌲 🌲 Projects for the Amateur Naturalist

1. Relate soil erosion to trees. Locate erosive situations. Are any trees near? Are tree roots exposed? Do they hold the soil? Pull back some soil that has "held" and examine it for roots, some perhaps so fine that a hand lens is required to see them. Inexpensive hand lenses (10–15 power) are available at college bookstores, some hardware stores, and some sporting goods stores.

2. Collect, identify, and mount plant parts that show symptoms of disease (like wilted leaves or rotting wood) and/or the fungi that cause the disease (such as conks and blight-spotted foliage). Mounting will need to be in sealed, clear bags.

Black cottonwood—another riprap tree—along the stream, and spruce and fir trees up the slope of an Idaho mountainside (USDA Forest Service photo).

3. Learn the economic losses in low-value trees. In a stand of trees, determine the volume lost by crook (bends), disease, and ice breakage. Determine the volume in trees killed by insects or disease. (Use volume table in Chapter 14, Project 1.)

4. Compare relative humidity and temperature under various individual trees, under stands of several kinds of trees, and in the open. What effect do the trees have on the microclimate or the "climate near the ground"?

23

Toxic Defense
Black Walnut

Standing at the side of a rural road in the eastern mountains, a group of experts especially knowledgeable in various fields of forestry pondered the failure of pine seedlings in a newly established tree nursery. The soils had been analyzed for possible deficiencies of all the nutrients known to be required by plants. The possibility of toxic levels of elemental cations and anions had been investigated. So, too, had soil microbes—fungi, insects, and nematodes. Organic matter measured adequate, the pH was within an appropriate range, and soil texture analyzed all right for seedling growth. Everything, it seemed, was in good order. But the seedlings couldn't survive.

The team of experts, gathered around to consult with one another on what now should be done, appeared stymied when an elderly man in bib overalls sauntered by. The local farmer paused to take in the unusual grouping of strangers in his vicinity. Hearing the comments, the man—who knew nothing of Liebig's law of the minimum, cation exchange, and the term pH—volunteered a solution to the problem confounding the experts. "Years past," he said, "that land was a walnut orchard."

Allelopathy

American black walnut trees contain a tannic acid chemists call juglone. The reddish-yellow crystalline substance leaches from leaves and, some believe, exudes from roots. If roots don't release juglone, as seems apparent, the chemical at least flows to the outer bark of roots. There, tree physiologists agree, roots of other species that come in contact with those of black walnut trees die. But not only trees of other species: even black walnut seedlings won't grow under older trees of that brand.

If scientists debate whether roots secrete juglone, not to be argued is the assumption that the organic compound leaches from foliage. Experimenters boil the carbohydrate out of green foliage and then kill trees growing in soil to which the toxic juice has been added. The same chemical can also be washed from green shucks of walnuts by late summer and winter rains, thereby inhibiting growth of plants growing nearby. Tomatoes as far away as 80 feet from walnut trees are affected, and alfalfa for 60 feet. The naturally occurring herbicide also injures potatoes, apples, blackberries, rhododendron, and mountain laurel, as well as pines.

The word allelopathy describes this herbicidal behavior. Plants other than black walnut show similar traits. Many of the hundreds of species of Australian *Eucalyptus*, the ubiquitous tree of heaven known to many people as *Ailanthus*, yellow birch, and sugar maple seedlings are allelopathic. Foresters in the Douglas-fir region long thought seedlings of that species were injured by allelopathic extracts from parent trees. To their surprise, research showed that old Douglas-fir trees were not the cause but, rather, the species' usual competitor following

Black walnut, the American hardwood tree of high value for furniture (USDA Forest Service photo).

cuttings that make openings in the forest. Even the germination of salmonberry and thimbleberry was hindered, these woody shrubs seldom seen where western bracket fern, the real culprit, claims control of a cutover site.

Ponderosa pine seedlings in southwestern range lands, like the aforementioned Douglas-fir, are affected by allelopathic phenomena. There material leached from blades, juices that seep from roots, and winter exudates from dead Arizona fescue and pine muhly grasses diminish the ability of the pine seeds to germinate. Tree physiologists can't make up their minds which route the poison takes from grasses to tree seeds and seedlings.

Other examples of allelopathy occur when broomsedge grass grows in loblolly pine stands and, in the Delta country of Louisiana, where cherrybark red oak competes with sweetgum. Extracts of live and dead foliage and roots of the low-quality grass detrimentally affect the pine, while large cherrybark red oak trees grow without their kin nearby and with only a few other species. Sweetgum is notably absent because of toxic levels of salicylic acid leached from these cherrybark red oak crowns by rain. The chemical, tied loosely to foliage, can be leached with cold water. Peach trees, too, often need to be replaced because of toxic products released by the action of microflora in the decay of their own roots.

For the *Eucalyptus* trees, noted earlier, volatile terpenes serve an allelopathic purpose. Other excreted chemicals may be let loose into the environment through decaying vegetation. These include steroids, alkaloids, and sulfides. Sycamore is notably affected by this putrefaction. It seems that allelopathic plants occur from rain forests to desert climes. Sometimes they improve plant growth—Kentucky bluegrass grows better under certain trees that produce allelochems.

Influence on Succession

From the above, one can correctly suppose that allelochems play a role in ecological succession. Tree dominance for certain stems, species diversity, and site productivity could be controlled by these compounds rather than by the more commonly supposed tolerances for light, shade, nutrients, moisture, and pH.

"Definite" allelopathic potential contributes to the occurrence of Utah juniper and redcedar in the West, sugar maple in the East, and the antagonism that Norway spruce exhibits for heather in the heaths of northern Europe. Various poplars, trees widely distributed throughout the world, also seem to be affected by chemicals exuded from grasses.

If streptomycin and other major pharmaceuticals are products of chemical reactions in the soil, one should not be surprised at the ability of allelochems to control vegetative growth. Indeed it is a field ripe for research by the herbicide industry, so desperately in need of naturally occurring compounds to replace the synthetic ones often suspected of injuring human health.

Walnut Wood

American black walnut, with the possible exception of wild black cherry, produces the most valuable wood in the northern hemisphere. Prices of $1,000 are paid for 1,000 board feet growing in the woods. Logbuyers call this the stumpage price. A record $25,000 has been offered for a thousand board feet and $12,600 once was received at a timber auction. For perspective, stumpage prices for southern pine sawtimber run around $200, for post oak $20, and for pine pulpwood $20. So valuable is wood of this species that "rustlers" steal high-quality trees from residential yards and, where planted, trees must be protected from timber poachers.

For export, walnut wood is sold by the pound, bringing high prices in western Europe where it competes with English walnut for gunstocks, pipe stems, highest-quality furniture, wall panelling, and caskets. Airplane propellers, musical instruments, and veneer for many purposes are cut from black walnut. Wood of the species has high value largely because the dark heartwood contains flashes of pale-yellow sapwood. However, other equally important reasons are hidden from view: The wood is heavy, hard, strong, shock-absorbing, and durable. It warps little, withstands strains with changes in temperature, "works" easily, has straight coarse-textured grain, and appears lustrous and velvety—rather than slick—when finished. Most pieces of the wood have a mild, yet distinctive, curiously aromatic odor and taste. In cross section the pores appear distributed by size throughout a growth ring. For one or more of these reasons manufacturers seek black walnut trees to be turned into lumber for the products noted above.

In spite of the allegation that southern grown walnut is brash, fracturing readily, isolated trees harvested along with major hardwoods in the South are separated, stored, and shipped in carload lots to furniture and veneer plants. One of many fancy tables made years ago to refute the charge enhances, without a blemish, the living room of our home. Walnut trees grown in the South do make good wood.

The furniture industry especially prizes burls cut from knotty, crooked bolts, from limb crotches, and from tree stumps—often below ground level. Table tops are sawn from larger ones, exquisite gunstocks from others. Burls form when irregular grain combines with partly developed buds and streaks of darker-colored wood. Someone described the wood as having "quiet poise which marks it as one of the great gentlemen among American trees."

So valuable is this "gentleman" that the export trade was once controlled, though not for long. Balance of payment problems and the stubborness of America's walnut furniture manufacturers brought about the removal of restrictions. But what sickens a person who appreciates natural wood finishes is the painted black flecks squirted from spray guns at furniture plants and intended to add figure to already beautiful surfaces. Visit your furniture store: Can you find any pieces free of this faked "wear" imitation of an antique figure?

Today even the light-colored sapwood is sought, for it is readily darkened by steaming and staining to appear like the chocolate-brown heartwood that often exhibits purplish-brown to black streaks.

Veneer logs are at least 13 inches in diameter. From these timbers, first squared or lathed round, knives slice or peel sheets ⅟₃₆ inch thick. "Book-matched" sheets are kept together until glued into panelling or laminated onto tabletops. So treasured is the curly grain figure of black walnut that it is artificially created with special knives and heat presses.

Current industrial uses, apart from wood, include oil from the nuts for soap and paints. From ground nutshells comes an abrasive used for cleaning jet engines and as a filler for textured paints. Nuts ground into meal are fed to livestock, as they contain many vitamins, nutrients, proteins, carbohydrates, and fats.

Earlier Uses of the Tree

Not always has black walnut wood fascinated only those who appreciate exquisite panelling and furniture. Abraham Lincoln, no doubt in his youth, split boles for fence rails and posts. By the time of the Civil War, barns were strung on walnut beams, railroad ties were hewn from these tough stems, waterwheels were made from the rot-resistant heartwood, and charcoal was kilned for gunpowder. American antique furniture hides walnut wood in drawer bottoms while exhibiting chestnut and oak panels on exterior faces. This consumption in the land west of the Atlantic went on even while the "Age of Walnut" strained the coffers of the European princes and lords whose supply of the even-finer English walnut wood was then running out.

Pioneers used more than the wood of the tree a hundred-plus years ago. Of course, people and wildlife ate the kernels of the fruit; and from the husks of the fruit folks obtained black dye to color wool and cotton cloth. The hulls were soaked, and the "liquor" was boiled, then strained and cooled to a lukewarm temperature; the wool was then immersed in the dye bath, which was reheated to the boiling point and allowed to simmer for an hour. As the temperature gradually lowered, the cloth was rinsed several times. Adding sumac berries further darkened the dye. Each repeated use of the liquor lightened the color. For gray, the yarn was first dipped in lye water. Layers of leaves interspersed with strata of yarn in a kettle of water and boiled all day also produced black color for textiles.

In those days oil boiled from pounded nuts was used as butter and as a hair oil, boiled nut meats were dried and caked for food, and whole nuts (hull and all) were pickled. (Left to overripen, the oil in them turned rancid.) From green shucks came the chief ingredient of brown hair dye. Nuts were so important to a family's welfare that every child in walnut-growing country had hands stained brown in the fall of the year from the clubbing of fruit to remove the hull.

Pioneers claimed that the fragrant leaves repelled ants and flies, while poultices of damp walnut hulls capped a head to keep it from turning gray.

Some folks supposed that the juice of the hulls cured skin diseases and the inner-bark served as a physic (laxative), which indeed it did; while a nut was often carried as a preventive or cure of rheumatism. The sweet sap, like that of sugar maple, was boiled for syrup.

Civil War soldiers believed that the bitterly irritating bark stopped bleeding, the rind of the fruit removed ringworms, and an oil-soaked cloth, when applied, relieved the pain of an aching tooth or "tuberculosis" of lymph glands of the neck. Claimed, too, was the effectiveness of a salve made from a spicy scented leaf extract. Physicians noted that "perseverance will effect the cure," taking three weeks. Possibly the cure without the leaf and lard concoction would have taken but one week. Still, an older black walnut remedy was for mental illness which, or so it was believed, the meat of the nut could cure.

Walnut in Mythology

That eating nutmeats could cure psychological disorders probably was a rumor circulated in the days of Rome's greatness, for the association of the tree with the gods was early apparent. Tradesmen possibly carried *Juglans* species from the Orient and eastern Europe to the Mediterranean country, and from there to the isle called Britain. The word stem *wal* meant foreign, as in the German name for the tree—Welshnuss, or foreign nut. Taxonomists placed these trees in the *Juglans* genus, and that genus, along with hickories, in the family *Juglandaceae*. The European walnut is *Juglans regia*.

Juglans came from *Jovis clan*, Jupiter's nut, a name given by the ancients who stored seeds of the tree in the old city of Pompeii. Archaeologists discovered them there in the unearthing of the Mount Vesuvius-buried metropolis in their "dig" two centuries past. Perhaps the witches' brew fed to Glaucus by the blind girl in Bulwer-Lytton's *Last Days of Pompeii* was the nectar of Jovis clan, the god-of-the-sky called Jupiter. In the first-century A.D. setting, the witch was an alchemist: today's chemists isolate many nitrogenous compounds from the sap of the wood and acids from the seeds of black walnut. Chemical composition of the seeds supports taxonomic classification for members of the *Juglandaceae* family. (Traditionally, and especially since Linnaeus and his son, classification has been based on the arrangement of flower parts.) That is, chemical components of hickory seeds differ from those in walnuts; but all hickories (*Carya*) have the same organic compounds, as do all members of the walnut (*Juglans*) genus.

Appearance of a Noble Tree

Scattered stems of black walnut mix their crowns with ash, elm, oak, cottonwood, eastern redcedar, and dozens of other forest trees in twenty-five states of the eastern United States. Landscapers plant the noble stem in most of the others, often resorting to horticultural varieties that were first cultivated in the 11th century.

The fast-growing tree exhibits lower branches that spread widely (to 128 feet in a reported case). In the forest it stands tall, straight-trunked, and clear-boled. When open grown, it bears a large, rounded crown. Large trees top out at 150 feet in maturity. The champion, in 1975, was a tree 22 feet in circumference and 132 feet tall.

Looked at closely, the foot-long frond-like leaves, comprised of 15 to 23 pointed, yellow-green leaflets, grow on stout twigs. Heavy, upward turning branches exhibit coloration among the earliest of trees in autumn, the hint of yellow turning brown against the backdrop of the dark brown, deeply furrowed bark.

Because the flowers are small and colorless, as with most trees, they go unseen. In the spring male catkins, hanging in slender bunches on the previous year's growth, ripen about the time leaves appear. With the leaves' appearance, one now sees the short spikes of female flowers coming from the current year's growth. By fall, the ripened heavy fruit, a nut with a thick, light-green husk, is conspicuous in the leaf-barren tree against the sky. The shell around the seed remains there during germination, a period of about 2 months from seed-fall. Because the hull doesn't open and break away, rodents feed on walnuts long after the season's other mast is gone. The grooved shell makes a convenient handle for the jaws of squirrels.

Inside the twigs, tasting like sulphuric acid, is a light-colored pith separated into chambers by thin diaphragms after the first year. A sharp knife readily reveals the pith to the naked eye. (White walnut, or butternut, has dark pith.) The pith often doesn't show in the section of the twig that develops between seasons.

On the outside of the twigs one notes prominent lenticels, raised a little above the surface of the bark. These organs on deciduous trees serve for oxygen uptake in winter. Prominent too are the heart-shaped leaf scars, notched at the upper margin, where last year's foliage once clung. A small new bud rests in that notch.

A closer look at the leaf scar reveals three groups of smaller bundle scars marking the pathways of carbohydrate, nutrients, and water into and out of last year's leaves. The three clusters, in a U-shaped line, appear to some like the image of a horse's head.

Plantations

The high value of black walnut suggests investment planting of trees to replace the world's rapidly dwindling supply. Only 0.5 percent of America's hardwood resource is of this species. Genetically proven strains for wood quality and fast growth should be selected, planted at 18 × 18-foot spacing, and thinned when about 12 years old. At final harvest, perhaps in 30 years, the trees should be about 30 inches in diameter and have two merchantable logs of beautifully grained wood.

Intensive management is essential: pruning, thinning, pesticide application, cultivation, irrigation, and ditching for drainage. Soil for the stand should be rich and with a high pH; it must be mesic, moist but well-drained; and never subject to overflow nor drought.

For these hardwoods, the faster the growth, the denser the material, as the volume of the wood that is in pore space is not proportional to the gross volume of wood. Proportionately less pore space makes up the wood volume in fast growing trees. Thus there is a greater percentage of solid fiber.

Along the way, these open-grown trees produce nuts with kernels of unusual flavor. To encourage seed production, orchardmen beat trunks with softwood clubs, thus fouling the carbon:nitrogen ratio of the growing parts of the tree. This checks the descent of carbohydrate which, in turn, stimulates flowering. An insulting old rhyme tells the story:

> A woman, a watchdog, and a walnut tree,
> The more you beat them the better they be.

Either nuts, knocked from trees by shaking or flailing, or seedlings may be planted. Nuts when tested for viability sink if sound. Husks are removed while soft, using a corn sheller, and the seeds are then stratified for three months at 34°F. Cone-shaped screens prevent rodents from consuming seed and nipping newly germinated seedlings. Crows, jays, and robins want a share too. Until needed, husked seeds retain viability when stored in moist sand in cool cellars or in the open in pits a foot deep.

Silviculture

Black walnut, growing its best in Appalachian coves below 4,000 feet elevation and in Ohio River bottoms (never in swamps), usually occurs as an occasional stem, even when associated with climax vegetation. In no forest cover type is black walnut an important component, with a single exception: Groups of trees of this kind occur in former pasturelands where squirrels have cached and forgotten their winter food. Buried nuts illustrate the reputation of the species as a seed producer and the good viability of its seed.

Injured young trees sprout, but these new stems—usually from the root collar—exhibit poor quality. Fortunately the species has no serious pests, webworm and heartrot being the worst.

In the forest, growth typically tallies 9 inches dbh and about 90 feet in height in 30 years. Thinning is necessary, for trees die unless periodically released from overstory competition for light. Black walnut is a shade-intolerant species.

Individuals grow best in deep soil, 6-inch stems reaching to 30 feet in 6 years.

Patch clearcutting, taking out a few trees to make openings for the establishment of regeneration, requires silvicultural artistry. But it does work. So, too, does group selection where a seed source is available. The former gives even-aged stands, the latter a forest of several ages. Lighter-colored heartwood seems to result when trees are open-grown.

Though never dominant in the woods, American black walnut is a tree to which we should cater. The tree's presence reminds us that items and ideas of the highest value often do not dominate.

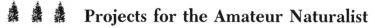 Projects for the Amateur Naturalist

1. Design a simple picture, then cut and assemble the picture from veneers of several woods. Names of suppliers of many species of veneer may be obtained from art stores and hobby shops. Black walnut of several shades is an ideal wood for dark figures in a picture. (See *Veneer Craft for Everyone*, by H. J. Hobbs (Charles Scribner's Sons, 1976).)

2. Following the instructions given in this chapter, prepare a dark dye from black walnuts and treat some cloth with the preparation. Use rubber or plastic gloves to protect your skin from the stain. How "fixed" is the color in the material?

3. Determine viability of seeds. Take a sample of seeds you collect, obtain from your state forest service (most such agencies will gladly send you an envelope of perhaps 100 seeds for this purpose), or purchase from a commercial supplier. Simply cut them through the middle with a sharp knife. Hollow seeds are not viable. Another way is to plant seeds that have been stratified or that do not require this treatment in a box with 2 inches of a mix of sand and peat moss at about 70°F. Count the germinated seedlings and note the number of days required for germination. Then compute the percentage appearing viable at several intervals of time (perhaps 5 days) until it appears that no more seeds will sprout.

24

From Cotton to Cottonwood

Cottonwood

Overflow bottoms along much of the South's river courses not so long ago produced an abundance of cotton. Cotton was king. Its production controlled the economy and, in turn, was controlled by the economy. The fiber once used in sugar sacks was replaced by paper, in clothing it was replaced by nylon, and in tablecloths by plastics. Those changes caused great withdrawals of land from cotton production. Much of the land of the rich, black fertile stream terraces has been taken over by cottonwood, that superb fiber producer of the poplar genus, *Populus*.

Or take the case of a factory, laid waste a hundred years ago in the Oconee River bottom of the Georgia Piedmont. The foundation bricks are yet there— deep in the woods, mute monuments to a significant industry. Paper was its product—high quality writing paper for fashionable folk, 100 percent rag content, and the rag fiber was cotton. As though to hide those crumbling pillars from the shame of failure, giant cottonwood trees now cover the land; from these, too, paper is made.

New Trees

Here we should note *Populus euroamericana*, the cross between *P. deltoides* of the southern United States and *P. nigra* of Europe. In the Po Valley of northern Italy, this hybrid exhibits fabulous vigor. Frequently trees of this cross, when vegetatively propagated, grow 3 inches in diameter in a year. Sixteen-inch trees in 14 years are common; in fact, that is the maximum age of managed stands there. This poplar cross has been established in many Mediterranean countries where it serves as raw material for paper, plywood, and lumber. Discovery of the "cross," considered a godsend in the days following

Fast-growing eastern cottonwoods in the South are used for paper, pulp, and lumber.

World War II, enabled relatively quick availability of wood for the rebuilding of Europe.

Another close relative is the famous Lombardy poplar, really a clone of a particular strain of black cottonwood (*P. nigra* var. *italica*), and also originating in Europe. Lombardy is now a popular poplar in the Western World. Another poplar coming to North America from Europe is a variety of the Carolina (*P. canadensis* var. *eugenei*). This once common street tree is believed to be the result of hybridizing of an unknown poplar with Carolina poplar. Only the male of the species is known to now exist. It was in a French arboretum in 1832 that the original tree was noted. It was still vigorous according to a 1913 report, but the effect of artillery shelling in two world wars upon this famous stem is unknown.

Ecological Characteristics

Pure cottonwood stands, usually of the species *deltoides*, are found on formerly cultivated fields and in well-drained flats and "ridges." Throughout their life, these stems tolerate flooding. Associated tree vegetation includes boxelder, hackberry, elm, and green ash, all entering the ecological successional pattern after the poplars and willows (Chapter 22) have become well established. The late comers eventually take over the site because the pioneer species are short-lived. Foresters consider the rotation age no more than 30 to 35 years; after this period the stands fall apart from disease and insect attack, leaving the forest to later arrivals if nature is unmolested.

Eastern cottonwood (*P. deltoides*) occurs on newly formed land built up by floods, in old-fields subject to flooding, and along river courses. New land forms as a meandering river cuts its banks and deposits on a "point-bar" down-stream the soil that has caved away upstream. Succeeding floods deposit coarse sediments near the bank of the river, building high, well-drained ridges or natural levees. These new-land soils, moved by the force of the river, are generally sandy. Fronts, on the other hand, are deposits of fine silt and clay material that have settled out of suspension. The water carrying these sediments of almost colloidal size—and having many physical properties of colloids—either filters into the soil and percolates through its profile or evaporates to the atmosphere. In both cases, the mineral particles accumulate in the soil or on the surface of the land.

Tolerance to Flooded Land

Of all southern bottomland hardwoods, eastern cottonwood probably has the greatest ability to withstand and recover from water-saturated soil. Roots die when soil is soaked for over a month, but extensive adventitious roots quickly develop from dormant buds in the inner-bark of the main stem. Some height growth may be lost, and the foliage may be slightly chlorotic, but it regains its green color and the trees resume growth after flood waters recede. When cottonwoods have been completely submerged for a brief period during the growing season, damage is slight; and if the flood is so severe as to deposit as much as 3 feet of silt or sand at the base of the trees, a new root system develops—in one case 4 feet above the original.

An exception to the high-water tolerance of cottonwood is found when newly planted stock, especially cuttings, are flooded. A couple of weeks to a month is the limit beyond which seedlings and vegetatively propagated stock of this species survive complete inundation. Seeds, however, germinate after being under water for a month, perhaps encouraged by high water temperatures—up to 93°F—at the time of year of seed-fall.

Tolerance to Arid Land

Cottonwood is found in the arid west too—often the only plant attaining tree size. The ability of cottonwood to develop drought resistance is appreciated by ranchers of the Rockies. Once established, the trees live on, furnishing shade for cow and cowboy, shelter from the wind for house and barn, and living riprap along the intermittent streams. There, too, the roots grow fast to form a network to hold the soil and thus to conserve soil and improve water quality.

Soil Moisture Regulates Growth

The importance of eastern cottonwood as a commercial tree, growing easily an inch in diameter and 10 feet in height a year, brought forth the need for evaluating the quality of land for forest production. Foresters developed two techniques for estimating capability of mid-South soils to grow this species. One is based upon soil texture, internal drainage in the surface or upper 2 feet, and an ocular estimate of the inherent moisture condition of the soil. Soils of clay texture, both buckshot and gumbo, are composed of fine particles so minute as to be almost of colloidal size. Sandy soils, in contrast, feel coarse-textured to the touch, while silts are in between. The soils are internally well-drained if no distinct gray zone or reddish-brown, yellow, and blue mottling occur within 2 feet of the surface. Should the colors of iron oxidation, hydration, and reduction appear nearer the surface, drainage is poor. Those soils on a slope or ridge, enabling floodwaters or heavy rains to drain off, seem inherently dry. Good sites, indicated by silt loam soils, appear well-drained.

The other method for relating the average total height of dominant and codominant trees at 50 years of age—called site index—requires identification of soil series. Series are soil names, classified by parent material (as limestone, granite, or water-laid sands) and the causes of origin (as by weathering, blowing wind, or flooding), and with horizons or strata similar in arrangement, thickness, and texture. Hence, land productivity can be mapped according to the soil description. For example, a homogeneous, alluvial, undifferentiated surface stratum of 2 to 4 feet is indicative of high-quality land.

Ecological Succession Begins

The life cycle of this pioneer hardwood begins in late February or early March when male and female flowers develop on separate trees as young as 10 years of age. Eastern cottonwood seeds, produced annually, mature and usually fall between April and July, but for some seeds it is as late as mid-August. A freeze after flower buds begin to open destroys seed crops. The small seeds are carried by wind and water to moist sites. Short-duration floods aid germination, water on the land depositing a fresh layer of silt in which the cottony seeds settle out in white masses to germinate. Favorable soil moisture conditions must prevail, for seeds remain viable under dry conditions only a few days. Some say that a few hours after release they will die if dry, and germination must occur within a few days. While moist sites are essential for germination and juvenile growth, the trees are relatively drought-resistant later on.

As many as one-half million seedlings per acre appear. Delicate the first few weeks, many are lost to hard, blowing rains and hot sun. Seed germination occurs on any site, but reproduction is adequate only on open areas where mineral soil is exposed and sunlight reaches seedlings for much of the day. The combination of factors—seed source, exposed mineral soil, and large openings—accounts for the abundant regeneration on old-fields, sandbars, and other river deposits subjected to frequent showers or flooding. Sites must be nearly devoid of leaf litter and ground cover for establishment of reproduction. As dominance is asserted early, weed trees seldom are a problem. Indeed, except on very wet areas, cottonwood, if seeded-in with black willow, crowds the latter out. The species, extremely intolerant of shade, will not develop even under sparse stands of trees.

With suitable markets, cottonwood plantations along the upper Mississippi River can be commercially thinned when 8 years old. Thereafter, cutting 3 to 4 cords per acre at 3-year intervals is possible.

Prior to the final harvest, intermediate harvests—to thin and remove diseased and inferior stems—maintain optimum growth and enable establishment of succeeding higher quality forest species. Foresters may clearcut cottonwood in the final harvest with the expectation of replacement by other species, such as sycamore, sweetgum, and ash, all usually present in the understory.

Where new cottonwood forests are sought, two seed trees per acre seem adequate for riverfront areas, providing as many as two million seedlings on each acre. Silvicultural treatment may also be by harvesting groups of trees, perhaps an acre in area, or strips, perhaps a hundred feet wide, if regeneration to the same species is desired. However, normal natural succession to a mixture of valuable hardwoods is usually preferred.

New Forests Not From Nature

Foresters often employ artificial regeneration where a seed source is not available, as in abandoned fields and where lands have been repeatedly burned, overgrazed, and overcut. Nursery-grown cottonwood seedlings, wildlings, and cuttings have been successfully used.

Wildlings dug from the forest for transplanting may be 4 to 7 feet tall and have 10-inch roots. They make satisfactory stock. In an early study, first-year growth and survival were better for wildlings than for cuttings, foot-long sections of stems inserted vertically into the ground. Today cuttings are the recommended practice.

Cuttings, growing more than 16 feet in the first growing season at the rate of an inch a day, are especially effective for propagating cottonwood forests.

These sticks, cut from 1- to 3-year-old trees, are dipped in plant hormone or growth regulator solution overnight to increase rooting ability before insertion into the soil.

Cottonwood does best when introduced on moist, well-drained, fine sandy loam or silty soils in the battures, those bottoms between rivers and levees which usually flood yearly. However, heavier clays on gentle slopes bordering swamps and sloughs are also acceptable sites. Heavy clay "buckshot" soils, recognized by the absence of trees and by sparse grass cover in times of drought during growing seasons, are not recommended cottonwood sites. They dry out and crack under the moisture stress typical of late summers. Ridges of coarse sand and swampy areas, where backwater likely submerges seedlings for several days, are also unsuitable planting chances. In abandoned fields where row-cropping has removed the moisture-holding organic matter and where planting of cottonwood cuttings is frequently prescribed, a tree starts slowly and grows poorly. Seemingly vigorous trees die suddenly in midsummer when free water is unavailable. When bottomland clays reach the wilting point, soil may still feel moist to the touch; feeling wet doesn't guarantee adequate moisture.

Management Matters

Confronted with this situation, one might

1. restore organic matter before planting by turning under several cover crops,

2. control moisture-competing weeds, vines, and shrubs by disking or bull-dozing just prior to planting,

3. use a subsoil plow to break through the plow sole and thus enable water stored in subterranean aquifers to move to the surface horizon of soil by capillary action, or

4. irrigate until trees are firmly established.

In any case, several cultivations during the first growing season may be essential for young trees to outgrow competition. Later, when grass no longer inhibits growth because either the cottonwood roots obtain nourishment below those of the grass or the tree's roots are more plentiful, cultivation may not be needed.

Cottonwood can be successfully grown from seeds in the nursery bed, producing 2½-foot seedlings in one growing season. Large vigorous stock has an advantage over cuttings when heavy vegetative competition is a factor. Cuttings still seem the best recommendation when combined with intensive culture, such as cultivation.

Turning under the sod improves rooting through aeration enhancement as well as through nutrient cycling. Sod, however, reduces overhead compe-tition for light, hence an equally important reason for cultivation.

Further improvement in growth may be obtained with applications of fertilizer applied following planting. Extra cultivation must accompany fertil-ization to control the weeds that otherwise severely compete for soil moisture.

Usefulness

Cottonwood's value is in its high-grade pulp. It is a poor-quality wood otherwise. Disadvantages for structural use include its softness, weakness in bending, low shock resistance, and a disagreeable odor when moist. A chipped, fuzzy grain occurs when one works the wood with tools. Add to this its capacity to warp, shrink, not stay in place; its low nail-holding ability; and its low durability when exposed to the elements; and it becomes a wonder any paper chemist ever hypothesized anything good could come from *P. deltoides*. Oh, we should mention that the Indians made fire by friction with the rubbing together of cottonwood sticks. And, too, its light-weight logs could be readily hoisted into place for stockade construction. More modern uses, in addition to paper, include excelsior, veneer (core and crossbanding stock), boxes, and concealed furniture parts.

Some Pests: Insects

The twig borer is the most serious pest of young eastern cottonwoods in the Mississippi Delta. The insect attacks terminal twigs much the same way that tip moths injure pines: the adult punctures the bud and lays eggs in the hole, the larvae then hatch and tunnel through the bud and into the nearby stem. Height growth is stunted, resulting in branching and distortion of the main stem. Lesser pests include leaf beetles, clearwing borers, and leafhoppers. All of these insects are controlled for a year by dipping vegetative cuttings or seedlings into a systemic insecticide just before planting.

Cottonwood root and stem borers damage plantations, larvae making tunnels up to 6 inches long in the pith and wood of young root crowns and lower stems. Sprouts are broken off at the tunnels. A hole kept open for the escape of the adult moth indicates an attack. The caterpillar is white or pink, with a brown head, and about an inch long when fully grown. Hopefully natural predators may be adequate to control this pest.

Cottonwood leaf beetles—larvae and adults—consume foliage, occasionally completely stripping trees. The ¼-inch-long adult has black and yellow stripes. Larvae, ½ inch long and black, give off a pungent odor when molested. Normally, lady beetles feeding on eggs and pupae check outbreaks of cottonwood leaf beetles. Aggravated attacks of these insects have been attributed to drift from cotton insecticides that kill natural predators.

Other Pests: Fungi

The poplar canker, caused by a *Cytospora* fungi, frequently kills weakened young trees, especially on poor sites. The fungus disease, entering dead tips of twigs, appears as lesions or cankers that develop as more or less circular areas on trunks and large limbs. Young infections are recognized in smooth-barked shoots by brown, shrunken patches. The pycnidia, one of several spore stages, appear in the dead bark as pimple-like pustules. Sprouts often develop just below cankers, and the diseased inner-bark blackens and emits a disagreeable odor. Control is effected, in part, by cultivation, release, and avoiding improper sites for growing this species.

A *Melamspora* rust, which forms yellow spores on lower sides of leaves and dead patches on top, defoliates cottonwoods. Reduced growth and death occur where winters are severe. Hybrid poplars and cottonwood clones differ in resistance to leaf rust of *Melamspora* but, thus far, none has been found wholly resistant.

Still Other Pests

Insects, disease, and animals of farm and forest do not work alone in attacking cottonwood. *Homo sapiens* takes his turn too. To him, cottonwood is often a nuisance, kicking up walks (my driveway), obstructing sewer lines (I moved mine to save a tree), and piling masses of silky seed a foot deep in midwestern gutters.

Livestock exclusion is mandatory because of severe browsing of valuable young trees. Deer, rabbits, and rodents may require control to protect seedlings and saplings from the animals' gnawing of twigs, trunks, and foliage. Piney woods' rooters, those mean, wild razorback hogs, dig up young trees that have been fertilized, perhaps for the more succulent and nutritious roots or perhaps for the salty savor of the chemical.

The Future

Fast growth of hybridized cottonwood and its usefulness for high-quality magazine paper, light-weight but opaque, are signs of the tree's increasing importance. In America, as now practiced in Europe, foresters soon will be row-cropping vast acreages in tree-farms. Human cotton-pickers will be ill at ease between these rows, though they once labored on these lands. Now, elaborate combines harvest the crops for the papermakers' giant fourdrinier machines.

🌲 🌲 🌲 Projects for the Amateur Naturalist

1. Convert the volume of wood from Chapter 14, Project 1, to value, using the following figures:

Sawtimber

southern pine	$ 200 per thousand board feet (MBM)		
black walnut	1,000 "	"	" "
post oak	20 "	"	" "

Pulpwood

southern pine	$ 12 per cord	
spruce	1 "	"
cottonwood	16 "	"

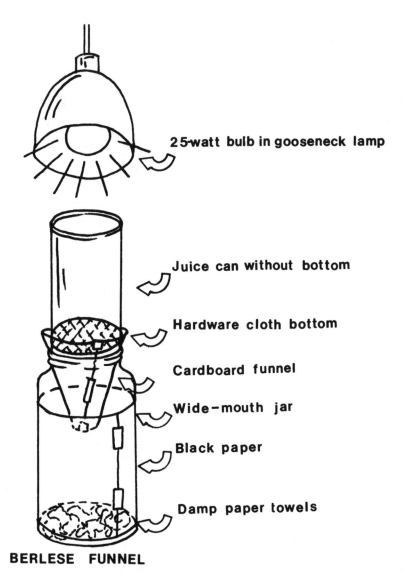

25-watt bulb in gooseneck lamp

Juice can without bottom

Hardware cloth bottom

Cardboard funnel

Wide-mouth jar

Black paper

Damp paper towels

BERLESE FUNNEL

FIGURE 24–1. A funnel for collecting insects. A flashlight can provide enough light in an isolated place.

2. Collect insects in the woods with a Berlese funnel (see Figure 24–1).

3. Root cottonwoods. Most varieties of *Populus* readily root, thus they are used in many parts of the world for fiber. Simply take foot-long pieces of living branches or the main stems of small trees. Stick them in a hole in the ground, pack firmly, and keep moist. You soon should have a new tree. Sometimes cuttings from branches form crooked trees.

25

Species Proliferation

The Oaks

*T*he oaks—perhaps three hundred species of them in nine genera—split into two main groups. The red oak group generally contains those species that have little sharp bristles at the ends of the lobes of their leaves; those of the white oak group do not. Red oaks have flesh-colored heartwood; for white oaks it's darker. You can see the pores in the summer-wood of a cross section of the wood of the red oak group; for white oak, they are barely visible with a hand lens. But the most reliable distinction is the open pores in the sapwood of red oaks, while gummy tylosis fills these voids in white oak wood.

Casks and Pipes

The reddish-brown gum that plugs the pores of the wood makes members of the white oak group useful the world over for holding liquids. The barrel staves of Missouri Ozark white oak supply the distilleries of St. Louis so effectively that the demand for barrels from the trees of those woods extends to Europe.

Long ago, in Colonial America, casks were assembled and disassembled, prefabrication style, and shipped abroad. Some made the journey several times with various liquids. So aggravated was a defiant Englishman named Maverick about his troubles with government over stave trade that he marketed his material to an agent in Spain. The agent sold Maverick's cargo, and forwarded the receipts in Spanish coin to an English merchant who gave Maverick credit for English goods needed, and not otherwise available, in New England. So the word maverick entered the vocabulary. In those days Massachusetts merchants politicked to get access to vast storehouses of white oak forests beyond the Bay Colony.

Coopers split the barrel staves from radial sawn bolts in such a way that

Willow oaks on a bottom-land site (USDA Forest Service photo).

the ray tissues in the wood stopped the flow of liquids. Otherwise alcohol seeps through the wood. Not only are the staves made of white oak, so too are the headings. Hoops, also, are shaped from white oak saplings. In addition to cooperage, this wood once supplied pipes for a primitive industry and civilization.

198

Other Uses for White Oak Group Woods

Chestnut oak, also called tanbark oak, long found use in the leather industry. Tannic acid from its bark preserved and dyed the hides. (That chemical, sometimes called gallic acid, reacts with iron in nails and screws to discolor white oak wood.) The industry steeps air-dried bark in water for tannin extraction. In times past, bark for the chemical trade often had greater value than the wood of some species of oak.

Durability of post oak heartwood encourages its use for fence posts and rails. Heartwood lasts for two decades or more in the soil of the warm, moist Southland. Some white oak species shrink, warp, check, and are difficult to kiln-dry. Yet boat builders use the wood. And cabinetmakers capitalize on the "mirrors" exposed when the wood is quarter-sawed. Those silvery flecks, split rays that reflect light to show wood of two colors, form prized patterns for high priced furniture. Quartersawing, which began in earnest in the 1880s, utilizes oak logs to their greatest advantage.

Axles for heavy wagons and knees for sailing ships came from live oak, among the toughest of all northern hemisphere woods (see Chapter 27). Oregon white oak, the only timber-producing oak of the Pacific Northwest, is used for insulator pins for utility poles, saddletrees, and stirrups. Its splintered wood

Ozark Mountain forest of white oak, black oak, and hickory trees (USDA Forest Service photo).

makes good baskets. The "old oaken bucket" of Sam Woodworth's lines, heavy for easy dipping in the well, joins rugged oxbows, plow moldboards, guitars, oil tanks, and handles (boiled in oil to toughen further) in the inventory of uses. Shingle oak, as the name suggests, readily splits for roof shakes. Perhaps the most unusual commercial use of any tree of the genus *Quercus* is that of the Mediterranean country cork oak (*Q. suber*). When the tree is about 30 years old, strippers carefully peel the bark to supply the sponge-like material for bottle stoppers. Restripping occurs at 10-year intervals for 100 to 500 years. The cork is cut at right angles to the lenticels to give air-tight plugs; if parallel, the cork is permeable. Boiling the bark in water removes impurities and softens the cork. Although *Q. suber* has been introduced into California, most of the world's supply of cork comes from Spain, Portugal, and Morocco. A single tree may produce nearly a thousand pounds in a single crop.

Red Oak Group Wood and Its Uses

The reason that red oak group species can't be used for tight cooperage is also the reason that they make better railroad crossties and mine props. They take preservatives more effectively because their pores are not filled with gum. You can actually blow through a section of red oak wood for some distance along the grain.

Red oak wood has no odor nor taste. That makes it useful for slack cooperage (barrels that hold solids and not liquids) for food containers like flour and sugar barrels. Readers must keep in mind that the odorless character is for dried wood. Once I had cut fresh firewood and, for convenience, stacked it near the house. But I had neglected to note the proximity of the bedroom window, always open at night, to the pile of wood. Shaken from my slumbers to "go wash your feet again," I knew the problem. That's the smell of unseasoned red oak. (The wood was moved the next day.)

Woods of the many species of the red oak subgenus, unable to be separated by any particular characteristic after removing the bark, are heavy, hard, strong, and stiff. The wood splits readily and case hardens with age to a toughness approaching steel. Its high shock resistance makes it in demand for tool handles. Much shrinkage occurs in drying and some species split and check in use. Bridge builders use a lot of water oak on rural roads because the species, so prone to such defect, has no higher value.

While fence posts are an important use, they must be treated with preservatives, for even the heartwood does not resist decay. Because the wood machines well with cabinetmakers' tools and resists wear, caskets and furniture are milled from it. Much now goes for pallets, especially wood from low-grade trees. Barbecue enthusiasts know something of the importance of oak charcoal, but it is even greater in industrial chemistry because of its absorption properties. Blackjack oak makes some of the best for back yard use. Yellow dye, commercially produced from the inner-bark of black oak, is called guercitron.

The Wood of Both Groups

For both oak groups, the fine, shiny silver-like grain, formed by wood rays, takes a high polish, thus encouraging use of the wood of these trees for furniture, especially for decorative inlays in the surfaces of other woods. The oak is often stained brown by a chemical reaction that occurs when mycelium of a bracket fungus infects the tree's bole. A deep emerald-green results when the mycelium is that of a cup fungus. This green pigment is a rare natural dye called xylinden. Another color, from which a red dye is obtained, is gleaned from a scale insect that attacks wood of the kermes oak, a Mediterranean shrub.

Common blue-black writing ink originates with tannins extracted from the gall of a wasp that attacks oak trees. From galls too come tannins with which to work leather. Like bark for that purpose, the galls are chopped into fragments, cooked, and the tannic acid extracted by steam.

How important are these gall-forming insects? More than 800 species attack oaks, almost all of which are wasps. Grubs of the insects, hatched from eggs laid in various parts of the tree, feed on normal plant tissues. Cell division is stimulated, forming hypertrophied red, shield-like disks on twigs or leaves.

As growth rings are distinct, aging trees is easily done, provided you have a stump. (The wood is so hard that I broke more than one forester's increment borer, made from the best Swedish steel, in penetrating boles of these trees, before I learned that greasing the bit with beeswax solves the problem.) Rings are distinct because summer-wood pores are more abundant than spring-wood pores: they are also smaller and lighter in color.

The wood is always porous. For some species it is diffuse porous, the minute holes distributed throughout the growth ring; for others the wood is ring porous, the tiny openings following the curvature of the ring around the bole.

Outward Appearances—Form

Oaks are named in Latin *Quercus*, from the Celtic *quer*, meaning beautiful, and *cuez*, tree. Especially in the fall, when leaves of deep rich reds, oranges, browns, and russets color the land, is the genus' name appropriate.

No single silhouette distinguishes the oaks, or almost any species of oak. Indeed, within a species one sees various forms, depending upon the site and whether the trees grow in the open or in dense shade. Sometimes oaks have short, dividing trunks; other times there is a single central stem, with or without heavy side branches. Often they display symmetrically spreading crowns or pyramidal drooping branches.

Some species, like pin oak, develop short, sharp spur branches low in the trees that persist so long they eventually are swallowed up by the expanding bole to become knots that degrade logs. For open-grown black oak, limbs grow close to the ground; for swamp chestnut oak, you may need to look up fifty feet to see the first branch. Lammas shoots, or water sprouts, cover the trunks of some species under some site conditions; others exhibit clear boles.

Some oaks, like canyon live oak of the West, readily coppice following fire—fortunately for the folks of southern California. Many evergreen oaks of that region, like coast live oak, form chaparral. (The Mexican-Spanish word means evergreen live oak brush.) There the oaks grow with manzanita and ceanothus, together loosely called chaparral.

Other oak species are shrubs; some, like bur (or burr) oak, may be either tree or shrub. Some grow at sea level, others at tree line in the mountains. Some are most vigorous on dry, rocky ridges, while others hug the overflow river bottoms.

Leaves

Leaves are of course the principal distinguishing characteristics of the many species of oak trees. Yet variety within species is dramatic: the shape and number of the lobes and bays are so erratic that some taxonomists believe hybridization between species is common, but this is hard to prove. For all the tropical American oaks, only one case of true hybridization is acknowledged in the scientific literature.

Red oak trees, for example, have leaves of two main shapes: either a finger with a single lobe or a curve like that of a scythe blade. (Its scientific name is *falcata*, meaning scythe.) Willow oak leaves resemble those of willow or peach trees, while foliage of water oak looks like spatulas. Dendrologists say that if even one leaf on the tree appears like a spatula, call it water oak, though all the rest are long, narrow, and unlobed like willow oak.

Most leaves have pinnate veins (the vascular framework arranged on each side of the midrib); they may be entire or toothed, their teeth rounded to sharp, broadest above or below the middle, with veins raised or depressed, and either hairy with tomentose pubescence or "clean shaven." Some are thick and some are thin. Some are smooth; one is like sandpaper. All appear alternately on the twig and with distinct petioles that do not significantly differ between species.

Among the trees of *Quercus* are leaves that form crosses, that look like hands, or fingers, or turkey feet. Some display unusual pigmentation: white oak foliage, for instance, colors the tree a violet tint when the buds first open in spring. Some species like live oak remain green, holding their leaves for several years; others, such as willow oak, lose a portion of their leaves in the fall; but most are deciduous, dropping all of their foliage in the autumn.

Twigs

Twigs of oak species are each distinctive, in winter being readily identified by their individual peculiarities. Many are fluted, the valleys and ridges caused by shrinkage of young twigs as they dry. Some have a pubescent fuzz. Lenticels—minute openings on the surfaces for exchange of gases—are conspicuous; buds differ by size and shape; stipules—small growths associated with leaf petioles—appear in pairs, one on each side of the bud, and these may hang on a long time; and buds crowd toward ends of twigs. Inside of the twig, in a neatly sliced cross section made with a knife, shines a star-shaped, light-colored, soft pith.

Flowers and Fruits

Female flowers whose ovaries become acorns occur in small clusters, called spikes. Nestled with leaf buds along the twig, they appear with the unfolding leaves in spring. In the ovaries are six ovules. Five of these usually abort, the one remaining forming the seed enclosed in the nut and in turn in an acorn cup. Wind disseminates the pollen from the showy clusters of male catkins that hang from near the ends of twigs, that method of distribution possibly encouraging hybridization. These staminate flowers, produced on separate branches but on the same tree as the pistillate organs, often veil the whole crown of a tree.

Acorns, common to all species, vary greatly. Overcup's cup almost completely encompasses the fruit; others by degrees less so. The cupule forms from tightly compressed ill-formed leaves that fuse together and harden. White oak group acorns mature the year of pollination; for the red oak group it takes two years. White oak seeds generally germinate in the fall; for the red oaks it's in spring; white oak seeds are sweet, those of red oaks bitter.

Some fruit appears every year, bumper crops sporadically, the vigor of deer, squirrels, and feral hogs often being directly related to the size of the crop. Other wildlife dependent upon oak mast for overwintering food include turkey, grouse, bobwhite quail, pheasant, bear, and songbirds. Even small wrens eat acorns. A woodpecker drills holes in trunks of California blue oaks into which the bird drives acorns. Hidden there, the thick bark holds the fruit safe from thieving squirrels. Some say the bitter red oak acorns serve wildlife as cathartic medicine.

Animals, particularly the gray squirrel, and water currents distribute seeds of oak trees. And gravity plays a major role in distribution.

It is written that ground-up acorns, when roasted, make a good coffee substitute. In addition to acorns, people eat another product of oak trees. It is the beefsteak fungus, both looking and tasting like meat, that grows on oak boles as a bracket conk weighing up to 30 pounds. Health food enthusiasts gather the tender, juicy, red spore-bearing organ (called a sporophore) just as it ripens. While the fungus enters the tree in pruning wound infections, it does not cause rot. Rather, chemicals exuded by the pathogen stain the oak wood brown. (Veneers from wood with such color are valuable.)

Spiral Arrangements

Phyllotaxy, the arrangement of leaves on twigs, is ⅖ for all oak trees. Here's how that works: hold a twig vertically, and choose a leaf of a single season.

Now count the leaves above the chosen one, around the stem, until you come to a leaf in line with and directly above the chosen one. That number is the denominator of a fraction. Then count the number of times you had to go around the stem to arrive at your last-counted leaf. That number is the numerator. So for *Quercus*, go around the twig twice to find a leaf directly above one below, and you will find that to be the fifth leaf above. One often encounters this series, named Fibonaci for its discoverer, in nature. Each species has its own code, and all spiral arrangements in nature are coded with these fractions (elms are ½, alders are ⅓). While neither arithmetic nor geometric, it is not haphazard. Here's the series: ½, ⅓, ⅖, ⅜, ⁵⁄₁₃, ⁸⁄₂₁. Now note how the numerators and denominators add up (I've used the = sign for lack of an adequate symbol): ½ + ⅓ = ⅖; ⅓ + ⅖ = ⅜; ⅖ + ⅜ = ⁵⁄₁₃; ⅜ + ⁵⁄₁₃ = ⁸⁄₂₁.

Taxonomists' Fun and Games

The genus *Quercus*, to which the oaks belong, joins with beeches, chestnuts, and chinquapins in the beech family (*Fagaceae*). *Quercus* is one of nine (some say six, others eight) genera of that family worldwide. (Tanoak is in another family.) Some three hundred (up to nine hundred are claimed) species and possibly many hybrids provide puzzles for taxonomists. About eighty species grow in the United States, about sixty of which reach tree size. Unravellers of the puzzle deal with over one hundred fifty forms in the United States alone. Fifteen important species grow in the Northeast, seven important ones in the Southeast, and about twenty in the western states. No single species covers even most of North America, but white (*Q. alba*) and red (*Q. rubra*) inhabit much of the eastern half of the United States. They are the most widespread. Over fifty-five species have been described in Central America, lumped together from a couple hundred that at some time have been named by botanists.

To aid in cataloguing, two subgenera are usually recognized, but not always by the same names. The white oak group, identified readily by rounded lobes on leaves, is called *Leucobalanus* (or *Lepidobalanus*), while the red oak group (which some books call the black oak group) is *Erythobalanus*, most obviously recognized by the bristle tips at the point of each tooth or lobe. Specialists further label series within these groups, but we'll not do that here. Because of the great variation in foliage within species, mounted collections are not to be trusted if only a few leaves are shown. The same may be said of tree identification books. And what some people call hybrids could be natural variation within a species.

Leaf size varies, too. Usually foliage on sprouts or young trees is larger than on seedlings arising from seed and older trees.

Readers are introduced to splitters and lumpers among plant classifiers. One splitter, for instance, found a minor distinction in the size of seed-leaves in certain oaks and proclaimed a new subgenus (*Macrobalanus*), but it didn't stick. Other botanists gather together many "kinds" that some call species into a single category. They are lumpers.

Europeans claim natural hybrids in their "oak collections" of trees planted and cared for in arboreta in Britain and on the Continent. Thus, an appropriate comment about this genera is that "the only consistency is inconsistency." Everything in this chapter is likely a generality.

Among distinctives between red and white oaks not otherwise noted in this chapter are

1. the loosely oppressed scales at the base of acorn cups of white oaks. These are pointed at the apex and thickly corky. (It is the opposite for red oaks.)

2. broad stigmas on the ends of flower styles of white oaks (narrow for red oaks, observed with a hand lens), and

3. acorn shells within which is a thick, felt-like layer of matted creamy or silvery "hair" for the red oaks (white oaks do not have this hair).

Champion Trees

While large oaks are usually 100 feet tall and 4 to 5 feet in diameter (Shumard oak) or as little as 30 feet tall (blackjack oak), the American Forestry Association's National Register of Big Trees lists 52 champion oak trees. The largest is 150 feet tall and 29 feet in circumference. That California valley (white) oak (*Q. lobata*) has a crown spread of 110 feet.

Problems for the Genus

Trees of the genus *Quercus* are not without their problems. City smoke and industrial air effluents cause death. While bur and pin oaks seem especially resistant to smoke and gas, urban foresters do not recommend most species for city shade-tree planting in heavily industrialized zones. Gypsy moths, notorious hitchhikers whose caterpillars feed on leaves, travel on campers and cars to new areas to attack and defoliate trees. Fire injuries leave wounds into which fungi enter, the wood-rotting pathogens then decaying the trees. Oak wilt knocks out black oak within a few weeks of infection, the disease seemingly passing through root grafts from one tree to another.

Many oaks in the East are hosts to mistletoe, the semiparasitic flowering plant with sticky seeds that birds carry on their feet and leave on the bark of high limbs. There the seeds germinate and are nourished by the oak. In mythology, mistletoe is especially prized when taken from an oak.

How Foresters Regenerate Oaks

Most books say the oaks are intolerant to intermediate in their tolerance of shade. My experience contradicts that, finding these trees for the most part only slightly less tolerant than the very tolerant sugar maple and American birch (Chapter 29). Thus, while clearcutting to produce even-aged stands may be economically necessary, more appropriate are selection harvests to establish many-aged forests. New trees usually are already established from seeds and sprouts under the stems marked for cutting. Tolerance may be less in the drier border regions of the species' habitats, but here the intolerance is likely for the xeric site rather than for shade.

Foresters also employ a shelterwood system. This method, like clearcutting, develops even-aged stands of timber, but now three harvests, rather than one, take place. The first encourages seed production and seedling establishment, and the latter ones gradually release the seedlings from some competition for sunlight, soil moisture, and nutrients. Meanwhile, the uncut large trees put on growth while protecting seedlings from vegetative competition.

Similar to coppice (sprout-developed) forests are the pollard stands of Europe. There loggers cut trees at several-year intervals, perhaps 6 feet above the ground. From that high stump new sprouts arise which farmers later harvest for bean poles. Cross sections of old pollarded stems just below the top of the stump make beautifully figured wood for furniture.

The deep taproot of most oaks discourages transplanting. So too does nibbling by rodents of newly planted stock. When seeds are planted, they should be placed 2 to 3 inches deep to avoid theft by birds and mammals. When a new oak forest is desired, both white and red oak species should be planted together. The difference in season of germination thus enables some seeds to make it through to seedling size. Even then, it takes skill and luck with the weather for people to establish new oak forests.

Rotations for sawtimber run to about 80 years, for pulpwood about 40 years. On the way to these ages the stands are thinned, for while the trees grow in shade, best growth is where sun reaches crowns.

Biblical Beards

In ancient times people worshipped oak trees. Called "Jove's own tree" by poets, white oak especially has a sentimental charm. Zeus, the god of thunder, may have been on Shakespeare's mind when the bard wrote in King Lear of "oak-cleaving thunderbolts."

Then came the early English whose kings saw in the ownership of oak forests an opportunity for taxing. The panelling and rafter wood of castles and cathedrals was a source of wealth for owners of the forests from which they came. As a means of determining the tax, the number of swine that the forest could sustain by its acorn crop gave the assessor the needed clue. And in the early days of this Nation, taxes were assessed on white oak pipes and hogsheads.

In the American Deep South, garlands of Spanish moss in the low-lying forests are as Dixie as the region's hot sun and cool shade, both needed for the moss' growth. Oaks host strands of the moss, often called biblical beards because they look like the ill-kept facial hair artists hang on the images of prophets. This "air plant," not a true moss, gets its nourishment from air dust and rain water. It is therefore not a parasite upon the oaks; indeed, it grows on other trees and even on utility line wires. In fact, you can grow it on a clothes hanger in a warm, moist bathroom in northern climes. There it lives for years.

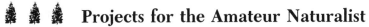 **Projects for the Amateur Naturalist**

1. Observe kinds of leaves on broadleaf trees. (a) At first, be satisfied with simply knowing that trees differ according to leaf shape. (If you find ten different trees, don't worry about what kind they are.) (b) Now, be satisfied that they are oaks or hickories or maples. (Don't be concerned about what kind of oak or hickory or maple.) (c) Finally, with experience, you'll learn to identify the species from the foliage. (Worrying about this detail often frustrates amateur naturalists.)

2. Make a tree identification key of at least three species that are members of one genus, such as oak, hickory, maple, or birch, based upon foliage. For example:

   A. Trees needleleaf—Go to N
   A. Trees broadleaf—Go to B
      B. Trees with lobed leaves—Go to C
      B. Trees with leaves not lobed—Go to L
         C. Leaves with toothed margins—Go to D
         C. Leaves without toothed margins—Go to K
            D. Leaves occurring opposite one another on twigs—Go to M
            D. Leaves not occurring opposite—Go to E
               E. Leaves with fuzz—Species X

3. Evaluate charcoal as a filtering material. Fill a bucket that has holes in the bottom (an old rusty one will do) with charcoal of the kind prepared for outdoor cooking. Break the charcoal into small pieces and leach through it (a) a smelly substance or (b) a cloudy substance. You could use concentrated onion juice for the first and muddy water for the second. Does the leachate after passing through the charcoal have the smell or the sediment?

4. Bake bread. Grind flour from the kernels of white oak acorns or hickory nuts (except for bitternut hickory) and follow cookbook instructions for baking.

5. Determine the phyllotaxy of ten stems each of three species of deciduous trees. How consistent is the Fibonaci series? Do any conifers exhibit phyllotaxic spiral arrangement?

26

Tree Legume

Black Locust

Sixty years ago a soil scientist noted that trees of several species found close to black locust in the forest grew much faster than stems of the same species growing apart from this tree legume. A. G. Chapman surmised that the nitrogen-fixing bacteria housed in nodules on the roots of the trees supplied the protein building nutrient for all the plants in the community, not just for the black locust trees.

How the Bacteria Work

Certain bacteria in the soil infect roots of legume plants. Infection takes place through irritated surfaces of microscopic root hairs or through injuries to roots. A prick of a needle simulates the irritation, a nodule then forming. At the point of infection, plant hormones, or auxins, are produced that, in turn, stimulate growth of root cells, much like the chemical changes that cause galls to form where certain insects attack tree twigs. As the cells enlarge, the tissues of which they are the building blocks expand to form swellings that appear as nodes. Nodulation, the name for the process, depends on how much and what kind of light reaches the ground and on moisture and lime in the soil. Adding lime encourages reproduction of the bacteria, the microbes then "fixing" or, better, converting molecular nitrogen in the soil atmosphere to a chemical compound that plants can use for their growth.

These nodules contain hemoglobin, the only place in the plant kingdom where physiologists find the ingredient of animal blood. Hemoglobin seems to play an indirect role in nitrogen-fixing by controlling oxygen concentrations. Nodules store carbohydrate, the energy source for bacteria feeding. For black locust the particular bacteria are of the genus *Rhizobium*.

Other members of the *Leguminosae*, the family sometimes called pea or bean and to which the pod plants belong, also have nodules that house bacteria. Kinds of microbes, some being aerobic and some not, differ for the various species.

Nonlegumes join in the action. Nodules form on roots of species of other families. Libocedrus, a gymnosperm akin to the conifers, and snowbrush, a shrub, both nodulate. So, too, do red and white alders (Chapter 2). The alders depend upon rod-shaped bacteria called actinomycetes, rather than rhizobiums.

Nonnodular species close to nodulating ones are affected by nitrogen-fixing bacteria. Ponderosa pine trees nearby Scot's broom benefit as though treated with commercial nitrogen fertilizer. Douglas-fir growth is enhanced where red and white alders live on the land. Alder actinomycetes, one report states, fix 150 pounds (though much less would be typical) of nitrogen per acre

Black locust, a principal tree planted in windbreaks and shelterbelts in the otherwise treeless prairies and for stabilizing the spoil of surface-mine sites (USDA Soil Conservation Service photo).

each year. And nitrogen in soils under pines may be fixed by unknown organisms. Hence, the symbiotic (mutually advantageous) relationship between nodulating trees and other plants is important in wildland ecosystems.

Symbiosis works both ways: it's a mutual relationship, the trees—in this case black locust—need the bacteria, and the microbes require the black locust. If no rhizobium are present, inoculation of the soil with the bacteria is necessary for black locust survival. Up to 250 pounds per acre are fixed each year by these bacteria in a black locust stand, though most accounts report much less.

Soil scientist Chapman's evidence for nitrogen-fixation was deductive. He noted that the more nitrogen the soil contained, the greater was the improvement in the growth of plants. Since the days of his observations, radioactive isotope N^{15} data support that conclusion.

Roots, a Tree's Brain

Roots, once called the center of biological activity, could have been what Charles Darwin had in mind when he said, "If the plant had a brain, it would be in its roots." The root zone and, thus, the locale of nodulation, is the rhizosphere. From the rhizosphere comes antibiotics; it is also the home of rod-shaped rhizobium bacteria that make a friendly attack upon black locusts.

The rhizosphere, too, is where decomposed foliage becomes incorporated into the mineral soil. For legumes, the incorporation of the decaying organic matter is especially desirable, as these leaves contain much nitrogen. Decomposition occurs quickly, the released nitrogen feeding other bacteria engaged in the destructive process. Though shade-intolerant, black locusts sprout profusely from their roots; in the arid Southwest some lateral radicles measure 25 feet long.

Nitrogen Is Not a Mineral Fertilizer

Nitrogen is unique among "mineral" plant nutrients, for it does not occur in rocks. All nitrogen in plants, and in the soil that nourishes them, comes from the atmosphere. Eighty percent of the earth's nitrogen supply, continually recycled, is in the air. Some 12 pounds of this gas permeate the atmosphere above every square foot of the earth's surface. There it is inert, not available for plants and thus not usable for manufacturing animal protein. Nitrogen's uniqueness extends to its availability to plants as both a cation (ammonium) and an anion (nitrate) in the soil. Both forms in time become a gas as they return to the atmosphere as ammonia and molecular nitrogen, respectively.

Nitrogen reaches the ground in rain and by lightning strikes. About 5 pounds per acre each year are leached into the soil in a readily available state from rain. Several times that much makes it to the land's surface by electrical discharges. Some of the element is then converted to nitrate for plants to absorb. Quickly plants take it in and convert the nitrate to amine, a building block for proteins and alkaloids. The latter compound occurs in toxic quantities in *Leg-*

uminosae wood, as those suffering from a skin rash from handling it will attest. Bark especially is high in nitrogen protein.

Nitrogen leaves the soil via leaching into underground drainages, dissipating into the air through fire that returns it to the atmosphere as gas, and through plant absorption. Nitrogen applied to a lawn generally leaves the site in a few weeks by one of these mechanisms. The element nitrogen is cyclic, some returns to the air and some to the soil as plants decay.

Leaching into streams is especially notable for a short time after clear-cutting of forests. Nitrogen levels in the water mount as trees are no longer present to utilize the nutrient. Within a few years, however, new trees and shrubs absorb the excess of released nutrients and the creeks are back to normal. Then, as the climax forest is approached, relatively more ammonium and less nitrate is consumed by the forest.

Wood of Black Locust

"One of America's most durable woods" aptly describes black locust. While I was researching this chapter, a delightful book by the master housewright of Colonial Williamsburg came my way. In *The Woodwright's Companion*, Roy Underhill explores traditional woodcraft, including the use of black locust. Posts of this species, he says, are "reputed by some to last two years longer than stone. Others say that it will last twice as long as the hole (into which the post base is buried). One man even claimed it will last two lifetimes—and says he knows cause he's seen it."

The longer the yellowish-orange wood is exposed to the air, the harder it is. Woodworkers refer to this phenomenon as case-hardening. The combination of hardness and durability encourages the use of this material for boat building, especially of the upper works of the frame and its ribs. So, too, its use for insulator pins for power lines. Tree nails, dowels used to hold planks of another species of wood together, have been lathed since colonial times from black locust. Conestoga wagons, crossing the prairies to the west, no doubt were held together with these oven dried pins that, as they swell and grip the sides of the hole in the board into which they are hammered, truly outlast the wood of the hole.

Useful qualities of black locust caused its export to foreign ports and its introduction (for a time) as the most widely planted North American tree in Europe. One report tells of its establishment in Germany in 1601. In the earliest days of New World colonizing, Jamestown's pioneers recognized its value and its resemblance to the locust trees of the Eurasian East. So they named it locust, and later botanists clarified its taxonomy by terming it *Robinia pseudoacacia: pseudo*, meaning false, and *acacia*, for trees of similar characteristics of biblical fame (which are usually evergreens). New World settlers were planting it too by the mid-1800s; now it's found in all of the 48 contiguous states.

American Indians carved bows from the shock-resistant wood. They taught early settlers to use the timber for corner posts for houses and barns. So important to the Native American was black locust wood that colonists found the trees planted by Indians in the lower Coastal Plain of Virginia, far beyond the species' natural range. Some wonder: Did the Indians transplant the trees or plant seeds? Maybe Indians taught colonists to boil a yellow dye from the wood. Maybe, too, they showed white men the wood's usefulness for heat in primitive industries.

Black locust's color and grain, displaying dramatic alterations of light and dark shades in the early- and late-wood of each season's growth ring, make attractive furniture. The surface appears smooth and satiny, the abrupt transition from early- to late-wood making a striking contrast. Contrasting too is the creamy white sapwood and dark-brown to yellow-green heartwood. Alas, its hardness forbids much use for commercially built furniture as the cabinet-maker's tools dull quickly.

The colorful wood is hard to distinguish from Osage-orange. The latter is darker when first cut, and water poured on shavings dissolves the leached color onto a cloth.

A variety of black locust is called shipmast and referred to as a clone. Its tall, straight timbers make excellent poles.

Identifying Characteristics

Trees are not tall, 40 to 60 feet, and seldom over 18 inches in diameter. Each generation seems to inherit its form, some straight and others crooked, from its parents. Black locusts grow best in rich, moist limestone-derived soils, but endure almost any situation, serving well for controlling erosion and as shelterbelts in dry lands. In the woods, its frond-like foliage and feathery, irregular, and open crown stand out among the tuliptree, maples, pines, and other species of a mixed forest.

Robinia, the genus to which black locust is assigned, was named for Jean and Vespasien Robin, a French father and son team who sought plants with pharmaceutical properties for Henry IV. I know not of their success, but young shoots and the deeply fissured bark of the tree are poisonous to livestock. Children have been sickened from chewing the inner-bark.

These trees are notorious for the half-inch-long sharp spines that extend from each side of old bud scars and new leaves at the nodes on twigs. Botanists call these thorns modified stipules. Ordinarily stipules are soft, temporary appendages, but not so for black locust. A related tree, honey locust, produces such long, brown spines that they served as pins to fasten the coats of Civil War soldiers. On water locust the thorns are dangerous daggers. Heaviest thorns appear on young wood; hence, grafting generally carries this character to scion material. Notorious, too, is the odor of the roots when severed.

On the plus side, one notes the showy hanging chains of droopy flowers and the way the shape of the tree's crown with its graceful foliage appears like the plume of a drum major's giant headdress.

Leaflets of black locust (some 7 to 21 make up a leaf) fold or droop on dark or rainy days. Sometimes this occurs in the evenings. Readers may know the small herbaceous forb called sensitive plant, the leaves of which, when barely touched, fold and droop. Sensitive plant, too, is a legume.

Black locusts display perfect flowers, both sexes occurring in the single white pea-shaped blossom. By fall the ovary of the flower has developed into a kidney-shaped bean within a pod, the most revealing characteristic of all legumes. These plants, we've noted, are in the pea or pulse family, pulse coming from the Latin *pollen* and eventually suggestive of the fine flour ground from the beans. Some botanists call the pulse family *Fabaceae*.

Seeds in pods rattle all winter as they flutter upon the tree in the breeze. Those hard beans with the nearly impermeable seedcoats inside a flat, papery fruit play an unusual role. They have some green color in them. That's chlorophyll. While most seeds are for storage of carbohydrate and protein to nourish a new plant upon germination, legume seeds photosynthesize as well. The green chlorophyll, as in corn leaves, is the chemical that, with the catalytic aid of the sun, produces starch and sugar. Photosynthesis begins about four days after the little roots, called radicles, emerge. I know of no species that begins to produce sugar and starch as early as those of the *Leguminosae* family.

Black locust trees are among the last to leaf in spring, displaying a "filmy shifting veil," and the first to drop their foliage in the fall. Possibly this relates to *R. pseudoacacia* being among the long-day trees, those that bloom in the late spring, as the days lengthen, but before leaves form.

Mesquite Story

The story of the extension of the range of black locust's close relative is worth noting. Mesquite, it seems, once was confined to that part of Texas hugging the Mexican border, or at least was much less extensive than is its habitat today. Cattle, as they were marched to market to the north, consumed the highly nutritious peas in the pod. Each year those animals browsed on the pods and several days later passed seeds in cow paddies. Soon the seeds germinated. A couple of years later, other bovine fed upon the seeds of the trees "born" earlier in those manure piles. These seeds, too, softened by acids in animal stomachs, dropped to the ground ready for germination. In time the range widened. Now mesquite (*Prosopis juliflora*) is found in dense nuisance stands in East Texas and north into Oklahoma, Kansas, and southeastern Colorado. So much a problem is it that costly mechanical and chemical methods must be used to control the weed trees and to maintain grasses on the range.

Black Locust for Spoil Banks

For fifty years foresters have sought species of trees that could survive and grow on mine spoil, the piles of soil, subsoil, and rock removed from the top of seams of coal or valuable minerals. From the first, black locust has appeared especially useful for reclaiming these and other disturbed lands.

R. pseudoacacia exhibits aggressive behavior, quickly producing cover to hold the soil on ore lands. It survives and grows well on acid soil. Foresters have introduced it to near-eastern and middle-eastern countries for reforesting droughty as well as abused lands. In spite of the fact that the optimum pH for the species is about 7, neutral on the acidity-alkalinity scale, black locust does well where the pH is as low as 4 (very acidic).

Soil scientists say that all nutrients save one essential for plant growth occur in most mining overburden, the material between the ground surface and the mineral seam. Sometimes nutrients suffice for good growth; sometimes they undergo chemical reactions when exposed to the air and become toxic. But nitrogen is the exception. It's always in short supply because the organic matter, the principal way soil stores nitrogen in available form, is gone—removed by oxidation as it is exposed to the air. Even with the nitrogen-fixing bacteria connected with black locust, the element may be inadequate to support growth of this species. But the more nitrogen the bacteria can fix, the better; for they cannot be accused of environmental damage, as leaching of synthetic commercial fertilizer may be.

Even before the American Civil War, England introduced black locust for reclaiming mined lands. Wherever introduced, it escapes to take over open fields.

Shale barrens, not necessarily abused by man's activities, fortunately are readily reforested by this species. Thousands of trees cover the land, and a pleasant aroma attractive to bees permeates the air. In America, the tree serves as a shelterbelt species where precipitation is as low as 12 inches a year.

Environmental Concern

Some innovative trials use municipal waste water for fertilizing forest trees. The waste collected from household and industrial sources is piped or trucked to fenced woodlands, there to be sprayed on the land through sprinklers. The soil under the trees serves as a filter for the germ- and organic-laden effluent. Of the many trees tested, black locust exhibits the best height growth and survival. It seems, therefore, to be tolerant of an abundant supply of nutrients. Foresters anticipate considerable acreages being set aside as living filters for human waste.

Fortunately the species appears resistant to air pollutants. Neither ozone, given off by electrical motors and manufacturing processes, nor oxides of nitrogen from industrial effluents—as measured by leaf sensitivity—damage the tree in air-contaminated locales.

Wildlife appreciate the tree. Deer browse its twigs, quail consume its seeds, and bees produce a good grade of honey. Rabbits eat sprout bark when snow is deep; otherwise they prefer other plants.

Black Locust Problems

All is not well even for the hard and hardy black locust tree. Aggravating is the borer (*Megacyllene robiniae*) that enters tree trunks just as they approach fence-post size. One simply can't get a staple to stay in the hollow space of larvae tunnels. As the beetle works most industriously on weak trees, stems growing on reclaimed land suffer greatest. And economically those are the stems needed to assure rehabilitation of the land.

A moth (*Parectopa robinella*) is another nuisance. The female lays eggs on leaflets, and the caterpillar that hatches burrows into the leaflet, and thereby "mines" the upper layer of cells. Then it chews a hole in the lower layer, defecates in the hole, and falls to the ground to pupate. The dark defecation spots appear as blotches on the leaf.

A caterpillar folds and pleats a leaflet to form a silky tent. The silver-spotted skipper cuts a hole in the tent in order to slip out to feed at night.

Longhorn beetles, aristocrat among bugs, trouble black locust trees on shale barrens. And a rot caused by *Fomes rimosus* enters through borer wounds to decay the wood of living boles.

Final Note

Rugged trunk but dainty flowers; durable wood but wrecked by borers; armed with thorns, but inviting in its durability. That's black locust, intriguing in its inconsistencies.

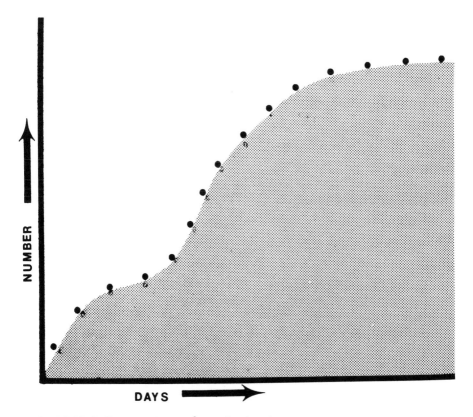

FIGURE 26–1. Determining seed germination times.

🌲 🌲 🌲 Projects for the Amateur Naturalist

1. Determine germination time for black locust seeds. Soak seeds in dilute sulfuric acid. (Your pharmacist can supply you with the acid. Seeds may be purchased through a farm supply store.) After 24 hours, place the seeds in a 2-inch-deep pan of moist sand in a cool (but not cold), dark place. Every day note germination of the bean-like seeds and graph the time of their appearance (see Figure 26–1).

2. Measure the effect of forest upon water evaporation. Do forests reduce evaporation? To find out, put a washtub or large dishpan of water under a stand of trees and another in the open, at least 50 feet from an obstacle to the wind, like a building. Carefully mark the water level in each. At 24-hour intervals, until the next rain, measure the depth of water evaporated and convert the data to inches per acre.

3. Observe nodules. Find the bacteria-housing nodules on the roots of locust trees (legumes) and red alder (a nonlegume that supports nodules that also contain nitrogen-fixing bacteria). Use a hand lens to see the nodules.

27

Ship Timbers

Live Oak

*L*ive oaking, they called it. From colonial times until the likes of the Confederate ironclad Merrimac replaced the wooden vessels on the seas of the world, live oaking supplied much of the timbers for boats. Other nations also utilized live oaks from America's southern forest, many a timber sawed and hewn from these crooked boles serving a shipwright's special need in his shop in some port town abroad.

In recent times I have seen the same technique used near the Aegean seacoast city of Thessalonika. Here the trees harvested were alepo pine (*Pinus halepensis*). Stacked in piles of various shapes where small fishing boats were built, the craftsman selected from the inventory of logs the shape best suited to his peculiar need. Perhaps this one for a keel, that one for a knee, and another for the stern posts to which the rudder would be fastened.

In America's live-oaking days, the wooden parts taken from the coastal forests of the Atlantic and Gulf shores were mostly used for knees, typically the structural midside supports for deck beams and to which the side wood of shiplap planking was fastened. Some trees were selected for keels, others for keelsons (structural timbers above the keel), and still others for the associated futtock or frame.

In a word, naval architects supplied skilled artisans with the measurements of the parts needed for a vessel. Cutters carried these drawings into the swamp border stands of live oak, located a stem whose dimensions and configuration met the specifications, cut the tree, hewed it on the site to a more precise fit, and dragged it by mule, oxen, and high wheels to the landing. Boatloads of these timbers were hauled to the shipyards of Philadelphia, to Falmouth for the Boston trade, and to Maine for structural assignments in tall ships for military and merchant fleets. Schooners carrying these odd-shaped

A remnant live oak near the Gulf coast. Note the branch curving away from the stump for the ship's knee (Texas Forest Service photo).

pieces of wood, many lost in stormy seas, were destined for Great Britain or France.

What Kind of Tree Is Live Oak?

Quercus virginiana, named for the state of Virginia, was called *Q. virens* at the time of the Civil War. Virens, meaning green, was an appropriate name, for, unlike most oak species, its foliage persists through the winter. Leaves generally fall after 2 years with new foliage sprouting in the spring of each year.

Two kinds of egg-shaped, edged-curled leaves characterize live oaks: thick and thin. Thick leaves persist; thin ones drop just before spring foliation. Both are shiny above and whitish below.

Botanists argue whether live oak is a member of the white or red oak group. It has some characteristics of both (Chapter 25). Its fruit, like that of the white oaks, ripens in one year; but the inner surface of the acorn cup is matted like the red oaks. Nor is the nut bitter, like the red oak acorns. Some leaves have sharply pointed bristles at the ends of lobes (red oaks), and some don't (white oaks).

The majestic tree with its round-headed full crown, seldom more than 50 feet above the ground, is a choice ornamental. From colonial time till now landscapers and homeowners have chosen one of the many varieties to grace the grounds of mansions and shanties alike. Spanish moss, draped like biblical beards, festoons the many branches that form where the trunk divides just above the ground. Garlands of the *epiphyte* hang like veils to give the shiny and whitish leaves a sad and eerie semblance of a weeping woodland. Scarves of the stringy strands may hide the clumps of mistletoe that tenaciously hook to the branches of live oak trees.

Shorter-lived than most observers expect live oaks to be because of the great girth and extravagant spread of the crown, oldtimers may be but two— maybe three—hundred years of age. A hand lens helps distinguish the nearly invisible growth rings to show diameter increment of an inch or more a year.

Live oak trees can rightly be called oldtimers, for chartered in Louisiana is a society to which only live oak trees belong. In typical blue-blood fashion, restrictions for membership are tight; only stems at least 100 years of age and 17 feet in circumference join the club.

If live oaks are short and not so old as they look, the trees do grow to massive sizes in trunk diameter and crown-spread. Trees 6 feet across at breast height and with foliage extending a hundred feet from drip-line to drip-line are not unusual. The American Forestry Association's national champion live oak in 1976 tallied 37 feet in circumference, was 55 feet tall, and spread over a circle of land 132 feet across. That big tree record-holder is one of the blue bloods of the pelican state of Louisiana.

And seagoing pelicans enjoy the comfort of the live oak habitat. Stands of these trees are not likely to be found more than 20 miles from salt water. Built into their genetic makeup is the ability to resist both foliar damage from salt spray, toxic to most trees, and overly ambitious tides that, in times of storm, inundate the soils with salt water miles inland. Often, apart from storm water, ordinary high tides inundate roots without deadly effect. Tolerance to salt, which other species do not exhibit, enables live oak stems to express dominance, even though they exhibit intolerance to shade.

Not only do live oaks endure salt, they also withstand sand blasting and sand burial, common phenomena in coastal lands. Flood, drought, fluctuations in temperature, and low nutrient levels of bleached coarse sands seem not to be formidable to the life of stems of this species. Thus, a tree's physical shape (for structural use) as well as its vigor appears to be controlled by groundwater levels.

Ecological Relationships—Dunes

Q. virginiana does more than endure these trying sites. The tree stabilizes dunes once vegetation initiators successfully, though tentatively, grasp the sand. Typical plant pioneers found along the shore include sea purlance, a low-spreading annual, and its successor, sea rocket, whose stiff stem traps debris that builds up the organic-matter content in the sand. Then come the dune builders, usually green grasses and forbs. Ordinarily scrubby shrubs follow them, forming windbreaks. Finally, after a long period of soil development and protection, a forest of live oak becomes established. It endures, and in its endurance the tree plays an important role in estuary protection for wildlife. Of these dark live oak hummocks, John James Audubon, the ornithologist, noted, "The air feels cooler, . . . songs of numerous birds delights, . . . flowers become larger and brighter, and a grateful fragrance is diffused."

In the Forest

Outer banks and bayheads, as well as coastal dunes—in short, sandy soils of recent origin—are typical sites for live oak. These situations extend along the coasts from Virginia to Mexico and on the isle of Cuba. Noted earlier, trees of the species endure salinity, but only where drainage is good. Pure stands are prominent on coastal ridges and on natural levees and frontlands near the mouth of the Mississippi River. Seldom is the tree established more than a few hundred feet from a watercourse—never more than a mile.

Climax forests occur in ridges along the edges of salty marshes, but a difference of 3 feet in elevation determines the occurrence of this site-particular species. Its leaf waxes protect the tree from desiccation on droughty sites as well as during periods of moisture stress on wetlands. Protection from cold is also afforded: while temperature never as yet has dipped to below − 7°F in its natural range, the typical variety has endured to − 15°F where planted to the north.

One doesn't find live oaks in river bottoms, but rather on the sandy well-drained soils adjacent to them. It is rather intolerant of floods. However, intermittent inundation, even for a short term in the growing season, seems not to injure the tree.

Sprouts from stumps and roots, at first forming a scrubby ground cover, grow to become massive live oak trees. And the old extensive root systems no doubt effectively prevent windthrow during coastal storms of hurricane force. A natural brace also occurs to protect the trees from being toppled by wind. The brace, layers of dense wood laid down on leeward sides and absent on windward sides of stems, displays asymmetrical growth. That lack of symmetry, incidentally, adds to the value of the wood for knees. Wood anatomists, however, note that for broadleaf trees tension wood ordinarily develops on the windward sides. In that event, the wood would not be desirable for ship timbers.

Because live oak acorns are sweet, turkeys and mammals (especially hogs) crave them. The mammals, along with gravity and water, carry the egg-shaped seeds to new planting sites. Often the nuts occur on trees that are but a foot tall. (Indians made cooking oil from these acorns.) High and prompt germinative capacity generally guarantees a new forest. One peculiarity is that the root (called a radicle), shortly after its emergence from the acorn, grows extraordinarily large just below the ground surface. Generous transfer of starch and protein from the seed-leaves (cotyledons) causes this. Possibly it is the reason buttressed bases, and even roots, later become so oddly shaped. That form encourages the usefulness of both of these parts of the tree for ship timbers.

Often found alone, but more often with other species, live oaks join water oak, southern magnolia, and yaupon on better-drained sites. Where soils drain poorly, green ash and American elm are likely associates in the forest.

Q. virginiana retains dominance because it has few enemies. Fire is its worst, injuries from scars enticing insects and disease-causing fungi to infest and infect. Its immunity to natural disorders carries over to the unnatural: synthetic herbicides don't faze live oak, which is disconcerting to foresters attempting to upgrade stands from low- to high-value forests.

Drought-hardy varieties, like *fusiformia*, have a range that extends into westernmost Texas, while the dwarf variety *maritima* hugs the Gulf coast.

Farmland Competition

Unfortunately, live oak stands are rapidly losing ground. Agriculture replaces considerable forested acreage and much more land goes for levees (and their "fill") to control water levels. Nor do the trees find ready markets in today's economy; thus, their care is not among the high priorities for foresters and owners of the lands on which they grow. Where farms have been abandoned, *Q. virginiana* follows in ecological succession the coming and going of annual weeds, perennials, and waxmyrtle shrubs. Not 10 years will pass before we see some live oak trees; in less than 50 years their dominance of the site will be expressed if the locale is one for this species.

What Kind of Wood Does Live Oak Have?

The shape of its trunk and branches is not alone among the characteristics of live oak wood that make it desirable for shipbuilding. The wood is dense, hard, strong, tough, and among the heaviest of American woods. It's close-grained and durable when in contact with soil and water. Because it has no characteristic odor, people confined to the holds of ships did not suffer with nausea. This was important, for vessels of most other species, their timbers always rotting from fungi attacks, became intolerable for habitation with their hatches battened down. Nor does live oak wood exhibit any peculiar taste.

Until discovery of this timber for boat construction, a ship's natural life expectancy was but about ten years. Understandably, shipping merchants were "happy" to learn that "Old Ironsides," nickname for the U.S.S. Constitution, was expected to be seaworthy for well over a hundred years.

The addition of live oak to the inventory of some 20 species of American woods for shipbuilding seemed a predestined mercy for a nation newly independent. The lowland oak joined black locust, several cedars, bald cypress, and other specialty woods in the shipwrights' timber bins.

Here's how Virginia Steele Wood, naval archivist, described the situation:

> In theory, the United States had a virtual monopoly on the world's supply of live oak; most of it was publicly owned by 1831. But as Europe's timber resources steadily shrank, American live oak became a commodity more and more coveted by Britain, France, Spain, the Netherlands, and Denmark. Even Czar Alexander I of Russia showed interest by ordering several barrels of acorns to plant in the Crimea. The congressional acts of 1817, 1822, and 1831 were all designed to safeguard the needs of American naval and merchant vessels by imposing fines and imprisonment on those found guilty of illegally cutting or removing timber on the public domain. Between 1817 and the end of 1831 the government spent a paltry $3,500 a year to prevent trespass on these lands, to have surveys prepared, and to support the Santa Rosa project. The country was, as a result, ill-prepared to protect itself against continual plunder of its timber; in December 1832, as directed by the House of Representatives, Secretary of the Navy Woodbury presented a lengthy "Historical Statement" with facts and figures to prove it. Recommending that the Navy Department continue to obtain live oak of the best quality, he confirmed that: "The wood is superior in strength, resistance, and hardness to the celebrated British oak that forms 'the wooden walls' of England."

Of course live oak wood had other uses wherever tough wood was needed. The rugged wagon axle is a notable example.

For comparison, live oak wood has a density of 0.8, white oak 0.6, and southern yellow pine 0.5. Weights of a cubic foot in the same order are 75, 56, and 44 pounds. Not unusual, then, for live oak timbers to sink in the sea. (Wood technologists, when determining wood weight, note the amount of moisture the wood contains. In the above cases, the woods contained about 45 percent water, typical of freshly cut or green wood. Similarly, the density of a sample of wood depends upon the amount of moisture in it at the time the piece of wood of known volume is weighed. This contrasts with other materials for which weight and volume are always determined under identical and specified conditions.)

North Carolina's surveyor-general described in 1709 the toughness of the wood of live oaks, but it wasn't until surveys of St. Marys River in 1770 that ship's carpenters searched there for proper pieces to fit the diagrams of the naval architects. Live-oaking was then underway.

The Live Oakers

Hundreds of Yankees went south "to the live-oak fields" even before John Bartram, the British royal botanist, reported to the king in 1766 that this tree had better grain than English oak for shipbuilding. The industry, according to the fascinating book by Virginia Wood, seems to have been well established for the Atlantic trade by 1700 in the old city of "Charles Town," only three decades after the settling of the South Carolina coastal community.

Here's a bit of her description of a live-oaking operation:

> For those directing the operation, it was easy enough to sit comfortably in Philadelphia and demand the finest live oak; however, it was quite another matter to drag it from the malarial swamps of Georgia. In early June of 1794, John T. Morgan, shipwright of Boston and "master builder of considerable abilities," who had been provisionally appointed constructor at the Gosport yard, was detailed to Charleston and Savannah by Tench Coxe, Commissioner of Revenues. Since all the land was privately held, Morgan was to seek out property owners, search along the coastal islands to determine what live oak and cedar was available, estimate the cost of standing and cut timber, and report on its proximity to landings convenient for loading onto scows or coastal vessels. He was not to make any agreements; others would attend to the contracts. He was, however, to take copious notes and perform his duties with dispatch "as the public anxiety is much excited by the circumstances (which) have occasioned this naval armament." After all arrangements were made, Morgan was to superintend the cutting and hewing of timber and to see that it was shipped to the six ports where construction on the frigates was to begin. In addition to expenses, his annual compensation was $2,000, . . .

Conditions were terrible in the swampy, mosquito-infested, and alligator-inhabited live oak stands. One diary reported "feveuorer . . . in all my Lims." The Yankee artisans worked with slave labor, usually felling trees in winter, when the sap is down, in order—or so it was believed—to prevent twist and check that occurs with too-rapid drying of the wood. Some craftsmen were convinced that the timbers were harder when trees were harvested in winter.

Pit saws, remnants of which have been found along the Altamaha River where fresh water collects, suggest some mechanical assistance for those who hand-hewed with broad axes this tough material. Rot and wind shake, apparent after trees were opened, caused the waste of much wood.

Moving the Wood Pieces

Logging boats plied the rivers upstream to sources of supply. Oxen, cleated to be able to stand on boats and lowered in slings over the vessel's sides, were shipped—in one case from Maine—to work these southern woods. Hobbled, they traveled in the holds of the boats, canvas hammocks under their bellies to protect them from falls and injuries on the rolling vessels.

Upon harvest, skidding, and hewing, live oak pieces were hauled by boats to yards and docks. From these wharves, commercial agents dispatched them to the Orient or the China trade or around the Horn for ships in California service as well as to the eastern markets. As naval archivist Woods describes, "Many a 'soft wood' ship was oak or better from shoe to broad teak rail, while few clippers had less durable stuff than the heavy hard pine of Georgia with generous white and live oak timbers at the critical points."

Freighting the heavy timbers had its risks. Tall ships would be "logy" on one tack, but sailed as though enthusiastic to arrive in port on the other. A ship would, when out-of-true, carry barrels of oil on one side of the keel to balance the heavy, odd-shaped pieces of wood on the other.

At boatyards, men buried the beams in bogs. Total submergence gave them protection from aerobic pathogens that rot wood. Soaking also prevented hardening of the wood so that tools dulled less rapidly when pieces were shaped. Wood stored this way came in handy a few years ago when Old Ironsides was restored for display in Boston Harbor: divers found seven hundred pieces in the mire of the sea at Pensacola on the Gulf coastal side of Florida.

Naval archaeologists lifted wood stored over a hundred years from the ooze of Portsmouth, New Hampshire, in 1945 and recovered more in 1957. But aged this long, the beams split, checked, cracked, and were so hard they damaged the saws. And worse, the stench of the wood when exposed to the air, as though waiting to decay, was nauseating.

Live Oak Trees and Politics

Live oak was first classified in 1696 by a botanist of London's pharmaceutical plant-introduction garden (where gardeners later, but unsuccessfully, introduced the tree); a hundred years passed before the economic significance of live oak became obvious. So obvious then was its importance that the U.S. Congress, now independent of the crown, at the urging of the President, appropriated funds for the purchase of timber for the nation's navy in 1799. At that time, too, two small islands off the coast of Georgia were set aside as live oak reserves. A few years later lands of The Public Domain were set aside by presidential proclamation as reserves to assure an adequate wood supply for the future. These forests, by 1868 totaling 268,000 acres, were mostly in Florida, Alabama, Mississippi, and Louisiana.

Earlier President John Tyler, on behalf of the oakers, ordered that a contract be entered into between them and the Federal Bureau of Construction. The agreement assured boat builders that they would have ribs for ships and straight pieces up to 40 feet long for stern posts. A worried government assigned federal agents to establish nurseries to grow seedlings to be planted to replenish depleted stands.

Inevitably, it seems, when government controls, scandal erupts. The House of Representatives heard complaints of alleged fraud participated in by landowners and live oak procurement personnel. Thieves, too, robbed the woods and storage bins. Navy secretaries got involved, frantically hiring agents to keep the pressure on to provide wood for ships and not for rustlers. In 1831, Navy schooners patrolled the coasts for poachers, the cut-and-run live oak gangs who lived in palmetto-camouflaged lean-tos near their valuable prey. By 1820, legitmate and stolen harvests had taken all the trees of value from islands off Georgia's coast.

As the Confederate ironclad, the Merrimac, marked the end of live-oaking, steel replaced the wood that gave Old Ironsides her title. Navies all over the world turned to metal vessels, driven by screw propellers, and boilers replaced the masts of tall ships. Live oak reservations were returned to The Public Domain, opened to settlement, and, because the soil is often rich, soon farmed for food or cotton.

Live Oaks as Monuments

I suppose no other species—within the range of the twenty or so varieties of live oak—commemorates military, political, and cultural events, and people and places, as prominently as does this tree. Churches were founded, treaties agreed upon, and charters signed under them. Criminals hung from, and spies perched in, their branches. Its endurable wood was, and is, often the "stone" to mark the grave of the humble. Alleys of planted live oaks still guide the visitor to many mansions of the Old South.

My favorite account tells about the tree in Georgia that owns itself. In 1820 the owner of the land on which the tree stood in Athens willed to the tree in courthouse-recorded documents all the land within 8 feet of its crown on all sides. In time the tree died. Promptly on the plot someone planted acorns from the old monarch, one of which today, as the legal heir, grows on land it owns. I'm told that's the only case in the world of a tree-heir to have this privilege.

In Louisiana's Creole country of the early 1800s, hot-tempered gentlemen settled their disputes on fields of honor with pistols or swords. These episodes frequently are commemorated by a live oak tree.

That the live oak tree *is*, is monument enough. Long has it been appreciated, as evidenced by North Carolina's surveyor-general, writing in 1709:

> Live-Oak chiefly grows on dry, sandy Knolls. This is an Evergreen and the most durable Oak all America affords. The Shortness of this Wood's Bowl, or Trunk, makes it unfit for Plank to build Ships withal. There are some few Trees, that would allow a Stock of twelve Foot, but the Firmness and great Weight therof, frightens out Sawyers from the Fatigue that attends the cutting of this Timber. A Nail once driven therin, 'tis next to an Impossibility to draw it out. The Limbs therof are so cur'd, that they serve for excellent Timbers, Knees etc. For Vessels of any sort. The Acorns therof are as sweet as Chestnuts, and the Indians draw an Oil from them, as sweet as that from the Olive, tho' of an Amber-Colour. With these

Nuts, or Acorns, some have counterfeited the Cocoa, whereof they have made Chocolate, not to be distinguish'd by a good Palate. Window-Frames, Mallets, and Pins for Blocks, are made therof, to an excellent Purpose. I knew two Trees of this Wood among the Indians, which were planted from the Acorn, and grew in the Freshes, and never saw any thing more beautiful of that kind.

🌲 🌲 🌲 Projects for the Amateur Naturalist

1. List everything in your home that is a product of a tree. The tally may surprise you. Some items you may overlook that contain chemicals manufactured from wood are paint, varnish, soap, ink, drugs, dye, celluloid, waxes, crayons, shoe polish, and chewing gum. You may also find vanillin, leather-dressing, greases, electric insulators, tars, alcohol, and glass cement. On the farm or ranch may be explosives.

2. Collect wood samples, identify, and mount. This may be done by taking limbs of 1 to 2 inches diameter and cutting an end to show cross, radial, and tangential views (see Figure 27–1). Or visit retail and wholesale wood-yards where willing salespersons will let you have samples of the ends of boards. A 1″ × 1″ × 4″ sample will suffice. You can then cut it to show the three faces (Figure 27–2).

3. Look for old plow furrows and contour terraces in forests established naturally or by planting on abandoned farmlands. Can you trace the "hills and valleys" from presently cultivated land into a forest? Do you observe any differences in growth between those trees that, as seedlings, were established on the hills or in the furrows?

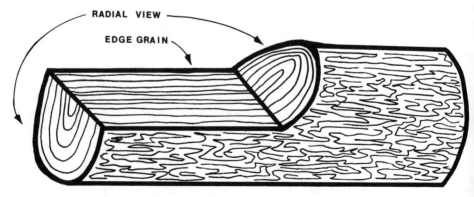

FIGURE 27–1. Cutting to show cross, radial, and tangential views.

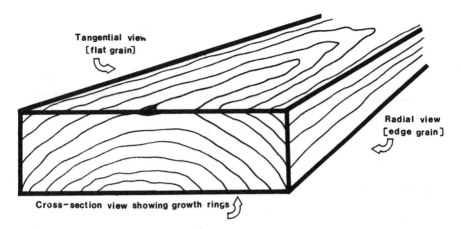

Tangential view
[flat grain]

Radial view
[edge grain]

Cross-section view showing growth rings

FIGURE 27–2. Board cut to show three faces.

28

Stink-Bomb Tree

Ginkgo

Ghetto kids in the city of Washington know well the Ginkgo tree by another name. The stink-bombs produced in the fall of the year, to be squashed underfoot on the concrete walks, give off a sickening smell like that of rancid butter. So tenacious is the foul odor that only diligent washing of hands and clothes eradicates the aroma.

If, dear reader, you are ever in the Nation's capital city, check out Ames place, a mile from the Capitol building. The one-block-long alley is lined with these trees planted perhaps 80 or 90 years ago. They provided quick shade. No doubt urban planners and landscapers of that time introduced the stink-bomb because of its tolerance to smoke and dust. The tree's resistance to disease and insects and its endurance in infertile, compact soils and in areas where the air is greatly polluted encourage its use in city sites. Few trees are as insensitive to dioxides of nitrogen (NO_2) and sulfur (SO_2); and drought and floods seldom affect it.

In the ghetto, the tree's small plum-like fruit, changing from green to yellowish-orange with the progress of the season, once gained importance in initiation rites. In your author's boyhood every new resident under the age of ten, unless brawnier than the citizens of longer tenure, was obliged to consume a plum. No way could a kid retain the mushy, putrid fruit high in butyric acid.

Yet inside the globe-shaped fruit is an edible kernel that is food for man in southeastern China, the region often considered the tree's natural range. Buddhist monks there and elsewhere in the Orient cultivate and preserve groves of these trees for their "silvery apricots," used in sacred rites. Ginkgo's Chinese name means white nut: when roasted it is tasty.

Botanists call this tree *Ginkgo biloba*. They consider it an oddity in the classification system. Often referred to as a living fossil, *G. biloba* is the only

Ginkgo, an Oriental tree of biological antiquity, planted in the British Kew Gardens in 1762.

species of its genus, of the family *Ginkgoaceae*, and of the order *Ginkgoales*. Though with broad leaves that are deciduous, the tree is strangely catalogued by some plant taxonomists as a near relative to the needle-bearing evergreens. It all seems deceptive, for the fruit—like the foliage—bears no resemblance to a conifer. To suggest that the male or female flowers are cone-like or that the seeds are naked, like the conifers, and therefore belong to the group called gymnosperms (meaning naked seed) also lends cause for debate.

Tree of Antiquity

Paleontologists believe *G. biloba* remains the sole survivor of a genus that contained many species thought to have been found in early prehistoric times, as recorded by geologists. Apparently the tree first appeared in Permian time, was abundant in the Triassic and Jurassic periods (when dinosaurs dominated the earth), then receded during the Cretaceous era (something more than 65 million years ago) as other flowering plants became established on the planet.

Ornamental ginkgo tree, full view.

Rocks of Permian time, which geologists date at 150 million years ago, contain leaf outlines unmistakably like those of this tree.

G. *biloba's* primitive status in development and its position in the geologist's calendar are considered related, both associated with the species' lack of contemporary botanical relatives.

Maidenhair tree, a more decorous name for the stink-bomb tree, describes the fan-shaped leaves similar to those of ferns called maidenhair. (I found no reports of any scientist questioning whether the paleontologists' discoveries could have been those of a fern!)

Among the reasons for attributing antiquity to this tree are its ecological requirements. Those requirements, in turn, led to the presumed extinction of wild populations. However, few hardwood trees, ginkgo's supposed competitors, appear in the fossil records, possibly because the broadleaved angiosperms (clothed seeds) were less abundant in those distantly historic times. And obviously the species has few ecological requirements now; yet—to add a bit of mystery—foresters won't find it as an escaped exotic in the woods. Nor will managers of a city's tree-shaded park be pestered with it as an uninvited guest.

And if this species is so tolerant of poor soil conditions, disease infection, and insect infestation, would not its relatives have been also? Of course that G. *biloba* could endure, and it alone, among the presumed trees of the ancient record suggests an answer. Too, it is clearly a temperate-zone tree while other broadleaf gymnosperms of antiquity (such as Norfolk Island pine or monkey puzzle tree (*Araucaria* spp.)) are tropical or subtropical. Wood structure is much like the conifers, though—we note again—G. *biloba* is broadleaved and deciduous. Along with the southern baldcypress and the sequoias of western North America and Asia, and possibly several broadleaf species, ginkgo escaped extinction in those times of geologic catastrophe.

A Matter of Mating

Nowhere does G. *biloba* now occur in the wild. Never mind its chance for extinction. No need to place it on the Smithsonian Institution's endangered- or threatened-species lists. Stink-bomb trees have been planted in many areas in North America and in other temperate-zone lands around the world. It is the oldest cultivated nut tree on earth and has become an "intriguing novelty for landscape use." Landscapers plant it as far north as Maine. A large specimen, reportedly a remnant of a group of trees planted by a princess in 1759 in London's famous Kew Gardens, survives to this day.

The uniqueness of sexual reproduction of this species rates notation. In reproduction the ginkgo behaves like cycads, palm-like stems that are not true palms. (The sago palm is the most common example.) A delay in sexual orientation of the dioecious trees (two houses: one house (tree) for each sex) may extend to 50 years. Female stems may not set their fruit until that time. So too may there be a delay in male flower development. Until orientation is apparent, the selection of cuttings for vegetative propagation is extremely risky.

The cuttings will root without delay, but the tree arising from the cutting may be a near-mature, soon-to-bear, stink-bomb-producing female parent.

Free-swimming antherozoids floating loosely in pollen tubes interest botanists. These male sex cells, when mature, swim through the moisture on the plant's flower to the female cell, there to fertilize the egg. That, to add to taxonomic "confusion, worse confounded," is a characteristic of tropical cycads, but not of conifers.

Leaf Spigots

Tree physiologists consider with fascination the leaf structure and processes of the two-lobed foliage of G. biloba. Leaf stomata (the slit-shaped minute openings on leaf surfaces through which water is released to the atmosphere) on yellow-colored autumn leaves open during the day and close at night. For most trees it's the other way around, so that water is retained in the heat of the summer sun. For this species, too, the stomata occur only on the abaxial (lower) surface of foliage, rather than on all surfaces, as typical for conifers. These stomata, again in contrast to most trees, are few and large, and that in turn affects resistance to water loss. The microscopic spigots control the amount of water passing from soil to root to leaf to atmosphere.

The size, number, and location of the stomata may play a role in the insensitivity of this tree to high nitrogen dioxide and sulphur dioxide concentrations in the air of large cities. Landscapers plant it around Tokyo because of the high SO_2 levels in the atmosphere there.

Out of the leaf surfaces pour pure oxygen molecules to replenish the air of diminishing supplies brought about by the respiration of people and other animals. As with all living things, plants, too, breathe, consuming oxygen and dumping carbon dioxide into the atmosphere. In the oxygen cycle, the carbon dioxide enters foliage through stomata, to be utilized in the photosynthetic process, and oxygen is given off. About an acre of vigorously growing trees is necessary to supply the oxygen needs of eighteen people.

Living Scissors

Leaf shedding in the fall of the year is considered to be nature's technique for enabling plants to survive low temperatures. Just before abscission, nutrient elements and compounds are transported to branches and roots for storage until needed the next spring for leaf growth.

The abscission layer works like a living scissors. Special cells are triggered by autumn's weather and length-of-day, growing and dividing at the base of a leaf. As these cells progress across the base of the petiole, they separate the leaf from the twig. Leaves don't simply die and fall in autumn. In one sense they are very much alive with the growth of abscission rows of cells.

Some readers will know that leaves don't *turn* red and yellow. Those brilliant autumn colors are present all summer, but masked by the green of the chlorophyll molecules in foliage. In the fall of the year the chlorophyll breaks down, exposing the red and yellow pigments of carotin and xanthophyll, and mixtures of those chemicals. Some other color-producing compounds also form as the abscission layer cuts off water and nutrients to the leaves.

Ginkgo's pyramidal crown with its sometime erratic branching habit, displaying the double-leaf trace of the fan-shaped foliage, spreads wide with age. It is a reminder in the cities of many parts of the world that this living fossil is an encompassing tree for all peoples.

▲ ▲ ▲ Projects for the Amateur Naturalist

1. Count the numbers of different kinds or species of trees used along city streets within a certain area, perhaps a square mile (ordinarily 10 blocks × 10 blocks).

2. Using tree identification books, determine the genus and species of the trees in Project 1. Some tree identification books and their publishers:
   a. Elias: *Complete Trees of North America*. Van Nostrand Reinhold.
   b. Preston: *North American Trees*. Iowa State University Press.
   c. Little: *Audubon Guide to North American Trees*. Knopf.
   d. Brockman, Zim, and Merriless: *Trees of North America*. Golden.
   e. Phillips: *Trees of North America*. Random House.

3. Count and chart the sidewalk cracks made by trees of certain species and sizes (see Figure 28–1).

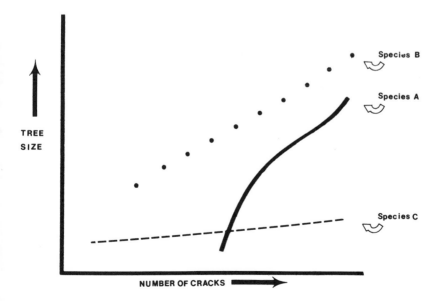

FIGURE 28–1. Relating tree size to sidewalk damage.

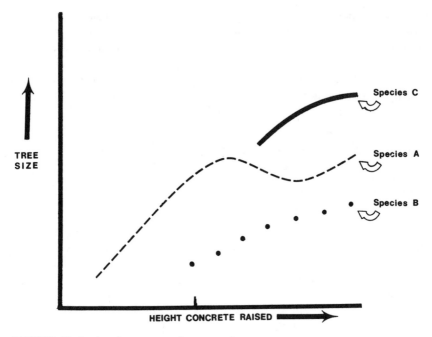

FIGURE 28–2. Another way to chart tree damage to pavement.

4. Determine the height that a concrete sidewalk (or nonreinforced pavement of the same thickness) is raised by tree roots (see Figure 28–2).

5. From 3 and 4, suggest species to be preferred and rejected for urban planting.

6. Determine the number of trees required for a city of 250,000 people to restore to the atmosphere the oxygen consumed by these people, assuming no other green plants or animals live there. See text.

Two tree species for landscape planting: the screen of hybrid poplars, blocking out noise and intrusion is about 4 years old; the 6-year-old white ash prefers deep fertile soil.

29

Forests to Fine Furniture
The Northern Hardwoods

*F*armers and merchant settlers, beginning in 1790, encouraged the harvest of the northern hardwood forests. Their interest was primarily agriculture. For under these broadleaf trees they found high-quality soils, rich in nutrients, and permeated with organic matter. The decaying vegetable material recycles nutritional elements and aids in holding moisture during droughty seasons for vigorous growth of food crops.

Alongside the farmers and merchants were the loggers and lumbermen who, out of economic necessity, "cut-out-and-got-out" of the forests of American beech (*Fagus grandifolia*), yellow birch (*Betula allegheniensis*), and sugar maple (*Acer saccharum*). They moved livestock and equipment from one tract to another, felling every merchantable stem, until much of the northeastern United States had been cut over. Their harvests provided wood, including fuel and construction material, for a growing nation. Much was exported to Europe.

Ofttimes the loggers, led by the foreman—the bull-of-the-woods—returned to harvest stems of lesser value left from earlier cutting. Then, as the last logs of fine furniture woods were skidded and sledded to the mills, entrepreneurs shipped men, mules, and machinery to the Lake States, there to begin anew to cut-out-and-get-out of the forests of northern hardwoods.

It took three-quarters of a century of logging in the Northeast to leave the land barren. Only 40 years were required for the Paul Bunyans of the Lake States to take the quality beech, birch, and maple, along with structural softwoods, from the region's forests to its mills. Cutting began in the upper thirds of Michigan, Wisconsin, and Minnesota in about 1860. At the turn of this century, loggers and punchers sold their tools and oxen to a new breed of lumbermen in the South or West. Some moved with their animals and axes to

An old-growth northern hardwood forest (USDA Forest Service photo).

begin anew to cut-out-and-get-out of the pineries of the South or the majestic softwoods of the Pacific coastlands.

Just about the time the clearing of the northeastern forests was complete and the logging industry moved to the Lake States, by uncanny coincidence, farmers began to abandon land. Throughout the region, exasperated by the exhausted soil that was worn out from cultivation abuse, farmers left their homes. In time trees returned. In time, too, as we shall see, quality stands of beech, birch, and maple would again cover the ground. Land census-takers record that, until very recently in the densely populated Northeast, forested acreage continued to increase each year as farmers abandoned their land.

Climax Vegetation

Foresters call beech, birch, and maple trees, when found together and without appreciable numbers of stems of other species, a cover type. It is written thus: beech—birch—maple. In America's forests only one species of beech occurs; the birch of greatest value is yellow; and the main commercial maple is sugar, also called hard or rock maple. Of course other kinds of trees intrude. Among these are deciduous trees, often of even greater value for furniture, like ash, wild black cherry, and black walnut. Occasionally conifers, such as pines, red spruce, and fir, or soft hardwoods like basswood enter into the climax forest of beech, birch, and maple.

The word climax tells much about a particular stand of trees. It suggests that if nature is left alone, man refrains from cutting trees, and there are no blowdown storms or fires, these same kinds of trees perpetuate themselves forever.

If young trees become established under existing stands before a harvest, as often occurs for this shade-tolerant type, the new trees are called advance reproduction. Because beech—birch—maple seldom invades burned over, cutover, or blowdown sites, trees of these species enter the forest as seedlings after ecological pioneer species are well established.

In nature, as with man, the only consistency is inconsistency. To the above rule about the beech—birch—maple type, exceptions occur: birch may be sub-climax, even seeding-in on burned over sites, then remaining to comprise a part of the canopy of the mature forest a hundred years later.

When stands are opened by thinning, epicormic branches or adventitious shoots sprout from the boles. Heat from the sun probably triggers the breaking of dormancy of buds lying just beneath the bark. Similarly, coppice may form as many sprouts appear at the base or surface of stumps of felled trees. Root suckers, trees arising from below ground, occur often. Vegetative growth depends upon the severity of thinning, species, and an inherited capacity that varies within a species.

Where These Trees Grow

Beech—birch—maple as a forest for producing wood for fine furniture is limited to the northern tier of states, from the Plains eastward, in the United States. The type grows far beyond these bounds, however; mixtures of trees of these species extend south and westward to East Texas. In the latter locale one finds the type along the bayous. There it is river birch (*Betula nigra*) rather than yellow birch as in the North; and southern sugar maple—sometimes called Florida maple (*Acer barbatum*)—substitutes for the sugar maple of northern climes. In the South the type prefers the hammocks and stream banks with deep and fertile humus-ladened soil.

The best stands for this type in the North are found on the rich soils of glacial moraines. These piles of rock, left behind by retreating sheets of ice sometimes a half-mile deep, provide a variety of essential nutrient elements in the mixed mineral till. Freezing and thawing, wetting and drying, and acid exuded from plant roots cause the release of nutrients about as rapidly as utilized by trees. Mid-slopes of the Adirondack, White, and Green mountains in the Northeast are ideal situations. Soils similar to these relatively fertile materials, lying between the ridges and swamps, cover vast areas in the Lake States. There the beech—birch—maple type occurs between the deep coarse sands of ancient lake beds and the fibrous, organic surfaces of present-day swamps.

The type, exacting in its site requirements, takes much in the way of nutrients from the soils in which it grows. Leaf mold, fungi, and insects form a mull humus layer in which elemental-rich organic matter is mixed with the mineral soil, in turn fueling a multitude of microflora and microfauna. Soil scientists call some of these soils weak podzols, the latter word from the Russian language suggesting an ash-gray color. Podzols result from the leaching of mainly iron and aluminum from horizons near the surface to those below, leaving the silicates—like the quartz of beach sand—just below the surface of the ground. Leached materials collect in a band below the gray layer. With weak podzols, however, the ash color is not likely to be apparent.

Good precipitation, amounting to 40 inches evenly distributed throughout the year, in a region of low evaporation also encourages vigorous growth. However, flooding can be disastrous to these trees. Beech may grow on poorly drained sites, but dies if its roots are submerged for about 2 weeks. Birch may make it on swampy lands. If it does, it is because the seed fell on rotting stumps and on hummocks that formed where wind-tossed trees have rotted and faded into the undulating land.

Seeds and Seedlings

To know how the stands of these species reproduce, students need observe the natural order. Without a time machine, we must look at forests of various ages to recognize essential periods in ecological succession. Ordinarily, mature stands are uneven-aged—trees from seedling age to over a hundred years old thoroughly mixed among the several species. It takes long periods of natural ecological succession to arrive at these conditions.

The devastating hurricane of 1938, clearing a swath of forests 80 miles wide from the Connecticut coast to the White Mountains of New Hampshire, showed what can happen with forest destruction. The beech—birch—maple type covered vast acreages within this zone at the time of the big blowdown. That storm behaved like a monster clearcutting machine. It felled much of the climax forest, levelling vast stands of beech, birch, and maple.

Pioneer species like gray birch, pin cherry, sumac, and a hundred others promptly invaded the blitzed landscape. That's nature's way of avoiding disastrous erosion and flooding in the interim before valuable stems cover the land. In time the climax species reappear, taking over the temporary forest-cover types. Slowly the shade-tolerant hardwoods encroach, seeding-in or sprouting from roots and stumps left from the earlier woods.

The heavy triangular seeds of beech, falling in autumn, are carried by mice, squirrels, jays, and turkeys. Tasty and sweet to man, so too are these seeds to wildlife. Stomach acids serve as a pregermination treatment, enabling ready sprouting of the seeds when disgorged in the droppings of woodland animals.

Foresters have their own technique for breaking dormancy in beech seeds for nursery tree production. They dry seeds to 25 percent of fresh weight and then store them in sealed bags at about 35°F for 100 days. When that is done, germination is prompt, else the seeds would be consumed by wildlife.

The one-seeded nuts, called mast, a little more than an inch across, are nested in pairs inside small prickly burrs. Both male and female flowers develop on the same tree. That makes beech trees monoecious, meaning one-house, or one tree for both sex organs.

Female catkins of the yellow birch appear cone-like. Good seed crops, producing a million two-winged nutlets per acre, cover the ground every year or two. These must come to rest on bare soil, rotted wood, or in thin leaf litter if seedlings arising from them are to survive. Often the seeds collect in pockets in the snow. The clumps of seedlings that form from nature's cache tell about it. When seeds fall and germinate on stumps or logs that later rot away, the new trees in time appear stilted. Roots of the seedlings and saplings grow down and around the decaying stump or log. Then when the dead underlying material completely decomposes, a cavity remains.

Under artificial light, birch seeds will germinate in a wet medium without further treatment. Nursery managers stratify them in moist sand or peat at 40°F for a month to assure sprouting when planted.

Many birch catkins and seeds are consumed by wildlife. The ruffled grouse, especially, appreciates this food.

While maple flowers bloom within a week after emerging from the bud, ripening requires 12 weeks. Leaves reach full size about three weeks after buds begin to swell, the flowers coloring the trees before the leaves appear. Some 50 male flowers occur for each female; bees carry pollen to receptive females. Generally the sugar maples are monoecious.

The long-winged seeds of maple, paired like forked keys, are carried by wind or water to their destination in the fall of the year. Only one of the pair is viable.

Uses of the Wood

From the earliest harvest, when pit sawyers laboriously converted logs to lumber, these trees have provided for a variety of necessities and luxuries. So good was the furniture made from the birch and maple that its value today on the antique market is unexcelled. The dense hardwood of all three species served, as it does now, for panelling, and the sap of the maple tree remains prized for its sugar. In colonial times, charcoal and potash, from the burning of the wood, provided export goods for a primitive economy.

A Civil War report entitled *Resources of Southern Fields and Forests*, by a physician named Porcher, noted the use of beech tar for "paraphine." Chemicals from the bark of the tree were used for tanning, ashes of its wood for potash, and its seeds for oil "little inferior to olive oil, and fit for burning." The record of that day spoke of the fat of hogs that feed on the mast as soft, readily boiling away, while Porcher called the pulp from those seeds sweeter than wheat flour. Yet it was said that eating of the fruit by humans produced vertigo, perhaps from fagine, a narcotic in beech-nut husks. The aromatic leaves were often used for filling mattress ticks. The inexpensive and elastic stuffing also repelled vermin.

Beech wood takes a high polish, so builders today put it down as flooring. Basketball players like the resiliency of these playing surfaces. That resiliency makes it useful for ax and hammer handles too.

Medical people once made alcohol from the sweet sap of birch trees, concentrating the liquid by evaporation, fermenting the exudate with yeast, and then distilling the fluid. Boiled or crushed birch leaves and bark have an aromatic wintergreen-like flavor. Probably the extract was used a hundred years ago in pharmaceuticals and food.

Birch wood's rosy tint when first cut, deepening in color with exposure, gives it high value in the marketplace. Today many kitchens have birch-wood cabinets, and dens are panelled with its veneer. The optimum growth rate for trees from which good furniture is made is 12 rings per inch. Furniture-wood trees are likely to be at least 22 inches in diameter, breast height.

(Another tree of the *Betula* genus, paper birch, provided the birch bark of Indian canoe fame. Native Americans stripped the waterproof bark from living trees, stretched it over frames of northern white-cedar, sewed it with thread woven from tamarack roots, and caulked the seams with the resin exudate of pitch pine or balsam fir. Because stripping bark leaves unsightly scars on paper birch, only the bark of fallen trees should be used.)

Maple trees, as noted, provided a principal source of sugar for pioneer families. The quality of the syrup depends upon the soil and climate of the region of origin. In fact syrup today is "boiled off" in one state and then shipped to another, where the reputation is higher, for packaging and marketing. By law, syrup is now graded to protect consumers.

In early times hollow elder or sumac branches were inserted into tree trunks to collect sap. Later metal pipes in the trees served like spigots. Now plastic tubes run from the trees directly to central collection points, eliminating the need for carrying the sap in buckets.

At the sugar camp—locale of the collection vats and evaporating pans— sap is converted to syrup. Trees of the "sugar bush" are tapped in the early spring when a combination of factors—like warm days and cold nights—produces good-quality syrup. One tree may produce 5 to 60 gallons of sap each year. Thirty-two gallons of sap "boil off" in the pans to provide a gallon of syrup or a little more than 4 pounds of sugar.

From the earliest days of its use for furniture, the birdseye figure of maple has been in demand. I've been told that some folks are able to tell that a tree contains birdseye grain before it is felled, thus encouraging the sale of single trees on home lawns in the region. "Fiddle-back" patterns in the grain are especially appreciated for veneers. And the silky lustre grain of maple wood, contrasting with the dark dull tone of mahogany, enhances its use for inlaying in surfaces of the latter.

One should note that it is the forest cover type and not each tree and all species that produce fine furniture woods. Indeed the beech often contains rot, limiting its usefulness to short pieces of solid wood for hidden parts of upholstered furniture, panelling, and flooring.

Lest we neglect, readers should know of the use of all of these species for paper manufacturing. They produce a rather high quality sheet.

Injurious Aspects

Human nature being what it is, stands with beech and birch trees suffer from abuse by people as well as by wildlife. Not enough that deer browse young trees and rabbits clip seedlings. The smooth light-gray, speckled, or blotched bark on beech trees lends itself to the carving of initials and cupid hearts. I have observed these markings, legible for more than 30 years, and, in one case, located a squirrel hunter's widow who, decades before, had roamed that beech bottom. And, as noted above, people cut the bark from birch trees as souvenirs of visits to the woods.

Woodsmen are always looking for bee trees in stands of beech. They set fires in hollow trunks to smoke out the singing, stinging insects and then rob the hive of its honeycomb. Sometimes it's literally bittersweet.

Nature has her way too. Paper-thin flammable yellow curls of the bark of birch stems hasten destruction by fire of all trees in the forest. Rot then enters fire-caused wounds. A fungus often follows an insect attack on beech trees while the wooly beech scale and birch dieback take their toll. Unrelated to biological damage is the frost crack that ruins much beech wood in northern climes; the best beech wood comes from forests in the Southern Appalachians.

Conflict Over Trees

Rounded crowns of beech trees, shiny silver-gray or yellow bark of the birches, and the brilliant multicolored maple foliage in autumn join to inspire artists and photographers. No group of forest trees is more spectacular to the beholder's eye. The beauty of this forest has led to many encounters between forest managers and local citizens. In one case in New York, Dr. Bernhard Fernow, a German-born and educated forester, was head of the new Cornell University forestry program. This was before 1900. The well-respected Fernow had already headed the fledgling Bureau of Forestry in the U.S. Department of Agriculture. He, with his students, began to convert the low-value, second-growth and poorly formed old-growth hardwoods, including young stands of beech—birch—maple, to higher-value softwoods. The coniferous softwoods—pines, spruces, and firs—were needed for the rapidly growing population centers of the Northeast. The brush was burned; Lake Placid's playground was periodically clouded with smoke; and the clearcut areas were ugly. So aggrieved were the residents and absentee owners of lands in the Adirondack Mountains over what they considered mismanagement that they prevailed upon a State Constitutional Convention, then in session, to hold forever inviolate public lands within the Mountains. Soon New York State added to its preserve, and a line on maps delineated the zone in which the law prohibits tree cutting on State lands. Fernow in the aftermath was discharged and the forestry program at Cornell terminated. Some of today's best stands in the Adirondacks are those planted by the professor and his students. Perhaps, just perhaps, it was the loss of fall coloration, not the altering of the forest species composition, that so greatly perturbed the citizenry.

In a 1970s case, in the Monongahela National Forest in West Virginia, government foresters were clearcutting stands of northern hardwoods. Their aim was to convert many of these forests to construction softwoods, expected to be in short supply in the early 2000s. Injunctions followed law suits. Federal district and appellate courts ruled against the U.S. Forest Service. Only an act of the Congress enabled national forest managers to utilize the most effective and efficient means for regenerating stands of timber. Before their management plans are approved, the law requires that they be subjected to public scrutiny. No argument, clearcutting is ugly. No argument, too, that beech, birch, and maple trees display a spectacular palette in the autumn. The debate rages over whose woods these are and for whom the trees shall be grown.

Pilgrims and pioneers moving inland and westward from America's northeastern coast began an ecological process that yet goes on. The trees they cut were needed by men; the lands they cleared were used for growing food for men. The forests returned. They again serve men for fuel, for furniture, for pulp, and for recreation. They illustrate the rehabilitation by natural processes of unintentionally mismanaged land.

🌲 🌲 🌲 Projects for the Amateur Naturalist

1. Make rock sugar candy from genuine sugar maple syrup. A letter to a New England, New York, or Lake States' department of agriculture should obtain for you a list of suppliers of maple syrup, their product straight from the evaporating pans at the edge of the sugar bush. To make delicious rock candy or sugar cakes, heat syrup to 32°F above the boiling point of water (212°F at sea level), stir while cooling slowly to 155°F (using a candy thermometer), and pour into molds.

2. Observe mammals or their signs in the forest or woodlot and suggest the relationship between their presence and the type of vegetation. For example, squirrels hang around pine forests where seeds are abundant, while rabbits enjoy the inner-bark of maples, clipping young stems near the ground line. Teeth marks may be a clue.

3. Observe how sprouting starts a new forest. In a forest of hardwoods, harvested at least a year ago, count the sprouts that arise from stump tops, from the bases of stumps, and from roots extending from the stump. Which of these kinds of sprouts will make a worthwhile new forest?

30

Tropical Hardwoods

The Dipterocarps

*T*he deepest trench in the South Pacific Ocean, called "The Wallace Line" by geographers, marks the eastern edge of the range of dipterocarps. To the west of the great inverted divide, on thousands of islands in the Philippines, Indonesia, Malaysia, and in the tropical zones of the sub-Asian continent of India and Indo-China, dipterocarps are the species of preference for international commerce. North Americans know them as the veneer of hollow-core flush doors, those interior doors without panels that, because of their low cost and attractiveness, grace the houses of commoners. Millions of square feet of plywood and solid-wood panelling from various species of this "false mahogany" decorate American houses and offices. Importation of the wood or products made from it began in the late 1940s and continues to the present.

Two Wings

As entomologists call insects with two wings, like houseflies, *Diptera*, so botanists call the family of trees with two-winged seeds *Dipterocarpaceae*. Taxonomists classify nine genera with the double-winged carp, or fruit, in this family of some 400 species. Most of those of commercial value are in the *Dipterocarpus* genus. The great variety in appearance and other characteristics of the trees within the *Dipterocarpaceae* family and the proliferation of other species in dipterocarp forests make difficult their management for future timber supplies.

Foresters catalog the commercial dipterocarps principally as members of the *Shorea* genus. In Indonesia the common name is meranti; in Malaysia it is lauan; in the Philippines, mahogany (though not the true mahogany of furniture fame). Meranti woods are commonly called red, yellow, white, or dark red, depending upon the species of *Shorea*. Dipterocarps of the tropics also include kapur (*Dryobalanops lancelota*) and keruing (*Dipterocarpus* sp., the "sp." indicating an unnamed or unknown species).

Ecological Contemporaries

Tall trees, frequently more than 200 feet high, dipterocarp crowns rise above the surrounding forest, which is often a complex jungle of plants of many kinds. Two hundred and twenty species have been tallied in a 5-acre tract of such a mature forest. Another tract, less than 4 acres of lowland, supported 239 species belonging to 45 families and 122 genera. Never do less than 40 species of flowering plants occur on a 2- or 3-acre plot. Vines called "lianas" climb trees, sometimes weighing them down until they break, but the trees do not fall: the encapsulating vines hold them up. Rattan, one of these vines, is an important raw material for wicker furniture.

Within the forest of the many-aged dipterocarps grow other hardwoods of value, like the colorful ramin (*Conystylus* sp.), most of which has long been imported by Italian craftsmen for high-priced furniture. Important conifers within the stands of tropical broadleaf dipterocarps are many species of *Dacridium* and *Agathis*.

In fine silts of tidal swamps near dipterocarp stands, one finds mangrove trees growing, their buttressed boles resting upon natural stilts. The water-filled openings among the pitchfork prongs under the boles provide habitat for fish, crabs, and other crustaceans. The mangroves are used for fuel, in rayon manufacture, for tannin, and for charcoal.

Air plants grow high on the boles of trees of dipterocarps. These epiphytes, kin to pineapples, receive light for photosynthesis in an otherwise shaded forest. They also play a role in producing soil, high on the bole of the parent tree, in which to grow.

Dipterocarps produce leaves with drip tips, like pitcher spouts. This enables prompt transfer of rainwater from crown to ground. Otherwise considerable volumes of water would be held in the broadleaf crowns until evaporated by the tropical sun. Rain and sun here are intermittent. Rains often last only a few minutes, and the sun appears for equally short periods. Drip tips assure rainwater storage in the soil until needed for tree growth.

Reforestation Efforts

U.S. industries responsible for the harvest of some of the tropical rain forest following the Second World War attempted dramatic reforestation efforts. Where the hardwood dipterocarps were felled, foresters planted some thirty species of commercial timbers to assure future harvests. Eucalyptus, native to Australia, slash pine of the Caribbean islands, pines from California's Monterey peninsula, and cadam from continental southeastern Asia seemed most adaptable. Yet problems arose in their introduction.

While *Eucalyptus diglupta* trees reach harvest age in 20 years, stems erupt with cankers caused by a fungus. Tropical America's slash pine in the sapling stage exhibits foxtails, long terminal stems without branches that soon bend from weakness. A shoot moth accompanies the tree, infesting terminal buds and causing witches' brooms to form as the surviving competitive buds struggle for dominance. Poor flowering affects future regeneration of the slash pine stands, necessitating planting after each harvest. Monterey pine (*Pinus radiata*) may exhibit second-generation malady, as we have seen in Australia (see Chapter 14). Planted trees survive and grow especially well, but after their harvest, the next stand of the species on the same site, for reasons not understood, declines markedly in vigor.

Cadam may more than compensate for the failures of other introduced species. *Anthocephalus cadam*, named for an Indian forester who served in various parts of the world (including Texas), grows so fast that its age is often tallied in months. Its squarish bole minimizes trim waste at the sawmill. Especially useful for plywood corestock, cadam grows well in the Caribbean islands and in Central America as well as with the dipterocarps of Asian equatorial lands.

Natural Regeneration

Mixed dipterocarp forests quickly recover following harvest, but not to the same high-value species. Vines, bamboo, and scrub shrubs form an impenetrable jungle in these high-rainfall (80-plus inches), high-temperature woodlands. Precipitation is evenly distributed and the temperature constant throughout the year in this equatorial zone where seasons are so poorly defined that tree cross sections show no growth rings.

Rapid leaching of nutrients from the lateritic soils following harvests reduces soil fertility. Exposure of the soil in these openings encourages oxidation by the sun's rays of any accumulated organic matter, thereby excluding tree seedling establishment and hastening invasion of alang-alang, an *Imperata* grass that further impedes establishment of tree seedlings. Scattering rubber tree seeds on such depleted sites, a squatter-peasant practice on cutover lands, also interrupts ecological succession. Commercially valuable tree cover is delayed.

As dipterocarps are shade-intolerant species, liberation cutting is essential in order for them to reach merchantability within a reasonable time. Without access to light, maturity may require a hundred years. Selection harvests at 35-year intervals opens up a stand to enable residual trees to retain vigor. In these periodic harvests, loggers cut only stems above a certain size.

Big Fire

Pyrologists consider the great fire that raged in 1983 in the dipterocarp forests of Borneo the largest area conflagration in recorded history. Within a year, however, signs of recovery were apparent, with the crowns of tall trees above the general canopy greening with new foliage. Leaves budded, even though the freakish, drought-induced fire in the 8½ million-acre holocaust often crowned as it raced from ridge to ridge between the then-shallow rivers in a roadless land. Nondipterocarps first invaded the burned-over sites, the wood eventually being useful for pulp and particle board. In time the buttressed broadleaf and evergreen hardwood dipterocarps will capture their share of the charred landscape.

Socioforestry

Equatorial rain forests take on social, economic, and political significance as shifting agriculture retards regeneration. This slash-and-burn farming by peasant squatters on cutover lands expands in area as the cultivated sites support a crop for only a couple of years. Rice, corn, and grain legumes produced by landless and hungry people soon deplete the soil. When production falls, the farmers move to adjacent virgin or cutover forest to again machete and set fire to a tract of a few acres.

By this practice moisture is lost to the air and mineral nutrients are leached to streams. Both water and nutritional elements are important for sustaining a forest, but in the absence of perennial trees, recycling of nutrients and moisture does not occur. Baked, hard, infertile soils result.

Many fear that continuing the shifting slash-and-burn agricultural practices will hasten extinction of plant species indigenous to these forests. Many also fear the climatic consequences of the destruction of rain forests throughout the tropics. Nevertheless, governments encourage this transmigration, financing resettlement from crowded cities to remote islands of people ill-prepared for agricultural enterprises.

Exploitation and Government Edicts

Long before American lumbermen began the harvest of tropical trees, Europeans and Asians commercially exploited dipterocarps for their aesthetically pleasing grains of the wood. Aromatic oils and resins were also extracted from them, and gurjun balsam, a viscous yellow oleoresin called wood oil, "fixed" odors in soaps. Then, for three decades following the Second World War, logs from these forests were lashed into rafts a half-mile long and floated to river mouths where they were hoisted on to rusty WW II-vintage ships for transport to Japan, Taiwan, and Singapore. Victory and Liberty ships delivered the timber to mills that converted the logs into the doors and plywood panels previously mentioned.

Scarcity of these woods has resulted in government edicts that preclude shipment of logs abroad. Most countries growing dipterocarps now restrict shipment of raw wood to other lands. Rather, forestry agencies require the wood to be manufactured into products like plywood or doors before exportation. Whether government regulations will encourage silvicultural practices that will provide future crops of these fine trees remains to be determined. Edicts from state capitols were designed to encourage employment of nationals; forests for the future are a lesser concern.

Stands of *Shorea*, a dipterocarp in Indonesia. These trees, once marketed as logs to the industrial world, now are processed into plywood at island mills.

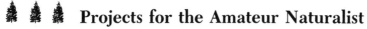 **Projects for the Amateur Naturalist**

1. Water pollution effect on forest trees. Follow a stream from its source through an urban setting, including a park. Note additions to the water from municipal waste, industrial effluent, and careless disposal. Are trees and other plant growth affected by this water pollution—how and how much? At various points, check foliage color, rates of growth of twigs, or evidence of fungus or insect activity.

2. Ecological relationships in wetlands. Search a wetland habitat (marsh, swamp, bog) for animals that find shelter there and that neither nest nor feed beyond the wetland borders. (Be cautious of sink holes and cottonmouth moccasins.) Chart depth of the water where various tree species grow. Observe the depth throughout a year. Is the changing depth related to the kinds of animals and trees growing there?

3. Acid rain influence on trees. Simulate acid rain by spraying some seedlings growing in a woodland or in a tray (perhaps in a greenhouse) with vinegar (a weak acid) and some others with tap water. Observe changes in leaf color, stem growth, and roots. Test the soil after several months for pH, using litmus paper or a pH kit.

31

Low-Mountain Shrubs

Chaparral

P yric holocausts year after year on the lower Pacific slopes in California burn through the chaparral. The word *chaparral* is Mexican Spanish (or more specifically Basque) for "evergreen scrub oak," vegetation easily ignited by lightning or human accident. We broaden the meaning to include other shrubby, multi-stemmed vegetation on the dry lower slopes lying below forests of true trees (woody plants with a single dominant stem).

Along with several species of scrub oaks (*Quercus* spp.) grow manzanita bushes (*Arotostaphylos* spp.), many kinds of shrubby, multi-stemmed plants of the genus *Ceanothus*, and the imported Scot's broom (*Cystisus* [*Spartius*] *scoparius*). The scrub oaks include Emory (*Q. emoryi*) and Mexican blue (*Q. oblongifolia*).

Some 50 to 60 species of the genus *Ceanothus*, of the buckthorn family, occur in the semiarid West. Here they provide browse for sheep and also hold the land together. Indians, some say, ate the seeds of several species, but livestock shun them, probably because of their bitter taste. Roots, bark, and leaves may have compounds suitable for medicinal use.

Scot's broom, a legume brought to this country by European immigrants, soon escaped to become a weed. In the Northeast it is a small plant. In the West, however, the pea-pod producer found a home, often outgrowing other species of chaparral. The scrub shrub easily exceeds 10 to 15 feet in height.

Many of the dry mountain ranges of the Southwest, today covered by chaparral, were likely once forested. Even now, pinyon pines, junipers, and ponderosa pines occur among or adjacent to the stems that comprise the brush. Sagebrush and grasses also invade, or are invaded by, chaparral. The particular associated species relates to the latitude, to the elevation of the slope, and to its aspect. Chaparral is usually found below juniper woodlands in the south

250

and above them in the north in the mountains of the West. At 4,000 feet on a west-facing slope, the assortment of species may differ greatly from those on an east-facing slope. Outcrops of serpentine rock, where naturally occurring toxic chemicals exclude commercially valuable trees, often support dense stands of these shrubs.

Fire and Development

As one-fifth of the state of heavily forested California, or 8 million acres, is chaparral, the significance of the vegetation type is apparent. Protected from wildfire for the past 50 years, dead twigs, leaves, and branches accumulate on the ground. In such a dry climate, decay is slow, because the insects and fungi that decompose organic matter require adequate moisture for sustenance. The scene is then set for the inevitable fire: a lightning strike or a careless person ignites the deep layer of tinder-dry fuel. Little short of a drenching rain can extinguish the blaze. Hazard-reducing fires, set by foresters under carefully controlled conditions to avoid some of the holocausts that periodically plague these woodlands, are now considered desirable. The process is called prescribed burning.

To many people, chaparral is aesthetically pleasing, especially so in contrast to hills of grassy cover where trees are scarce. Hence, developers in densely populated areas of Southern California and other western chaparral-covered lands punch roads through the brush, erect utility lines, and encourage home construction. Sadly, all such housing communities are high-risk ventures. For wildfires will, and do, occur. Yet, following the disastrous fires, chaparral promptly reinvades. In a few years, another developer will punch roads through the new brush, erect utility lines, and encourage home construction.

Chaparral ecology—seed germination, seedling growth, maturity, and fire—is like time-lapse photography. We observe in a short span of years the whole natural life rotation of a woodland.

Chaparral composed of evergreen live oaks, ceanothus, manzanita, and Scot's broom in the low hills of southern California provides fuel for disastrous fires.

♠ ♠ ♠ Projects for the Amateur Naturalist

1. Water use by trees. Determine transpiration rates for broadleaf and needleleaf trees in winter and summer. Tie a plastic bag tightly around a hardwood leaf or small conifer twig. After one, two, or more days, measure the water transpired by the foliage and collected in the bag. Using sample proportional arithmetic, estimate water loss (not solely water use; some water is retained in the tree as carbohydrate growth) by the tree or by an acre of such trees.

2. Decomposition of dead vegetable matter. Locate a log in a forest. Determine how decay is progressing. Listen for the sounds of insects nibbling on the bark and wood. Peel away bark and wood to locate insects and fungi. Identify them.

3. Impact power of raindrops. Locate a newly erected wall with bare ground adjacent. How high has the soil been bounced by rainfall of various intensities? Compare this with an older wall where vegetative cover on the adjacent ground has protected the wall from rain splash. Relate this to a forest cover over soil that has been, or presently is, eroded.

32

Tree-Like Monocots

Bamboos and Palms

*T*wo arborescent monocotyledonous plants produce a wood-like fiber. That's unusual, for arborescent means tree-like, but the monocots with which the reader is most familiar are grasses. Cotyledons are the leaves first put out when seeds germinate. Grasses, you recall from observing your own lawn, send out a single leaf from each seed. Dicots, typically deciduous trees, put out two seed leaves, opposite one another. Conifers are polycots, the small stem tip upon germination encompassing many needles.

Bamboos and palms are both monocotyledonous. From that point on they differ from each other. Bamboos are grass; palms belong to another family of plants.

BAMBOOS

Timber bamboo (*Phyllostachys bambusoides*), introduced into the southeastern United States from Japan, is a fantastic tree. With little exaggeration, it follows the rule of thumb that in 6 weeks it grows 6 inches in diameter and 60 feet tall. With some imagination you can hear the tree snap, crackle, and pop as it grows.

The tree's life, where planted, is begun by placing a 12-inch section of a bamboo stem just below the ground level in a horizontal position. Soon, from buds at the nodes, roots sprout and stems shoot upward. The first year the tree may be but 10 feet tall and an inch in diameter. Cut back to ground level, it resprouts the second year to grow 20 feet and 2 inches. Again cut back, and the new sprouts, fed by a now-extensive root system, tower further into the air. This continues, as does our "sixes" rule of thumb, for 6 years when height and diameter reach a peak. All this time the circle of bamboo stems widens as new shoots rise from the enlarged root system. The bamboo clump will continue to expand and to replenish itself upon annual cutting until the soil is exhausted of its nutrients, perhaps 6 years (again the rule) after passing the peak.

Wood-industry people, especially in wood-short areas of the world, justify annual harvests to supply blow guns, water pipes, furniture, poles, and scaffolding from the hollow-bored bamboo. In time, frequent cutting will be justified for paper production, for which *Bambusa vulgaris* seems preferred. Several decades past a private pulp and paper laboratory in Savannah, Georgia, successfully developed from bamboo grades of paper ranging from packaging kraft and newsprint to high-quality writing sheets. An issue of a local newspaper was printed on bleached kraft from the fibers of this super-hard wood. "Ah so," the Chinese made paper from bamboo in the first century A.D. The wood is used in the round, as the hollow boles cannot be sawed into lumber. Rayon too comes from this wood.

Stand of bamboo originating from a single piece of a stem placed horizontally just under the ground.

Natural and man-caused fires help in maintaining stands of the species of the several bamboo genera. Without destructive heat on occasion, the whole patch dies. Cleared ground, full sunlight, and warm soil stimulate bud elongation in the below-ground tissues to form new trees.

Synchrony, a Physiological Symphony

Bamboo species, all members of the *Bambuseae* tribe in the grass family (*Gramineae*), may number over a thousand. Any one bamboo species may have a natural range, perhaps exclusively so (no other bamboo growing there), of several thousand square miles. Within that range, in addition to a named species, may be "cohorts" of that species. Every stem that is a member of a cohort appears genetically related. All of the stems of a particular cohort arise from seed at the same time, produce flowers simultaneously, and drop their seeds together. The seeds all germinate at the same time. Thus, over a vast area, millions of trees that have never flowered suddenly bloom and then drop their seed. And soon all stems of that cohort die. Botanists call this phenomenon synchrony. Not now so obvious as it once was, for people now transplant trees, mix cohorts, and destroy stems before they flower. The cohorts of one Chinese bamboo, so the claim, flowered in 919 and again in 1115 and, when transplanted to Japan, flowered in about 1730 and 1845. Subsequently, plantings of stem material were made in England and Alabama where, in both places, flowering occurred in the 1960s.

That flowering occurs over such diverse climates for hundreds of years seems to justify synchrony as a genetic trait. Wind pollinates the flowers that soon become rice-grain-size seeds that germinate promptly upon falling to the ground. Prompt germination precludes total animal consumption of the seeds, for an assortment of mammals and birds (but no insects) swarm where the nutritious seeds fall. Where these animals in such numbers have been since the previous seedfall, perhaps a hundred years before, is a bit of a mystery.

Ranges for bamboo species vary with moisture, especially so in tropical mountains. One kind may be on a wet southern slope at a certain elevation but not on the dry northern aspect. Sometimes the trees seem not to be in clumps but, rather, as evenly spaced stems like a well-seeded field of corn. So it is that taxonomists named Kenya bamboo *Arundinaria alpina*, grass of the mountains. Some call bamboo simply woody grass.

An historic use of bamboo must not be overlooked. Thomas Edison found carbonized filament from a single fibro-vascular bundle from an internode of the tree the ideal material for his early incandescent light bulbs. Not till about 1910 was this cellulose material, that forms conduction tubes for moving liquids in trees, replaced in the globe by fine metallic wire.

Fishing poles and bean sticks are currently important uses for the canes. So, too, are the living roots for binding soil and, in many climes, the young shoots for food. And in those climes the traveller welcomes a rest in the shade of a dense jungle of bamboo, though the trees cast shadows that appear grotesque.

PALMS

Trees of the *Palmae* or *Palmaceae* family are among the tallest in the world. A species in Colombia exceeds 200 feet in height. The largest specimen in the United States, according to the American Forestry Association's big tree account, is a royal palm in South Florida which in 1973 tallied almost 7 feet in circumference and 80 feet tall. It displayed a 32-foot crown-spread.

Palms are among the earliest flowering plants to appear in the fossil records. Paleontologists read those records by the presence of pollen, readily identified in peat and muck swamps of various zones. These grains have been found in organic sediments dating to about 10 thousand years ago. Recovered seeds of one woody palm in the Mid-East date to 1400 B.C.E.

See How They Grow

Initial development of the tree begins below ground, the shoots of germinating seeds growing downward at an oblique angle before the stem becomes erect and displays phototropism (growing toward the light). Upward growth is from a single terminal bud; diameter growth is from many bundles of tissue located centrally within the tree's trunk. Hence outward extension goes along with the bud's movement toward the sky rather than as a separate physiological activity.

Monocot stems, unlike those of ordinary trees, are not divided into bark and wood. There is only an outer shell some may call bark and a central cylinder. Therefore palms do not lay down growth rings each year: no vascular cambium exists. The whole organism is primary living material. Palms don't even have a nodal plate like bamboos do.

First the juvenile bladeless scales appear and soon become leaves that are incompletely developed. After the vegetative core is firmly established, internodes form; from the last of these internodes a single apical meristem (living, growing tissue) produces a leaf. As the meristem thickens, each internode widens to achieve its maximum diameter before elongating. Now the tree, after accumulating an abundance of starch, expends its stored energy in the spring in a giant burst of flowering and fruiting. Wind and insects handle pollination tasks.

The energy sent to the inflorescence is in the form of a sap high in sugar. Even before sugar cane was cultivated, agile climbers cut open the flower stalk high in the palm tree's crown. Sap flow can be maintained for weeks by repeated cutting of the flower stem or even by pounding on the tree. But, as long as the reserves are sidetracked, the palm tree will not produce seed.

As the trees do not have the cambial conduction tissues of dicots, no additional channels to transport foods, nutrients, and water form with age. Thus, trees do not grow in girth with age. They also retain the same number of leaves. A section of the vascular system supplies nutrients, water, and sugars, but for one leaf at a time. Long-lived palm roots sustain continuous tension for liquids in the central column. This natural phenomenon is necessary in order for the tree to maintain vigor in the few, but large, leaves.

A palm tree of the subtropical United States, not far from the Gulf of Mexico (Texas Forest Service photo).

New growth of sawpalmetto following fire and arising from a bud deep within the protected tissue.

Other Uses of Palm

From the sap of the tree, natives of palm country ferment a low-cost wine. In an energy-short society, this fluid could provide a source of needed alcohol for fuel. Some species are used for lumber. Buttons carved from the "ivory" of some kinds of seeds, rattan from strands of fiber for wicker furniture, thread for weaving and for rope, and spines for sewing needles are products of palms. So too are leaves for thatching huts, hats, and mats. In tropical climes, laborers wear sleeves and hats woven from the leaves of palms.

The economies of tropical lands may depend on palm oil for foreign exchange. In Brazil, waxes come from boiled seeds and from leaves that are scraped and cut, the most notable example of the latter being the valuable carnauba wax from *Copernicia cerifera*. (Wax holds water in for drought-hardy palms; on shoes it keeps water out.)

Coconuts, dates, and betel nuts come from palms. No known wild stands of coconut or date palms are known to exist. Historians believe that the date was probably the first tree to be cultivated by man. Ancient writings listed hundreds of uses for it. Solomon of wisdom fame was so impressed with the tree he referred to a person's form as being like a palm tree, its columnar stature suggesting a high compliment.

Cabbage Palms

Cabbage palms find use as pilings for piers, as poles, and for brooms and baskets. Its logs don't splinter. The spongy stem makes good scrubbing brushes and the whole of the tree was once burned for its potash, an ingredient in soap.

Cabbage palms, as the name tells, are edible. The species is *Sabal palmetto*, meaning small palm in Spanish. The cabbage is the young leaf bud at the top of the trunk. Harvest of the leaf causes death of the tree. As far back as the Civil War, environmentalists of the time called for "state enactments" to protect the tree from cabbage poachers. Its form, incidentally, is displayed on the Great Seal of South Carolina.

In spite of its name, *S. palmetto* reaches heights of 80 feet and diameters of 2 feet. This northernmost of New World palms is probably the species pulled, in petrified form, from the edge of a slough near the Savannah River some miles north of where palms grow today. That section of the bole, about 6 feet long and 12 inches in diameter, dramatically exhibits the border cortex and vascular bundles of the cross section of the stem. Recall that in petrified wood, the wood doesn't turn to stone; it rots away, leaving the sediments that seeped into the pores of the wood as the solid matter.

The stiff leathery-textured cabbage palm leaf has a tough skin that folds into many segments. The close tufts of the sword-shaped leaves appear to be adapted both to store water for times of drought and to resist its loss when dry seasons occur.

Another edible palm, the California fan, grows along streams in the Palm Springs country made famous by presidents. Indians roasted the bud (killing the tree), ground the seeds into flour for bread, and sometimes burned and blackened the bole to improve the crop of nuts. The cabbage of some palm species is poisonous. The ill-informed should proceed with caution.

California fan palms, dressed in hula skirts of dead leaves below the wide-wave of living foliage, picturesquely display their leaves of radial symmetry in the desert sun. Leaves of fan palms really were used for fans. Porcher, a writer at the time of the Civil War, called attention to the fact that both mosquitoes and palm fans, "bane and blessing," were present in abundance in the same locale of the South.

Royal Palm

We must not pass without bowing to the royal palm (*Roystonea elata*), considered an endangered species in its South Florida habitat islands of isolation. State law protects it. Trees of this kind are planted in many places, the boulevards of stately spires adding elegance to the scene. Boles 100 feet tall display leaves 12 feet long, each weighing 25 pounds.

Washington Palm

Another palm rates our attention. *Washingtonia filifera* combines striking beauty with grotesqueness in the deserts of the Southwest. The species name reminds one of the many 8-inch long, thread-like filaments that extend from the margins of each segment of its single leaf.

Gulf Coast residents now enjoy the tree, transplanted to their clime, though they probably are not yet accustomed to eating the little black fruit enjoyed by desert-living Native Americans.

Canary Island Date Palm Problem

Thousands of Canary Island date palm trees (*Phoenix canariensis*) have been killed in the lower Rio Grande Valley of Texas in recent years. An organism invades the tissues in the wood-like substance through which nutrients and water move up the tree. Blocking the flow first causes the leaves to yellow and die. Soon the tree dies. Loss of a vast wood resource may be inevitable, as there is no known cure for the disease. While the wood is weak, fencing and house siding are appropriate uses for the dead stems.

Roundup

With rare exceptions among some four thousand species, all around the tropical and subtropical world, palm trees do not put out branches. The strong, columnar trunk is composed of bundles of long fibers. Boles seem to expand in diameter, but the added growth is really the heavy thatch of dead and drooping fronds of foliage of earlier years, hiding the "bark" all the way to the ground. The leaves live to produce carbohydrate but for a single year, though the tree is an evergreen. The thick thatch, because of its tinder dryness and fibrous texture, is at once a fire hazard and an insulation that protects the tree from excessive heat.

Some tropical members of the family *Palmaceae* have their feet in water. No injury occurs as long as the water moves rapidly enough for free oxygen to be replenished for palm root absorption.

Most palms are dioecious, male and female flowers occurring in separate trees. Men in early civilization knew this. Perhaps they pioneered tree-improvement techniques. Gardeners placed severed male inflorescences (flower stalks), when about to ripen, in the crowns of trees bearing female flowers to cross-pollinate them. Seeds produced by palm trees include the largest of all seeds (coconuts) as well as small ones the size of peas.

Palm trees so fascinate people that a North American group called the Palm Society is dedicated to their study and protection. Some 2,500 species have been identified.

🌲 🌲 🌲 Projects for the Amateur Naturalist

1. Collect, identify, and mount leaves. Large books are good plant presses. Mount on heavy paper or coated cardboard. Cover mounts with self-adhesive vinyl, available at book and office supply stores. (I have a collection made over 50 years ago by these methods, the plants still exhibiting colors.)

2. Make a water pipe from bamboo poles by drilling out the nodes and joining tapered ends of sections.

3. Locate a catalpa tree and count the worms on or under it. Then go fishing. Some wag suggested planting bamboo between catalpa trees: "Then you have the fishing worm and fishing pole side by side."

THE FOREST—
WHOSE WOODS
THESE ARE

Forests for the Future

The cake that you can have and eat is the forest. Woodlands, as renewable natural resources, can be used over and over again for timber, plywood, and paper. Or the land can be left as a wilderness—sometimes called a nonrenewable resource—forever. And in the East lands where stands of timber were laid bare 50 years ago are now desired wilderness areas because they appear as virgin, so rapid is the rejuvenation of the forest.

Recreation is but one use of the forests. America's Congress in the early 1960s tackled the problem of multiple use on national forest land. Even before preservationists were attacking intensive management of otherwise wild lands, legislators, sparked by professional resource managers, decreed that the 186 million acres of national forests should be used "for the greatest good of the greatest number in the long run" to grow fiber, wildlife, or grass; to produce clear, clean water; or to be enjoyed for recreation and aesthetic beauty. Industrial foresters followed this trend on private lands.

That doesn't mean that every acre will have five uses but, rather, that they may. Ordinarily two or three uses are typical, although, in deciding which use shall be predominant, all are considered.

We've listed the five functions of the multiple-use idea. These are also five components of the environment. There are three other principal components: air, noise, and waste. The woods are involved here because air is rejuvenated through CO_2 consumption and O_2 liberation by plant life. The trees only borrow the CO_2. Ultimately, because wood breaks down and rots "away" or is consumed by insects and pathogens, the CO_2 returns to the atmosphere.

Trees are planted to reduce the effect of noise, and, alas, the forests are used for garbage and trash landfills. But on top of that rubbish grow new crops of trees until a future miner excavates the fill to extract metals now too abundant as ore to warrant recycling.

In the act of managing forests, foresters may appear to use unorthodox means. We've mentioned earlier the use of prescribed fires for preparing seedbeds and controlling diseases. Controlled burning may also be employed to improve the range in multiple-use forests, as nutrient elements are quickly released in the process to fertilize a new stand of grass. Cattle will know, for the herds congregate where new lush grass has followed the burn. Fires may be prescribed to control brush and weed trees, for that's cheaper than silvicide chemicals and less likely to be damaging environmentally. Burning under particular conditions improves the habitat for game, especially quail. And prescribed fire is good for reducing the hazards of wildfire caused by careless folks or mad neighbors. Cheaper, too, than hiring towermen and pilots to continuously scout the woods that are floored with tinder-dry fuel.

"Timber famine" was the cry of the early 1940s. To respond to that slogan with the consequent challenge to participate in remedying the situation was the incentive for young people to enlist in the cause, motivated much as were other youths to enter the ministry or to desire the life of service of a statesman. The expertise of professional foresters has enabled the nation to overcome its threatened timber famine so that, at present, volume-growth nationally exceeds the harvested drain. Yet knowledge is available to quadruple annual volume increments when economics makes that feasible. Improved management practices to stimulate wood production also make it possible for certain scenic lands to be removed from production inventory and placed in parks and wilderness areas. More such lands can be set aside for aesthetic appreciation and for future study as funds are made available by the Congress for intensifying management on federal lands best suited for timber production.

Today's lay environmentalists may not be adequately aware of the charges

A nine-year-old stand of slash pine, an example of the "South's Third Forest," which now provides much of the nation's pulp for paper (The Langdale Co. photo).

by Congress to the resource agencies of government. That body, for instance, has directed that fiber production for the present and future needs of all Americans must be a principal reason for the government's ownership of public forest land. Foresters establish new forests now for the needs—spiritual and material—of our descendents. Harvesting Douglas-fir in blocks today means healthy stands of that high-value wood a century hence, whereas more aesthetically pleasing selection harvests now will likely result in ecological succession to less desirable species when the crop is ready for market in a hundred years. In the South, intensive management practices mean for the next generation higher-quality fiber, for wood and paper, produced on much less acreage.

Recent acts of Congress, specifically the acts of 1974 and 1976, mandate management procedures for the national forests and thereby emphasize the long-understood intent. Meanwhile American industries diligently improve management practices on their holdings.

Foresters *are* stewards of both public and private lands. The steward of King James's time was the manager of the estate. In the Greek, the term for steward or manager of the estate is *oikos* (latinized to *iconaea*), root word for both ecology and economics in today's English.

Happily for the managers of the public estate and for the vast industrial properties, these words are of the same derivation, for both environmental relationships and the material welfare of the nation must be considered in fulfilling America's destiny.

🌲 🌲 🌲 Projects for the Amateur Naturalist

1. Note changes in vegetation. Locate an old photograph of a nearby place—field, farmland, park, woods. Now find the photo point, take a current picture, and compare the two. List the changes that have taken place and try to determine the time the shifts took place.

2. Determine tree crown classes. The tops of trees in forests fall into one of four crown classes: dominants (sunlight on all sides), codominants (some light to some sides), intermediates (light only from directly above), and suppressed (no light penetrates the canopy to reach tree crowns). See if you can locate these classes in a forest.

3. Locate trees that have blown down in the woods or parks. If recently toppled, try to determine from local weather records the speed and direction of the wind that caused the damage. Study the roots, noting whether they are living or dead, broken or whole, large or minute, in the subsoil or in the surface soil. Why was the tree blown down?

Afterword
Forests: For Enjoyment and for Timber

There is an old dichotomy that partitions man's attitudes about the forest and its wilderness character into two compartments, labeled "friend" or "foe." The primeval forest as a thing of beauty is, like the company of a friend, to be enjoyed. Valued friends are protected from all who would destroy them. To the tiller of the ground and the pioneer settler fearful of two- and four-footed adversaries, the forest is the foe. And the foe must be eliminated to protect those who fear it. Loggers and their bosses cutting the forests of early America ofttimes have been classed with the latter group. Conservation historians picture them as ruthless barons who exploited the wilderness as a conqueror does his enemy.

Recent care of the forest resources of the nation, however, suggests that these lands, whether viewed for their aesthetics or used for their wood-fiber, are to be appreciated as a friend. Henry David Thoreau doesn't seem to have noted it, but certainly the philosopher would have recognized the inconsistency of the friend-foe argument, for he wrote of sylvan nature while hewing logs, from the very forest of which he wrote, for the walls of the cabin in which he would live.

Eric Sloane, another New Englander and a master with pen at both the easel and desk, entitled an historical novel *Reverence for Wood*. Interlaced with his prose are drawings of products from trees. Following a listing of things made from wood, he quotes Joseph Jenks, designer of the Massachusetts Bay Colony flag, "What better thing than a tree, to portray the *wealth* [italics mine] of our country?" Sloane, I believe, grasped the underlying attitude of our pioneering forebears who, while purchasing boards from the alleged barons, reverenced wood—thus the forests—for its practical usefulness for survival.

The dichotomy in attitude is older than the chronicler's first claims of land abuse in North America. Roderick Nash attributes various views in the biblical narratives to man's desire to enjoy for its beauty the wilderness while fearing for his safety when wandering therein. Joel (2:3) described Eden as a garden, and later—though after The Fall—as a desolate wilderness. Whether The Fall resulted in the dichotomy of attitude is a brief for another time, but the wilderness, either forested jungle or parched desert, would now "do you in" if not subjected to man's manipulation for man's benefit.

But, we like to think, we are more advanced in our reasoning than those who roamed Joel's garden both before and after The Fall. The forest can be enjoyed—though at different seasons in its ecological cycle—for its beauty, its utility, and the beauty of its utility. No question of the beauty of trees or a tree. Kilmer ("Only God can make a tree") and Longfellow ("Under the spreading chestnut tree") acknowledge for us this gift of pleasure. But the handle for a pick or the soft paper that replaced the rough cob may come from the trees in that same woodland cathedral. And are not a Stradivarius and a mallet from that same natural resource?

The forest is no longer the feared wilderness of Joel's time nor the pristine primeval woodland of Thoreau's lonely vigil and vision on the shores of a pond. Joel's jungle needed to be tamed, Thoreau's to be framed.

With wise management, the forest that is today harvested for the building of houses and the printing of books will, after a few tomorrows, be enjoyed for its beauty. And as population soars and the land base on which to grow necessary wood diminishes, the forest now loved for its scenic pleasure must take its turn in the rotation as a woodland to serve the material needs of man. Ugly for a while, but in the providence of a God who understands ecological succession far better than His creatures seem to, beauty will return. The cross was made of wood; so too was the manger.

Further Reading

Chapter 1 *Forest Cover Types of North America*, ed. by W. Eyre. Society of American Foresters. Washington, D.C. 1982.

Chapter 2 *Coastal Douglas-fir*, by R.C. Williamson. USDA Forest Service Handbook 445. Government Printing Office. Washington, D.C. 1973.

Chapter 3 *Regenerating Longleaf Pine Naturally*, by T.C. Croker, Jr., and W.D. Boyer. USDA Forest Service Research Paper SO-105. Southern Forest Experiment Station. New Orleans. 1975.

Chapter 4 "The Redwood Forest," in *Terrestrial Vegetation of California*, by P.J. Zinke. John Wiley & Sons, Inc. New York. 1977.

Chapter 5 "Forests in the Long Sweep of American History," by M. Clawson. *Science* 204, p. 1168. 1979.

Chapter 6 *Mountain Splendor*, by W.P. Keller. Fleming Revell Co., Old Tappan, New Jersey. 1978.

Chapter 7 "Influence of Eastern Redcedar on Soil in Connecticut Pine Plantations," by R.A. Read and L.C. Walker. *Journal of Forestry* 48, p. 337. 1950.

Chapter 8 "Mountain Climates of the Western United States," by F.S. Baker. *Ecological Monographs* 1. p. 223. 1944.

Chapter 9 *Silviculture of Minor Southern Conifers*, by L.C. Walker. Bulletin 15, Stephen F. Austin State University School of Forestry, Nacogdoches, Texas. 1968.

Chapter 10 *A Forest Atlas of the Northeast*, by H.W. Lull. USDA Forest Service Northeast Forest Experiment Station. Upper Darby, Pennsylvania. 1968.

Chapter 11 *A Bibliography of the Pinyon-Juniper Woodland Type*, by W.H. Johnson and D.R. Innis. Utah State University Agricultural Experiment Station Series 501. 1966.

Chapter 12 "The Fungus Causing Pecky Cypress," by R.W. Davidson *et al*. *Mycologia* 52, p. 260. 1960.

Chapter 13 "Foliage Symptoms as Indicators of Potassium-Deficient Soils," by L.C. Walker. *Forest Science* 2, p. 113. 1956.

Chapter 14 "Distribution of Fine Roots in Three *Pinus radiata* Plantations near

Canberra, Australia," by W.H. Moir and E.P. Bachelard. *Ecology* 50. p. 658. 1969.

Chapter 15 Ecology and Silviculture of White Cedar, by S. Little. Bulletin 56. Yale University School of Forestry. 1950.

Chapter 16 Regional Silviculture of the United States, 2nd ed., ed. by J. Barrett. John Wiley & Sons, Inc. New York. 1980.

Chapter 17 Silviculture of Subalpine Forests in the Central and Southern Rocky Mountains, by R.R. Alexander. USDA Forest Service Research Paper RM-254. Ft. Collins, Colorado. 1974.

Chapter 18 Utilization of the Southern Pines, in 2 volumes, by P. Koch. USDA Forest Service Agricultural Handbook 420. Washington. 1972.

Chapter 19 "The Tragedy of Chestnut," by C.F. Korstian. *Southern Lumberman* 117. p. 180. 1924.

Chapter 20 Prairies and People, by W. Droze. Texas Womens University Press. Denton. 1977.

Chapter 21 Aspen: Ecology and Management in the Western United States, ed. by N.V. DeByle and R.P. Winokur. USDA Forest Service General Technical Report RM-119. Fort Collins, Colo. 1985.

Chapter 22 Land Use Changes in the Southern Mississippi Alluvial Valley, by H.T. Frey and H.W. Dill, Jr. USDA Economic Research Service Report 215. Washington. 1971.

Chapter 23 Black Walnut for Profit, by B. Thompson. Graphic Publishing Co. Lake Mills, Iowa. 1976.

Chapter 24 Hardwood Management Techniques of Natural Stands (Proceedings of a Symposium), ed by F.W. Shropshire. USDA Forest Service State and Private Forestry Branch, Atlanta. 1971.

Chapter 25 Textbook of Dendrology, by W. Harlow and S. Harrar. McGraw-Hill Book Co. New York. 1964.

Chapter 26 Properties and Management of Forest Soils, by W. Pritchett. John Wiley & Sons, Inc. New York. 1979.

Chapter 27 Live Oaking, by V.S. Wood. Northeastern University Press. Boston. 1981.

Chapter 28 Urban Forestry, by G. Grey and F. Deneke. John Wiley & Sons, Inc. New York. 1978.

Chapter 30 The Tropical Forest, by M. Batten. Thomas Y. Crowell Co. New York. 1973.

Chapter 31 Forest and Wildlands in California. University of California Agricultural Extension Service. Davis. 1960.

Chapter 32 All the Trees and Woody Plants of the Bible, by D. Anderson. Word, Inc. Waco, Texas. 1979.

Forests for the Future "Ecological Concepts in Forest Management," by L.C. Walker. *Journal of the American Scientific Affiliation*. 32. p. 207. 1980.

Glossary

abscission Layer of cells that, in growing, separate a leaf petiole from its twig.

acidic soil A high hydrogen-ion concentration in the soil solution, acid reaction, below pH 7.0, referred to as "sour."

acorn Usually one-seeded fruit of oak trees, with a hard wall and generally partially enclosed in a husk.

adventitious bud Buds arising at positions other than where leaves or stems ordinarily arise, such as on roots, at the base of trees, and often as a response to wounding.

airplant Epiphyte; a plant growing upon another of a different kind, though not parasitic, deriving nutrients and moisture from the air.

alkaline soil Soil high in hydroxyl (OH) ions, associated with high calcium levels, pH above 7, hence basic or "sweet."

alkaloid Organic substance with alkaline properties occurring in plants.

allelopath In plant ecology, an influence, usually chemical, of one plant (other than microorganisms) upon the growth and vigor of another.

alluvial Soils developed from water-transported material and accumulated in delta-like fans or on lands of river overflow.

anaerobe Bacteria and other organisms that live in the absence of oxygen.

angiosperm Plants with seeds in closed ovaries, such as broadleaf trees.

anion Negatively charged nutrient element particle.

annosus root rot A fungal rot occurring chiefly in the roots of coniferous trees.

arboretum Place for cultivating trees and shrubs for scientific or educational purposes.

auxin Natural growth hormone in plants.

backcross Procedure for breeding a hybrid with one of its parents or parental types.

bacteria One-celled microorganisms active in fixing atmospheric nitrogen, producing disease.

basal area/acre Total area, expressed in square feet, of the cross sections at breast height of the trees on an acre.

batture Bottomlands occupying areas between rivers and levees and usually flooded yearly.

beta disintegration The decay of "soft" nuclear particles, as in the radiation of carbon-14.

biome An ecological community of inter-dependent organisms convenient to recognize and describe as a unit.

birdseye Figure produced in wood by small conical depression of fibers, appearing as little eyes.

board foot Unit of measure represented by a board one foot long, one foot wide, and one inch thick.

bog Uncultivated tract characterized by poor drainage, acidic peat, and low vegetation.

book-matched In veneer, sheets matched by turning over alternate slices of wood.

buckshot Clay soil structure appearing like large cubes or like the lead shot of shotgun shells.

bull-of-the-woods Supervisor of a logging camp.

bundle scar Mark left in a leaf scar by the severing of vascular bundles (within the petiole) at leaf-fall.

burl Hard, woody excrescence on a tree, usually resulting from the entwined growth of a cluster of dormant buds.

burr synonym for cone of a conifer.

C¹⁴ dating See *radiocarbon dating*.

cache A store of items for safekeeping, such as where squirrels hide acorns.

cambium Living tissues between xylem (wood) and phloem (inner-bark) of woody plants.

canopy All the green leaves and branches formed by the crowns of trees in a forest.

cation Positively charged nutrient element particles.

catkin Flexible, scaly spike bearing flowers of one sex.

cellulose Complex carbohydrate compounds occurring in wood and other plant material.

chaparral Thicket of shrubby evergreen oaks; now includes non-oak species.

check In wood seasoning, a longitudinal fissure caused by fibers separating along the grain.

chlorosis Yellowing of foliage, symptomatic of a nutritional deficiency.

chromosome Rod-like bodies regarded as the seat of the genes, ordinarily constant in number of the cells of any one kind of organism.

climax Final stage of ecological succession; the plant community that continues to occupy an area as long as climatic or soil conditions remain unchanged.

clone A group of plants derived by asexual reproduction from a single parent.

cohort In ecology, all individuals that function in synchrony, such as when all plants of the same inheritance flower simultaneously.

cone Fruit with overlapping scales.

conelet Immature cone.

colloidal Matter of small size (less than 2 microns) and having high surface areas per unit of weight.

competition Whenever several organisms require the same things in the same environment; "rivalry" between plant species for control of a site.

compression wood Abnormal wood formed on the lower sides of branches and inclined trunks of coniferous trees.

conk Visible fruiting body of wood- or tree-destroying fungus, often projecting from a tree trunk.

controlled fire Any deliberate use of fire on land whereby burning is restricted to a predetermined area and intensity.

cooperage Wood for barrels, consisting of two round heads and a body composed of staves held together with hoops.

coppice Method of renewing forest in which reproduction is by sprouting.

cotyledon First leaf arising from a seed; seed-leaf.

cover type Pioneer, temporary, or climax combinations of forest trees.

cupule A cup-shaped sheath characteristic of the partial cover of an oak acorn.

cutting Segment of stem cut from trees and used for vegetative propagation.

dbh See *diameter, breast height*.

dendrochronology The study of growth rings in trees to determine and date past events.

dendrology Identification and systematic classification of trees.

diameter, breast height(dbh) Diameter of tree 4.5 feet above average ground level, used for volume and growth determinations.

dicotyledon An angiosperm in which seedlings have two seed-leaves.

dioecious Trees in which male and female flowers are produced on different plants.

dipterocarps Trees with seeds in 2-winged fruit.

dominance Pertaining to the species most characteristic of a habitat which may determine the presence and type of other species.

dominant Trees with crowns extending above the general level of the crown cover and receiving full light from above and at least partly from the side.

dormancy Resting stage of a plant, when a tissue predisposed to proliferate or develop does not do so.

drupe Simple one-seeded, fleshy fruit with bony inner-wall.

duff Forest litter and organic debris in various stages of decomposition.

ecology The study of the interrelationships of living organisms to each other and to their environment.

edaphic Referring to the soil.

elfinwood Dwarfed trees at high elevations, caused by strong winds, deep snow, and other environmental conditions.

endangered Class of plants or animals in immediate jeopardy of extinction; more serious than threatened.

epiphyte A plant that grows upon another plant (or an object) nonparasitically.

escape An introduced exotic plant later found growing wild.

estuary Frequently flooded land where a river meets the sea.

even-aged Applied to a stand of timber in which relatively small age differences exist between individual trees.

face, naval stores See *face, turpentining.*

face, turpentining The exposed, debarked

surface of the tree from which oleoresin is collected. A tree may have one or two faces.

faller One who fells timber.

"fat" pine Conifer wood, usually heartwood of stumps and logs of the virgin forest, abnormally flammable because of high resin content.

fiber length The long dimension of fibers of which wood is composed.

fibro-vascular bundle Specialized conducting tissues in wood.

financial maturity Age at which it is advisable economically to harvest trees, individually or as a stand, in contrast to physiological maturity.

fire climax Species that will continue to be maintained on an area if fires occur at appropriate times.

fire, crown A fire that runs through the tops of trees.

fire, ground Where organic matter in the soil is consumed, especially in peaty soils; fire may burn for long periods entirely below the surface of the ground.

fire, surface A fire that burns only surface litter and small vegetation.

flatwoods Low-lying land, often moist but not inundated.

forb Non-grasslike herbaceous plant; herb or weed in stockman's language.

forester A person professionally educated in the management and wise use of renewable natural resources, including timber, water, range, recreation, and wildlife.

frontland slough Shallow depressions adjacent to the banks of former stream courses in which water temporarily collects.

frost-heaving Upward displacement of seedlings due to expansion of ice in the soil.

fruit Seed-bearing product of a plant.

fungus Plant, serving principally for decomposition, without chlorophyll, roots, stems, or leaves. Some do not play a decomposing role: mycorrhizal growths on roots and the nongreen component of lichens on rocks are examples.

gall Tumor or pronounced growth of modified tissue, caused by irritation by a foreign organism such as an insect.

gallic acid Organic compound in plants, especially in galls and teas.

geotropic Characteristic of a plant root to grow downward.

genotype Resulting organism of the sum of all the hereditary genes in an individual.

germination Rupture of seedcoat and concurrent development of rootlet (radicle) and leaves (hypocotyl).

glacial, glaciated Pertaining to the action of ice upon the land during the Ice Age.

glacial outwash Usually sand plains formed from water-transported material during the Ice Age.

glade Grassy, open space in a forest.

granite Coarse-grained, hard, igneous rocks consisting chiefly of quartz, feldspar, and mica.

gumbo A fine, silty soil, common in the southern and western U.S. that forms an unusually sticky mud when wet.

gum naval stores Oleoresin harvested from living pine trees by streaking or chipping the boles.

gymnosperm Plant bearing naked seeds.

heartrot Decay generally confined to the heartwood of living trees.

heartwood Inner core of a woody stem, composed primarily of nonliving cells and usually distinguished from the outer enveloping sapwood layer by its darker color.

heliophyte A plant thriving in, or tolerating, full sunlight.

herb Non-woody, flowering plant, including broadleaf forbs and grasses.

herbicide Chemical for killing plants; in forestry, sometimes dendrocide or silvicide.

high-grading Removal from a forest of only the highest-quality trees, leaving lesser-quality stems for future harvests and as a source of seed.

high wheels Large wheels, pulled by animals, used for transporting logs, by raising them off of the ground, from felling site to loading site.

host (biological) Organism upon which another organism feeds and develops.

hummock (hammock) Low area with deep rich soil.

humus Plant and animal residues that are undergoing decomposition in and on the surface of the soil.

hybrid Cross, usually between two species.

hydric For soils and sites, meaning wet conditions prevail.

hypsometer Instrument for measuring height.

increment borer Auger-like instrument used to extract radial cylinders of wood that show annual growth rings.

indicator See *plant indicator*.

inflorescence Character of floral arrangement.

Inland Empire Region between the Cascade range and Rocky Mountains in Washington, Oregon, Montana, and Idaho.

internode Portion of the stem between two nodes; the clear trunk between the zones where branches develop.

krummholz Crooked trees, due to harsh climatic conditions at high elevations.

lamma Shoot formed after a pause in growth; shoot formed on a tree bole when suddenly exposed to light.

larva The wingless, often wormlike, form of a newly hatched insect before undergoing metamorphosis.

lateral root Roots extending horizontally from the taproot or the base of the tree.

leaf scar Mark left on a twig at the point from which a leaf falls.

legume Dry fruit; product of plants of family *Leguminosae*.

lenticel Cells loosely arranged on the outer layer of twigs and serving for the exchange of gases through the otherwise impermeable surface.

lesion A circumscribed disease area on a trunk or stem.

levee Embankment, natural or manmade, to prevent flooding.

lianas Tree-climbing vines of tropical rain forest.

lichens An alga and a fungus growing symbiotically on solid surfaces, important in the weathering of rocks to form soil.

lignin Second most abundant constituent of wood, a part of the thin cementing layer in woody cell walls.

loam A mixture of sand, silt, and clay in proportions optimum for plant growth.

low flat Terrain between ridges, usually 2 to 15 feet lower in elevation, in river bottoms.

lumber Product of a sawmill or planing mill, and not further manufactured.

mast Fruit of trees considered useful for food for livestock and wildlife.

mature An individual tree or stand for which full development has been attained; may be physiological, economic, or sexual.

meristem Tissue capable of cell division and, therefore, of growth.

mesic For soils and sites, meaning moist but well-drained.

mineral seedbed Exposed soil exclusive of organic matter.

monocotyledon An angiosperm in which seedlings have a single seed-leaf.

monoecious Plant with male and female organs in different flowers on the same plant.

mor Soil whose upper mineral layer is relatively free of organic matter but above which is organic matter in various stages of decay.

moraine Deposit of glacial drift of rock and small sediment at the base or sides of a glacier.

muck Fairly well-decomposed organic soil material, containing mineral matter and accumulated under conditions of imperfect drainage.

mulch Material such as straw, leaves, sawdust, or paper, spread on a soil surface to retard water loss and weed growth.

mull Soil whose upper mineral layer is intimately mixed with organic matter.

muskeg A moss or peat bog, usually partly forested.

mycelium Collective term for minute hyphae strands or hairlike filaments of a fungus.

mycology The branch of botany that deals with fungi.

nematode Minute wormlike organisms attacking roots of plants.

nitrogen-15 Form of nitrogen that can be traced in vascular systems using radiation technology.

node (stem) Point on a stem that bears a leaf or leaves.

nodule (bacteria) A growth, as on the roots of legumes and certain other plants.

oleoresin Natural resinous substances and oils occurring in or exuding from plants.

osiers Willows having long, rodlike twigs used in basketry and fencing.

Outback In Australia, beyond the range of mountains near the east coast.

overburden Material overlying a former surface soil or a mineral seam.

pales weevil A beetle of the genus *Hylobius* that attacks the inner-bark of certain pines, especially seedlings, immediately following logging, as it breeds in freshly cut stumps.

pallet Wood platform on which material is stacked for convenient handling and transport.

particle board A solid wood product, usually manufactured in 4 × 8-foot sheets, consisting of compressed, ground, or chipped wood or sawdust.

particulate Minute solid and liquid pollution matter in the atmosphere.

pathogen Organism capable of causing disease.

peat Soil consisting largely of undecomposed or slightly decomposed organic matter, accumulated under conditions of excessive moisture, and containing little, if any, inorganic matter.

peduncle Stalk of a flower.

permeability, soil Relative rate of penetration by a solid object or by water, influenced by particle size, structure, and moisture content.

petiole Stalk of a leaf supporting the expanded portion or blade.

pH Logarithm of the reciprocal of the hydrogen-ion concentration, indicative of soil acidity or alkalinity (7 is neutral).

phenology Science dealing with the time of appearance of characteristic periodic phenomenon in a life-cycle of an organism, as in flowering of plants.

phenotype External characteristics of an organism due to the interaction of its genetic constitution and the environment.

phloem Inner-bark; principal tissue concerned with movement of carbohydrates in plants.

photosynthesis The manufacture of carbohydrate food from carbon dioxide and water in the presence of chlorophyll.

phototropism The tendency of a plant to grow toward the light, as a tree grows skyward.

phyllotaxy Arrangement of leaves on a twig.

physiology Deals with the life processes of organs, within living organisms, as the root of a tree.

piling Sound timber driven into the ground to support structures (buildings, piers, and so forth).

pioneer Those plants that originate successional patterns, as lichens and mosses on rock surfaces, or certain shrubs or trees following fire.

pistillate Pertaining to the female flower or inflorescence.

pitch pocket A concentration of resin, derived from sap, in wood of conifer trees.

pith Primary tissue in the central part of a stem, twig, or root.

pit saw Generally a two-man straight, flat saw for ripping logs in sawpits.

plant indicator Plants that, by their presence, denote site productivity for forest trees.

plow sole The depth to which the plow continuously turns the soil.

plywood Three or more layers of wood veneer joined, with grain of adjoining plies at right angles, with glue.

pocket gopher Short-tailed, burrowing mammal of the family *Geomyidae*.

pocosin Swamp in a slightly elevated area in the southeastern Atlantic states.

podzol Soil characterized by leaching of iron and aluminum oxides from a surface horizon to one below, leaving an ash-gray stratum near the surface.

pole (product) Round timber suitable for supporting utility lines or crude buildings.

pole (silviculture) Tree of median maturity and size (4–12 inches dbh).

pollard Shoot produced when a tree crown is systematically cut back beyond the reach of browsing animals and which has commercial value.

pollen Fine, powdery grains, also called spores, produced in male flower parts and disseminated, often by wind, to female flower parts where the sperm develops following germination.

pollination Transfer of pollen to receptive part of female flower.

polycotyledon A gymnosperm in which seedlings have many seed-leaves.

polytrichum moss Genus of mosses, chiefly of temperate and arctic regions.

popples Colloquial name for poplar trees.

pores, soil Space in the soil between solid particles, filled with water and/or air.

porous wood That which in cross section exhibits vessel or vascular elements, typical of dicotyledonous trees.

prescribed fire A controlled fire ignited under rigidly specified conditions of weather, soil moisture, time of day, and so forth, so as to result in the heat and spread required to accomplish specific silvicultural objectives.

Public Domain, The Land belonging to the government, formerly available for homesteading and other uses.

pulpwood Trees or wood suitable for manufacture into wood pulp.

pumice A porous, lightweight volcanic rock.

puncher Ox-, mule-, or horse-driver in a logging operation.

pustule Blister on the bark of a tree caused by fungal disease.

radicle Root of the seed embryo, from which develops the main root of a tree.

radiocarbon dating Technique by which the time of life of organic material can be ascertained by comparing carbon-14 content in the assayed material with that of currently living matter, C^{14} "decaying" at a rate of one-half of its mass in about 5,700 years.

rain forest Woodlands of high precipitation, generally over 80 inches and generally tropical.

resin Organic substance bled from trees, usually pines, for gum naval stores.

root nodule Swelling produced on root of leguminous and certain other plants in which bacteria convert nitrogen from the air into forms usable by plants.

root sprout Shoot arising from adventitious bud on exposed or buried root.

rosin Hard resin left after distilling volatile oil of turpentine.

rough Accumulation of living and dead ground and understory vegetation, especially grasses and leaf litter, sometimes with underbrush such as palmetto or gallberry.

sandhills A region of dunelike sand hills, specifically in western Florida and at the eastern edge of the Piedmont province from North Carolina to Georgia.

sapling Young tree beyond the seedling stage, usually 2–4 inches dbh.

sapwood Exterior wood, usually of pale color, in contrast to the more central heartwood of a tree.

sawpit A hole in which one sawyer worked in early-day mills, the other sawyer working on a scaffold above the log.

sawtimber Trees suitable for lumber or plywood.

schist Medium- to coarse-grained metamorphic rock composed chiefly of quartz and mica.

scion Unrooted part of a plant used for grafting to a rootstock.

second growth Trees that cover an area after the removal of the virgin forest, as by cutting or fire.

seedbed The soil or forest floor on which seeds fall.

seedcoat Hard covering that encloses the embryonic structure of a plant.

seedling Tree between seed germination and sapling stages; the product of a forest nursery prepared for out-planting in a field or forest.

seed trap Device used to catch seeds for analysis of abundance, and so forth.

seed tree Tree retained in silvicultural harvests to provide seeds for reproduction.

selfing In genetics, pollen from a plant disseminated to the pistil of the same plant.

serotinous Cones that remain closed on the tree unless subjected to high temperatures.

shade-tolerance Capacity of a tree to develop and grow in the shade of other trees.

shake Section split from bolt of wood and used for roofing or siding.

shelterbelt A strip of living trees and/or shrubs that provides protection from wind, sun, and snowdrift for open fields. See *windbreak*.

shelterwood harvest Removal of mature timber in several cuttings, extending over a period of years equal usually to not more than one-quarter of the time required to grow the crop, by means of which the establishment of natural reproduction under the partial shelter of seed-producing parents is encouraged, resulting in an even-aged stand.

shifting agriculture Farming practices associated with slash and burn agriculture, usually in tropical forests.

shingle Thin, oblong piece of wood with one end thinner than the other, for covering roofs and outer walls, usually sawed.

shiplap In lumber, a board with reduced thickness along the edge to receive the edge or tongue of another piece.

silviculture Art of growing trees in managed stands for the production of goods and services; concerned with forest establishment, composition, and growth.

site A particular area, denoted by specific biotic, climatic, physiographic, and edaphic (soil) factors; a reference to land productivity.

site index Expression of forest site quality based on the average total height of the dominant and codominant trees in a stand at 50 years of age.

site preparation Removal of unwanted vegetation, stumps, and logging slash prior to reforestation.

site quality Average height of all the trees in a plantation at 25 years of age.

slash-and-burn Agricultural practice, usually in tropical rain forests, that involves clearing a few acres, farming them until soil exhaustion, and moving to another site to repeat the procedure.

socioforestry Management of woodlands that considers cultural requirements apart from purely fiber production.

solifluction Slowly creeping soil and, with it, plants down a slope, usually occurring in cold regions.

spikes (flower) Floral arrangement consisting of a central axis bearing a number of sessile flowers.

spore Simple, one-celled reproductive structure in certain plants, as the fungi.

sporophore Spore-producing organ, usually the larger fungi or pollen.

stagnation Condition of a stand of timber that ceases to make height or diameter growth.

staminate Pertaining to the male flower or inflorescence.

standard Tree of good growth and form, usually 12–30 inches dbh.

steam donkey Mechanical rig for transporting logs from place of harvest to position for loading on rail cars, trucks, or wagons.

steroid Organic substance found in plant hormones.

stratification Method of treating seeds, often by placing them between layers of moist sand or peat, to overcome dormancy.

strobile Cone with overlapping scales.

stump sprout Shoot from dormant buds at the base of a tree.

succession Progressive development of vegetation toward its highest ecological expression, the climax.

sucker Shoot from lower portion of a stem or from a root.

sunscald Localized injury to bark and cambium caused by sudden increase in exposure of stem to high temperature and, perhaps, sunlight.

super-tree Phenotype believed to be especially superior in inheritance to a particular characteristic, such as growth or form; also plus-tree, select-tree, or superior-tree.

suppressed Trees with crowns entirely below the general level of the crown cover, receiving no direct light either from above or from the sides.

sustained yield Continuous production, achieving, at the earliest practicable time, an approximate balance between net growth and harvest.

synchrony In ecology, the simultaneous occurrence of an event by all plants of the same inheritance, regardless of location.

taiga Subarctic coniferous forests of small trees that form a transition zone between dense forests and tundra.

tannin Water-soluble compound in certain plants, used in leather tanning and dyeing.

taproot A large primary root, extending downward, usually providing support.

temporary species Plant that gives way to other species in ecological succession of plant communities.

texture, soil The relative proportion of the various size groups of individual soil particles, as sand, silt, or clay.

timberline Upper limit of arboreal growth in mountains or arctic latitudes.

tip moth An insect of the genus *Rhyacionia* whose larvae hatch from eggs deposited within terminal buds and which tunnel the interior of the twigs.

tolerance In ecology, the ability of an organism to endure under certain environmental conditions, as shade, light, drought, and so forth.

tree line See *timberline*.

tundra Biome of cold regions often having permanently frozen subsoil and a low vegetation of lichens, dwarf hardy herbs, and shrubs.

tylosis(es) In wood, outgrowth in a vessel wall from an adjacent cell, partially or completely blocking the opening.

vascular Tissues in plants that conduct food and nutrients, usually xylem and phloem in trees.

vegetative propagation Regeneration of plants by asexual methods.

veneer Thin sheet of wood of uniform thickness.

virgin forest Any forest not modified by humans or their domesticated livestock. Usually a mature or overmature forest uninfluenced by logging, although a young forest naturally regenerated following wildfire is also virgin.

white pine weevil An insect of the genus *Pissodes* that attacks buds and inner-bark of the leading shoot of white pine trees, resulting in deformed stems.

wildling Seedling naturally reproduced in a forest and transplanted for reforestation.

wilting-point, permanent Condition at which plants cannot recover turgidity, even when water is added to the soil.

windbreak A strip of trees or shrubs that provides protection for farmsteads from wind and cold. See *shelterbelt*.

windthrow Trees uprooted by wind.

woodwright Worker in wood.

xeric For soils and sites, meaning dry or adapted to dry conditions.

Index

283